THE TEAMS

I was putting out rounds from my XM148 as fast as I could load, aim, and fire. There wasn't any problem with targets—most of the hooches were small barracks, and I could put a round into the building and see guys falling out of them as the grenades went off.

The biggest thing right then was to suppress the enemy fire, using what rounds we did have to their maximum effect. I had my XM148 pumping out 40mm grenades as quickly as I had a worthwhile target. Another man in the squad had an M79 and he was also putting out 40mm fire. The two M60s we had were running hot with controlled but heavy firing.

We were way too far from the river to make any kind of break for the water.

The longer we stayed, the more enemy we would be facing.

"*THE TEAMS* HAS DETAILED AND EXCITING STORIES ABOUT SEALS STARTING FROM THE BEGINNING. THIS IS AN HONEST ACCOUNT FROM MEN WHO TAUGHT ME THE ROPES, MEN I LOOKED UP TO."

Harry Constance, U.S. Navy SEAL Team Two (Ret.),
co-author of *Good to Go*

Other Avon Books by
Bill Fawcett

HUNTERS AND SHOOTERS

Kevin Dockery

SEALS IN ACTION

POINT MAN
(*with James "Patches" Watson*)

WALKING POINT
(*with James "Patches" Watson*)

THE
TEAMS

An Oral History
of the U.S. Navy SEALs

Edited by
KEVIN DOCKERY and
BILL FAWCETT

AVON BOOKS  NEW YORK

AVON BOOKS, INC.
1350 Avenue of the Americas
New York, New York 10019

Published in hardcover by William Morrow and Company, Inc.; for information address William Morrow and Company, Inc., 1350 Avenue of
the Americas, New York, New York 10019.

The William Morrow edition contains the following Library of Congress
Cataloging in Publication Data:

The teams : an oral history of the U.S. Navy SEALs / edited by Kevin
    Dockery and Bill Fawcett.—1st ed.
        p.   cm.
1. United States. Navy. SEALs—History.   I. Dockery, Kevin.
   II. Fawcett, Bill.
   VG87.T43   1998   97-33133
   359.9—dc21   CIP

First Avon Books Printing: February 1999

AVON TRADEMARK REG. U.S. PAT. OFF. AND IN OTHER COUNTRIES, MARCA REGIS-
TRADA, HECHO EN U.S.A.

Printed in the U.S.A.

WCD   10 9 8 7 6 5 4 3 2 1

Dedicated to the memory of

George E. "Fast Eddie" Leasure
One story we missed

CONTENTS

INTRODUCTION

The term "Naval Special Warfare" covers a number of smaller organizations with greatly differing equipment and manpower but all oriented toward the same goal: using unconventional methods to take a conflict to the enemy from a maritime environment. Under the direction of the Naval Special Warfare Command in Coronado, California, are the Development Group in Dam Neck, Virginia; the Special Warfare Center in Coronado, where all of the introductory BUD/S training takes place; the Special Boat Squadrons; and Naval Special Warfare Groups One and Two.

The Special Boat Squadrons contain the Special Boat Units (SBUs). The SBUs are the direct inheritors of the missions performed by the Brown Water Navy in Vietnam and many of the actions engaged in by the PT squadrons of World War II. Besides the SBUs with their specialized small watercraft, the squadrons also are home bases for the new Cyclone class of patrol craft.

The Cyclone class is a 171-foot commissioned ocean-going craft with equipment and a crew capable of taking Special Warfare personnel anywhere in the world's oceans and many of the larger inland waterways. The Cyclone ships can support a Special Warfare detachment during an operation and remain on station conducting patrols for weeks at a time.

In the Special Warfare Groups, one on each coast, are the units best known to the public. The SpecWarGru has under its command the Naval Special Warfare Units, small organizations of men and equipment staged at advanced bases throughout the world. NSWUs are found in Guam, Spain, Germany, Puerto Rico, and Panama, each ready to support any operations by Special Warfare personnel in their area.

Also under the SpecWarGru command are the SEAL Delivery Vehicle Teams. The SDVTs contain the underwater vehicles and equipment that can deliver SEALs long distances underwater. Exiting from a submerged nuclear submarine, traveling far over the horizon to a target, arriving undetected, and extracting after the mission to arrive safely back at the submerged mother submarine is a normal mission profile for the men of the SDVTs.

The active heart of the SpecWarGru is its SEAL Teams. SpecWarGruOne in Coronado commands SEAL Teams One, Three, and Five along with SDV Team One, NSWU 1, and Detachment Kodiak, a winter warfare training center in Kodiak, Alaska. SpecWarGruTwo at Little Creek, Virginia, commands SEAL Teams Two, Four, and Eight as well as SDV Team Two and NSWUs 2, 4, 8, and 10. Each SEAL Team is made up of a headquarters platoon and ten operational platoons of sixteen men each. Each platoon is led by two officers, one for each eight-man squad. The squads are further broken down into two four-man teams.

These SEAL Teams today are trained to conduct a wide variety of missions. These missions can include observation and target designation, counterterrorism, hostage rescue, Combat Search and Rescue (CSAR), and Visit, Board, Search, and Seizure (VBSS) operations. The VBSS mission is conducted on the high seas aboard ships while underway and was performed many times by SEALs in the Persian Gulf.

All SEALs today are the inheritors of the reputation earned by SEAL Teams One and Two in the jungles and swamps of Vietnam during the 1960s and early 1970s. Platoons of ten men and two officers, later expanded to twelve men and two officers, performed operations that had never been conducted by U.S. forces before. Using the many waterways of Southeast Asia as their means of incursion and exfiltration, small units of SEALs, sometimes only one or two men, took the Viet Cong's methods of guerrilla warfare back to the enemy themselves.

SEALs would spend long hours crouching in the dark waters of Vietnam, sometimes with only their heads showing, waiting to trigger an ambush on VC boats moving through canals and streams. Terrifying minutes were also experienced by SEALs conducting audacious prisoner snatch operations in broad daylight deep in enemy territory.

Forty-nine men of Naval Special Warfare, thirty-four from SEAL Team One, nine from SEAL Team Two, five from the UDTs, and one assigned from SpecWarGru-Pacific, paid the ultimate price to develop the enviable reputation the SEALs have for "getting the job done." Among the losses should be included the dozens of men injured, some severely and permanently.

Though they refuse to consider themselves heroes—the term is an insult to the men of the Teams—Special Warfare personnel earned a remarkable number of awards and citations during the Vietnam War. Included in the awards are three Medals of Honor, seven Navy Crosses (eight including the South Vietnamese SEAL who also received the Navy Cross while on a SEAL mission), forty-two Silver Stars, 402 Bronze Stars, two Legions of Merit, 352 Navy Commendation Medals, fifty-one Navy Achievement Medals, and three Presidential Unit Citations. The list is even more amazing in light of the fact that there were never more than 125 SEALs in-country at any one time and often far less than that.

What of the background of the SEALs—where did they come from? The men of the Teams came directly from the Underwater Demolition Teams created first in the dark days of World War II. Those UDTs were themselves made up of men from the Naval Combat Demolition Units, whose primary operations were to blow the beaches of France open for the invasion of the Allies.

The SEAL Teams were first commissioned in January 1962 by the direction of the President of the United States, John Kennedy. The SEAL Teams' mission statement, still partially classified today, over thirty years later, reads in part:

THE SEAL MISSION PROFILE (NWIP 29-1)

1. PRIMARY: To develop a specialized capability to conduct operations for military, political, or economic purposes within an area occupied by the enemy for sabotage, demolition, and other clandestine activities conducted in and around restricted waters, rivers, and canals, and to conduct training of selected U.S., allied and indigenous personnel in a wide variety of skills for use in naval clandestine operations in hostile environments.

2. SECONDARY: To develop doctrine and tactics for SEAL operations and to develop support equipment, including special craft for use in these operations.

3. TASKS: Tasks may be overt or covert in nature.

   A. *Destructive tasks*—These tasks include clandestine attacks on enemy shipping, demolition raids in harbors and other enemy installations within reach; destruction of supply lines in maritime areas by destruction of bridges, railway lines, roads, canals, and so forth; and the delivery of special weapons (SADAM) to exact locations in restricted waters, rivers, or canals.

   B. *Support tasks*—The support tasks of SEAL Teams include protecting friendly supply lines, assisting or participating in the landing and support of guerrilla and partisan forces, and assisting or participating in the landing and support of guerrilla and partisan forces, and assisting or participating in the landing and recovery of agents, other special forces, downed aviators, escapees and so forth.

C. Additional Tasks:
   1. Conduct reconnaissance, surveillance, and intelligence collection missions as directed.
   2. In friendly areas train U.S. and indigenous personnel in such operations as directed.
   3. Develop equipment to support special operations.
   4. Develop the capability for small boat operations, including the use of native types.

For all of the secrecy of these missions, the men who have performed them share a brotherhood unlike that of any other in the U.S. military. Though any Special Warfare operator will readily acknowledge the qualities of many other elite military units, these men most respect those of their brothers who served in the SEALs, UDTs, or units that came before them. What matters most to these consummate professional warriors is that you served in the TEAMS.

THE BEGINNING OF THE TEAMS

In the early years of the 1960s, the United States of America had its youngest President ever and faced a decade of a new kind of warfare. John Fitzgerald Kennedy had served with the PT squadrons of World War II and knew personally what a highly trained unit of men could do in taking unconventional warfare to the enemy. Following his own knowledge and the recommendations of his advisors, President Kennedy directed all of the services to create unconventional warfare units. None of the services took the President's direction with any more enthusiasm than his own Navy.

The Navy had been working on developing new capabilities for warfare well before the Presidential directive arrived. Besides creating a new nuclear Navy, naval officers were working closely with the U.S. intelligence services to see just what would be needed in the way of men and equipment for this new kind of counterinsurgency, counterguerrilla warfare.

Almost a decade earlier, on the beaches of North Korea, the nucleus of the new unit was created when men of the Underwater Demolition Teams started conducting raids and demolition attacks well behind enemy lines. Working from the water that was their home and shield, Navy frogmen blew up bridges, closed tunnels, and moved guerrillas in and out of enemy areas during the Korean War.

The operations of these UDT men had not been forgotten, and their use was resurrected for the Cold War of the 1960s. After meetings in Washington, D.C., and elsewhere, it was decided to create a whole new Navy unit dedicated to conducting unconventional warfare. With the President's directive, plans went forward for the development of the new unit. When much of the higher planning was done, Lieutenant Commander William Hamilton, then both commander of UDT 21 and Commander Underwater Demolition Units (UDU) Atlantic Fleet, the predecessor of SpecWarGru Two, was to be the commanding officer of the new unit, at that time referred to as Special Operations Teams (SOTs), and Lieutenant Roy Boehm was to be his executive officer. During that time, Lieutenant Boehm was Hamilton's advisor on UDU matters and the operations officer of UDT 21. It finally came down to one man, Lieutenant Roy Boehm, to make the final decisions as to who would be part of the new unit.

A World War Two veteran of several campaigns, Roy Boehm was a direct-action kind of mustang officer who had come up through the ranks and into the UDTs. Though no small judge of men himself, Boehm also depended on others to help fill the ranks of the new unit, without being able to fully inform the men as to just what kind of a unit they were putting together, as he had been ordered to by Bill Hamilton.

JAMES C. TIPTON

J. C. Tipton was one of the very few individuals Roy Boehm confided in at all about the creation of the SEAL Teams, and what he confided was only enough for Tipton to complete his job. This made Tip, as he is known to his Teammates, one of the very few enlisted men to have a direct hand in the creation of the SEALs. Responsible for creating more than one legend in the Teams, J. C. Tipton helped write the beginning of the SEAL story itself.

In my whole life, I've only held about three real jobs, cowboy, sailor, and magistrate. The first job came easy, since I was raised in Arizona and my father and grandfather were both cowboys. The switch from a desert to the ocean took a little more work.

At the time of my joining the service in 1952, I was looking for a fast way out of town. I was more than a little tired of breaking horses, especially since the last one had almost broken me—twice. The Navy recruiting station was the only one open at the time, so it was the Navy that got me.

Even though I had not yet graduated high school, I did so well on the placement tests when I entered the Navy that I was selected for the NAVCAD [Naval Cadet] program and could have been sent to the Naval Academy in Annapolis. My career in the Navy would have been a different story and I would have been an officer, except that I just didn't do well enough on the later NAVCAD tests.

Instead of becoming an officer, I stayed in San Diego for a while pumping gas. Here I was, a seaman recruit, and all I had to do was fill up government vehicles at the base gas station. But that job wasn't going to last. They sent me to this office on the base where a lieutenant commander asked me what did I have against submarines.

"Not a thing," I answered. "What are they?"

That ended that conversation. The next day I found myself on my way to New London, Connecticut, to attend submariners school. That was quite a jump, from San Diego, California, to Connecticut. That was just about as far as I could get and still stay in the forty-eight states.

Submarine school wasn't any particular problem, and soon after graduation I was assigned to the USS *Trigger*. The *Trigger* was kind of a showboat rather than a working fleet submarine. The boat was the new *Trigger* and our commissioning skipper was Ned Beach. Beach was senior to the submarine squadron commander, but he had been made our skipper because he was the last skipper of the old *Trigger*.

The *Trigger* was one of the original fast attack subs, just a small boat but with plenty of legs and teeth. But we didn't get to use either her full power or torpedoes much. Instead, the *Trigger* spent most of her cruises testing gear for the new *Nautilus* atomic submarine. The *Nautilus* hadn't been finished yet, and a lot of the equipment we had on board the *Trigger* was experimental.

In between my time on the sub, I played basketball on the base, was pretty good at it, and managed to stay in fairly good shape. On one sub cruise down in St. Thomas, I had met Pat Patterson, Tex Hager, and a couple of other guys from the UDT. They were operating off our submarine for a while, and I managed to hit it off pretty well with them. The guys took me out fishing on one of their PRs [short for LCPR or Landing Craft, Personnel, Reconnaissance], we drank beer, and they gave me a face mask. I thought this was a lot of fun.

Pat Patterson and I were both torpedomen, only I still played with the steel fish and he just swam in the water. Flat out, I asked Pat, "Just what do you guys do, anyway?"

"You're looking at it," Pat answered. "We drink beer and fish."

That's for me, I thought, and decided to volunteer for UDT training. Back at the sub base I was putting in my volunteer chits regularly but never did hear anything back. Our basketball team did very well that year—we won the SUBLANT [Atlantic Submarine Command] championship and were all invited to a big celebration party. Tradition was that we would take our skipper and executive officer with us to the party.

Captain Calvert was the *Trigger*'s skipper by that time, and our exec's name was Adams. At the party, Mr. Adams asked me, "Well, how do you like the *Trigger*?"

This was a little odd, but I answered him, "I love it, it's a fine boat."

"I'm glad to hear that," Adams said, "and I knew you did. That's why I have been tearing up all of those chits you've been putting in for UDT."

That really set me off. I called that officer a bald-headed son of a bitch as well as a few other choice names. That isn't quite the way an enlisted man is supposed to address an officer, but nothing more was said about the incident after Adams walked away. But the next morning, I was told to report to the skipper's stateroom right away. That was the point where I realized I was walking to my court-martial and that would be the end of any Navy plans I might have.

Once in the stateroom, Captain Calvert said, "I understand something of the situation here. I knew nothing about any of this or what Mr. Adams was doing, and I am apologizing for him. I just happen to have an old friend that is a commanding officer at one of the UDT Teams in Little Creek. I have called him and there is a class starting next week. You're in it and I am having you flown down."

Whatever shape I thought I was in from playing basketball, it was nothing compared to how fit I was going to be in UDTR [Underwater Demolition Team Replacement] training. There isn't much room for PT on board a sub, but the UDT instructors soon made up for any shortcomings I might have had. Within two weeks of arriving at UDTR school, I think I went from 225 pounds down to about 170 or so. At least that's what it felt like.

Class 15 was the group I was with, and it started as a big class. There must have been 120 to 130 men at the beginning of training, but that number was whittled down fast. Only about twelve enlisted men and five or six officers were standing at graduation those long weeks later.

The thing I remember first from UDTR was marching along with the rest of the class to our first real PT. We were all wearing dungarees at the time, and the guy in front of me was a big fellow, with an even bigger name. Each of us had his last name printed across his back, and I could see where the man's name in front of me started on one sleeve and ended on the other. I tried to read his name as we marched along. It started with an A but kept moving as I tried to read. Harold Aschenbrenner did end up being one of the graduating few later on, well after I learned his name.

Stormin' Norman Olsen was the senior officer in our class. He was fresh out of the Merchant Marine Academy and arrived in Little Creek as a lieutenant (jg). Partly due to Olsen, and partly due to our own stubbornness, when the chaff had left the class, we were a very tight group. We were not UDT men yet by a long shot, but we had a feeling now for what it meant to be in the Teams.

One of the men from the Teams had gone down to Norfolk and apparently gone into the wrong bar. Frogmen are a tough bunch, but if you put enough people on the job, even the biggest man can get beaten. And that's what happened to this frog—he was beaten pretty badly.

Our class was down to a pretty tight group by the time of the beating incident, and we decided to see if we couldn't deal a little back to the boys at that one bar. The whole bunch of us, officers included, gradually wandered into this target bar. In small groups of two men each, we took up positions around the bar, just hanging around. On the word, each of us was to grab the local standing next to us and just punch him out. The plan sounded good in theory at least.

Several of the instructors were with us, including Eve Barrett. We intended to go through this bar, it may have been a local biker hangout, and be gone before anyone knew what had happened. But before all of the Navy men were in place, one of the locals said something to me that I just didn't agree with. As I said, "That's too bad," I reached out and rapped this guy right in the teeth. Seems I initiated the ambush just a little too early.

Things erupted quickly after I nailed the guy who spoke to me. Everybody who was with us hadn't gotten into the building yet before the fight was in full swing. When the last of our classmates arrived, the inside of that bar was a madhouse. But the plan did work after all. We cleaned house in that bar and got away without much in the way of casualties. We were back in the street and down the road before the riot squad arrived to really clean that place out.

At that time, I had a little four-string guitar I dragged around with me, but after the fight I needed to look for another one. Seems my little guitar got itself broke when someone smashed it over Barrett's head. But that guitar wasn't what I was watching when we left that bar. As far as we knew, nobody knew who we were to begin with. By the time we left they were all fighting with each other for no particular reason. But days later, my little smashed-up guitar arrived back at UDT 21. Somebody had known where we came from and they mailed the remains of my guitar back to me.

The hardest individual part of training was Hell Week, but I've never been able to tell anyone what it was that got me through it. Looking back on things now, the memory is just kind of a blur, I don't think I sobered up long enough to notice what was going on.

Actually, the one thing I remember from training back then was the weekly meetings where each student had to go in front of a board made up of his instructors and officers. Every week that board would list your strengths and weaknesses, mostly the weaknesses, and every week you ended up on probation.

The instructors always said the same thing: "You'll be lucky if you make it, and I don't think you will. You may quit now."

Probably all of the students received the same warning and invitation to leave. Mostly, I just didn't give it much thought. But there was one board meeting that did shake me up during training.

One week, I was told that I had to beat my best time on the obstacle course. During training, you had to constantly improve, to beat your best time, or you would be out. That situation had me thinking hard. I didn't see how I could speed up my completing the obstacles any faster than I was, at least not faster enough to make the time I had to. What I could do was shave the corners a bit on some of the obstacles.

There was one obstacle we had, among the twenty or so that made up the course, called the Slide for Life. The slide was a tall tower with a long rope angling down across a pond of water to a post. You climbed up the tower and slid down the rope to the ground. My idea to save time was not to slide down the rope, but once I was on it, just to drop into the water. The instructors didn't say you had to slide all the way to the end of the rope to complete the obstacle. It was about a three-story drop to the water from where I started, but I just limped out of that pond and continued on, beating my best time.

A lot of the students who started didn't make it through the course for one reason or another. There were some guys who were dropped because they couldn't measure up or complete some evolution. But there were some of the students who I thought would have been good men who quit. There was always something, some problem to be solved or evolution to be endured, that would just break these guys and they would leave. It wasn't just having ability that would get you through the course, there was always somebody who could outswim you or passed you on every run, but in the Teams, it was overall ability that counted the most.

It was overall teamwork that was pushed more than anything else in training. And we managed to push things a bit ourselves on occasion. When we did rubber boat drills, the boat crew would run with their boat held over their heads or sitting on top of your head. Any man who didn't work as part of the team—that is, he ran along and just looked like he was carrying the boat, but he really wasn't—well that guy increased your load that much more. There was more than one man on a boat crew who caught a swift boot in the ass from his crewmates for not carrying his share of the boat.

For myself, I just don't really know what it was inside me that got me through training. Maybe it was just that I was too dumb to quit. But there were times that I really enjoyed what we were doing, and other times that were very different. To this day, I hate running any distance at all. And I really didn't like swimming all that much either. Diving was a different story. If I was working underwater, you had to drag me out to get me to stop what I was doing. But just swimming from point X to point Y in order to cover distance, that I never enjoyed.

As the years went on in the UDT and the SEALs, slipping out of runs became something of an art form for those of us who didn't like to run. Of course, this was well after we had graduated from UDTR and were well established in the Teams. The bushes on Beach Seven were a good place to hide as the Team ran by. And Hoss Kucinski, Jim Watson, myself, and some others would take advantage of the cover whenever we could. It wasn't that we were ever really fooling Rudy Boesch, who always led the runs. I think Rudy always knew when we were sneaking out, and as long as we didn't make a big deal of it, neither did he.

There was one officer in the SEALs, I can't remember his name, who did raise a fuss about our sneaking off a run. As we slipped away from the end of the group, into the sand dunes and bushes, this officer would get all pissed off about it and go running up to Rudy at the head of the column.

"Men are slipping out of the run," the officer would

say. "They're not where they were at the end of the column."

Rudy would just keep running along and eventually say, "They're still there."

"No they're not," this officer would insist. "You look—they're not back there."

This conversation would continue throughout the run until, finally, the column was heading back to the Team area. As the runners went past the dunes, we slipped back in with the guys on the tail end. As we got back to the Team area, Rudy would point to us and tell that officer, "Is that them? See, I told you they were there."

Some of the real legends in the SEAL Team had come up through the ranks while I was in UDT 21, and Rudy Boesch was one I had kind of a hand in making. Rudy Boesch was a Boatswain's mate and always kind of a quiet guy in UDT 21. Rudy would just sit back in the Bosun's locker and do his thing and not mess with anybody. Later it came as quite a shock to some people that Rudy was the man who wanted to be the chief in charge of SEAL Team Two when it was first commissioned. Just proves that you can't judge by appearances. As far as Roy Boehm was concerned, Rudy Boesch was the very best admin man he had ever seen and would work the Team every day on PT, runs, and swims, leading by example. Roy met Rudy back when Roy was an enlisted first class and Rudy was still a third class. Roy Boehm thought Rudy was a good man when he first met him and had just gotten better.

But back in 1958–59, Rudy was anything but big on physical training. You didn't bug him and he didn't bug you. Half the time, you didn't even notice that Rudy was around. Whatever Rudy had to do, he did, but he wasn't very enthused about the running or daily PT.

We held the very first UDT pentathlon kind of competition at Little Creek in the late fifties. The events involved paddling boats, swimming and running, and all kinds of physical activities, and some of the guys we had in the Teams really excelled at these kinds of things. At the time, I had a busted-up leg and was hobbling around in a cast, so they made me a judge. R. A. Tolison and Stan Janecka were the other two judges as I remember. Each event of the competition was timed, and we would be spread out all over the base.

There would be short breaks between the different events as men would come into a check-in point and have their times written down. Nobody would know who the winner was until the end of the day, when all of us judges would put our notes together and declare the overall winner. The trouble was that we already knew who the winner was.

Before the competition, all of us judges got together and decided to mess with the jocks in the Team. All of these athletes were going to just tear this competition apart and show how good they were. As far as we were concerned, we were going to have Rudy win the competition and piss off all of the jocks.

For every event, we kept our scores in line and made sure Rudy was just a bit faster than anyone else. Rudy came out winning the competition, to everyone's surprise. From that day on, woe was me. Now Rudy became a runner and a jock big-time. He never slowed down or looked back after that win. Since that time, Rudy has been told the story, and he never believes it. "Naw," he'll say, "I won that legally." Hell, he never even came close to winning that thing legally.

But on the trophy at the Team, Rudy's name is the very first one inscribed. We never did actually figure out where Rudy really came in on the competition, we had doctored the logs so much. And we lived to regret it, as Rudy would lead PT, runs, and swims from that day forward, pulling me along with the rest of them.

Before that time you couldn't get Rudy to even go on a run if he could possibly avoid it. "Aw hell, I used to run," he will say now.

"Rudy," I answer, "we couldn't even get you on runs before then."

"That was only when I had a lot of work to do back in the Bosun's locker."

"Right, back when you could find a place to hide back in that Bosun's locker."

But for all of our kidding around, the Navy couldn't have found a better man for the job of chief of SEAL Team Two. Rudy went on to have the longest tour of duty of any man in Naval Special Warfare. In fact, toward the end of Rudy's time in the service, the President of the United States himself signed Rudy's extension to remain in the service.

But all of that was to come later after I was in the Teams. My class graduated in November 1955, and I moved over to UDT 21. But that was not going to be the last time I would go to UDTR. In the years that followed, during my time in UDT and the SEALs, I was an instructor at UDTR a number of times. I still never liked to run, and I especially didn't want to even move when I had a hangover, which happened more times than I like to think about.

When you're leading a run, as the instructors did, there were little tricks you could do to make the run easy on yourself, like when you had a hangover, and still run the students practically to death. What I liked to do was sprint out ahead of the student column, running fast until I could feel myself start to tire. Then I would go back to a real light jog. When the students saw me sprint out, they would try to catch up. That would spread out the line of students as the front ran harder and the rear finally caught on and tried to catch up. When the group had caught up to me, I would be ready to sprint out again.

The whole student body would be surging forward, never being able to set a decent pace for themselves. That is the worst kind of running to do and will just beat you into the ground. The students would be madder than hell at me but I would be doing just fine.

Finally, my legs just started giving out. My knees were pretty well shot by the time I was an instructor for my last class. Too many years of bad parachute jumps and worse. But when that last class finally arrived, there was no way I was going to miss the final eighteen-mile run.

The eighteen-mile run at Little Creek was from the base

down to the beach at Fort Story. I had always made that run with each of my classes, but on that last one, I just didn't get out of bed the next day. I would be aching and my knees were the size of softballs, but it did me good to hear the students bitch how that old son of a bitch had just run them to death.

But right out of my own training class, I had other jobs to do at UDT 21. Frank Moncrief and myself, along with George Walsh and Harry "Lump-Lump" Williams, who were already in UDT 21, all reported to sub ops together. Sub ops, for submersible operations, is where all of the underwater gear was stored, maintained, and prepared for the underwater work run by both UDT 21 and UDT 22. At that time, underwater work with scuba gear was still in its infancy and there wasn't much equipment in the Teams. Instead, all of the gear for both Teams was taken care of in sub ops, a small shed separated from the rest of the compound by a fence around it. So the men who ran sub ops were a little clique all of their own.

The four of us were, I believe, the last men to arrive at sub ops under what was called the blackball system. In the old blackball system, everyone who was already in the department voted on whether the new men would be allowed into the department. Our class had completed training at Little Creek and immediately went down to St. Thomas for scuba instruction. When we arrived at sub ops, each of us could operate the gear and work underwater.

But before we could come into the unit, each of the men there voted. And the system had gotten its name from the fact that each man had a white ball and a black ball to vote with. As each prospective sub ops man came up, the others put a ball into a container to vote on his acceptability. If there was one black ball in the box, you just didn't get in. We all got in and the blackball system was soon done away with.

But it was while down in St. Thomas during scuba training that I first got a taste of being underwater as a free swimmer. That was one hell of a lot different than my time in submarines had been. Scuba work was great, and I just loved it. For one thing, down in St. Thomas, you could see all kinds of things. Later, a lot of our underwater work in the Teams would be done at night, but even a dark dive was all right with me.

My enjoyment of underwater swimming stood out, and I was even used to test a lot of swimmers in the UDT and later the SEAL Team. A man could lose his nerve underwater, get "clausty," as we would say, and he just couldn't stay in the Teams. Over the years, I went out on a lot of check swims where my real duty was just to make sure that the other swimmer could make the grade and carry his share of the boat.

By the time SEAL Team Two was commissioned, I had spent a lot of time underwater, and doing a number of other things as well. It was only in the mid-1950s that the UDTs started parachuting and became airborne. Frank Moncrief had been with the first group from UDT 21 who went to Fort Benning and the Army airborne school. I went with the second group of frogs, only about ten or twelve of us, who made up the second class.

Even after there were a number of UDT men who had graduated jump school, it was a couple of years before we started jumping regularly in the UDTs. After graduating jump school, we still did some jumping at the Creek, but it was very limited static-line parachute jumps, and those only enough to stay qualified.

We were having a big problem with the parachute equipment we needed in the UDTs in order to conduct the jumps so that they could be part of our mission capabilities. For the most part, equipment and techniques for the kind of jumps we needed to do didn't even exist. We had to jump over water with scuba gear and even rubber boats. No one else knew how to do what we wanted, so we just developed the techniques ourselves.

There was one jump where Gordie Ablitt was going to carry a rolled-up rubber boat and jump it into the water. The technique involved having the heavy boat rolled up and attached to the lower front of Gordie's harness. As he got close to the water, Gordie would be able to release the boat to hit the water by itself and then he would land near it. At least that was the theory.

Though I don't remember the detail about the jump, Gordie sure does. Something about the boat I rigged not dropping away properly and sticking to Gordie's harness for the whole drop. As I have been told, Gordie cursed me all of the way down to the water on his jump. What could I say—it was an experiment. Better you than me?

We came up with all different kinds of designs and techniques jumping in with our equipment. And the experimentation continued in the SEALs after they were commissioned. Much of the SEALs' techniques came from our earlier trials in the UDTs. Besides the parachute jumping, we also increased the UDTs range of operations on dry land. Instead of just conducting reconnaissance and guerrilla-warfare type operations, we learned how to teach others to do the same things. The best way to learn something is to have to teach it to someone else.

The Company—the CIA—had been using men from the UDTs in the late fifties and early sixties to do foreign training and run other operations for them. My time with the Company turned out positive for me—it resulted in my being promoted to first class "at the convenience of the government." What that meant was that there had not been any openings in my rate for first class, but I was advanced anyway.

As early as 1957, I had been one of the UDT men who volunteered to work with the Company when they needed one of us. At different places and different times through 1957, '58, and '59, I volunteered and was sent off. Operations were taking place in South America, and Cuba was warming up as well. Some of us trained Cubans in southern Florida in handling rubber boats along with other skills. Sometimes we were sent out to look at something, come back, and report.

Exactly how the Company missions came down the line to the UDTs was not something I was ever told. But sometimes we would report for a deployment, and there would be a Company man there to brief us. "You and Jones are going to Miami next week," was what he might say. "Pack enough clothes for a couple of months." Just another deployment where the rest of the guys in the Team didn't know where you had gone to, and didn't ask when you got back.

All this hush-hush made for some funny moments. You could be working with a group in some swamp and along came another couple of guys from the Team to help out. They didn't know we were there and we didn't know they were coming.

This kind of thing went on for a number of years, with the program just kind of expanding over time. In part, this is what led to the commissioning of the SEALs. By 1961, we had almost a permanent group of instructors stationed down in southern Florida, training Cubans and running them in and out for operations. We had five or six men from the UDTs on station at any one time, running operations and the training.

There was an advantage in working with the Company—you didn't have to put up with the same kind of people every day. It seemed that the Company was made up of three different kinds of people. There were the Academy people who were in the Company for a career. Then there were the contract people who had been hired for a particular skill, whether flying a plane or whatever. Then you had the group I belonged to, the service people who were just pulling duty with the Company.

You could always tell the service people, even though you didn't know their names or even what service they were from. It was just something in the general bearing of a man, the way he held himself and the fact that he was usually more disciplined than the contract or even Academy types.

For myself, I enjoyed working with the Company during those years for the simple reason that you generally had things pretty much your way. When the higher-ups came around and started saying no, that you had to do this or that, I would always have the same answer: "I didn't ask to be here, I don't want to be here, and if you don't like the way I'm handling this job, you send me back."

Usually the guy who was making the trouble would just tell me to go back to what I was doing, and the way I had been doing it. Basically, the job we did was teaching everything we later did at the SEAL Team. We taught different things in different phases, but the subjects included combat swimming, rubber boat operations, small arms, guerrilla tactics, and demolitions. Everything was shown, including ambushes and body snatches.

We were running people in and out of the islands on a regular basis. And there was always one or two of us along on the ops. Officially, none of the instructors were to set foot on foreign soil, or at least that was always the saying down there. It did seem that there was a time or two an instructor was away from the camp for longer than seemed necessary to just drop someone off or pick someone up.

Roy Boehm and I were probably the first two people in the UDTs who knew that there was something going to happen to start a new kind of team. At least a year before the SEALs were commissioned, Roy was talking to me about this new organization that was going to be started and for me to go with him to meetings in Washington, D.C., to discuss the project. What I thought was that we were going up to D.C. to talk about a special kind of new boat we needed for special operations in the UDTs.

Experience we had gathered with our training in southern Florida and other Company operations had shown up the limitations of the small craft we had available for guerrilla-type operations. It had been decided that a whole new kind of boat needed to be designed with the features we wanted—shallow draft, self-bailing, light and fast. This was something the UDTs needed, and I had experience both in what we wanted and how we were going to use it.

So when Roy asked me to go to Washington with him, I didn't think anything particularly new was going to happen. But before we arrived at the meeting, Roy brought me up to speed about this new organization that was being planned. He gave me a rundown on just what was being planned and what the men were going to be able to do, leap over tall buildings, bend steel in their bare hands, all this good stuff. Then he asked me if I wanted in on this. There was only one thing I could say to this man. "Roy," I said, "you've been reading too many comic books."

The name "SEALs" didn't exist yet as far as I knew. But the idea for the organization wasn't any surprise to me. I don't know who first came up with the idea for the new Teams. It was Roy who was telling me about them. And Roy said that President Kennedy himself was behind the project. Who was I to argue with that?

For the last four or five years, we had been doing the same basic operation in the UDTs that Roy was describing for the SEALs. Along with a few guys from the UDTs, a few guys from the Army, and a couple of Marines just to balance things out, the operations we had done with the Company, intelligence-gathering, guerrilla and counter-guerrilla missions, were exactly what Roy had said was to be the job of this new organization. And it still looked like it would be the CIA saying to go here and do this.

Before we arrived in Washington, I had a pretty good idea about just what it was that was being planned. But the new organization still didn't have a name yet. I still don't know who exactly came up with the name SEAL. If I had to make a guess, I would say it was Roy Boehm. The first recollection I have of the name was after Roy came out of one of our D.C. meetings.

Roy had gone into the meeting with just the framework of the new organization and came out with a name. "SEAL, huh?" I said after I had been told what the new name was. "Sea, Air, Land . . . what's that E in there for?"

After that, we started setting up for the new Team in another building at Little Creek. Roy brought Hoot Andrews, a chief storekeeper, in right away to start putting together all of the gear, weapons, and equipment we would need to operate. Hoot had just become nuclear-submarine-qualified and Admiral Rickover didn't want to give him up. Roy used his Presidential priority, which was the same as Admiral Rickover's priority, and basically stole Hoot for the new Team.

"Now," Roy said to us, "you're going to have air ops and sub ops in this. Start making up a list of what you're going to need. Figure what you want and add about fifteen percent over that for what you'll need for each man."

The Team was now planned to be fifty men. For about one day, before the meeting where Roy came out with the name, it was only going to be twenty-five guys in the whole Navy making up this new organization. After the meeting, it was going to be fifty guys in the Team. By the next day, it was fifty guys in two Teams, one on each coast.

Now the new Teams had a name, but no commission or anything like that. What we did have was a few guys and a building at Little Creek. Roy had told us that we could get anything we needed. "Anything you think you will need," he said, "whatever it is, you can get it."

We had been pretty used to living out of Navy salvage in the UDTs. Our budgets hadn't exactly been the biggest in the Navy. In fact, the only time in recent years that we had any extra equipment in the UDTs was when we had stolen it from our CIA funds and brought it back with us from the training camps.

"Roy," I said, "man, that's great. How much money do I have to work with?"

"Well," he said, "try five million dollars, and if you run out, we can get more."

It was right about then that I fainted. Prior to that time, I had run submersible operations for the whole damn UDT on two hundred and fifty dollars a fiscal quarter! In UDT 21, we had been reusing our old baralyme [carbon dioxide absorbent for rebreathers] after drying it out. Instead of buying a new fifteen-cent silicone seal, that went in the J-valve of a scuba tank, we saved the old ones and heated them with a cigarette lighter and stuck them back into place. The diaphragms in our demand-valve regulators we patched up with rubber glue when they tore. Anything to save a buck, which we didn't have in the first place. Now the new SEALs were going to have anything they wanted.

That situation did cause a real rift between the new SEAL Team and the parent UDTs that first year. The UDTs were still operating with the dribbles that the Navy let them have, and these new SEAL pups were strolling about with the very latest and greatest. I probably would have been a bit jealous, only I was too busy working with the new gear.

It wasn't until years later that I found out Roy had lied to both Hoot and me. He wanted us to tell him what we thought going first class would be without any restraints. Then he evaluated the list and fought for the appropriations he agreed with.

The main thing I was interested in for the new Team was what diving gear we were going to get. That and the type of parachutes we would have. The big thing I wanted for the new Team was the paracommander, the hottest thing on the civilian skydiving market at the time. The paracommander parachute had a slow sink rate, high maneuverability, and a good forward glide because of the many slots and louvers built into the canopy. This was just the thing for special parachute insertions. But in spite of our money, we never did get paracommanders.

The Navy has a special five-year test plan for certain types of parachutes. That helped keep us from getting the paracommanders, but we managed to bypass that system in our own way. What we did was start modifying twenty-eight-foot canopies ourselves to make TUs [steerable parachutes] and anything else we might be able to use for our free-falling.

The original parachutes we got from the Navy were called Tojos and had thirty-five-foot canopies. They were fairly good chutes, but we continued to try and modify them to better fit our needs. Frank Moncrief came into SEAL Team Two after we had already been commissioned. Frank had been operating with the Navy Chuting Stars, the East Coast parachute demonstration team. So as soon as Frank arrived at Team Two, he immediately came into air ops with me.

With Frank's help, we tested the modified and unmodified parachutes we had, and I even made a film of our jumping them. I took the film up to the Navy powers that be to show them just what we wanted and why. At that time, the Navy didn't believe in sleeve deployments of the canopies. In a sleeve deployment, the canopy of the chute is packed inside a long cloth tube or sleeve. The sleeve is pulled from the canopy by the pilot chute, which pulls the entire package out from the harness. The neat thing about a sleeve deployment is that it eliminates most of the opening shock of the parachute.

For the pictures, I had this little plastic Kodak 8mm movie camera. I was going to jump out, drop next to Frank, and get films of the chute deploying. So we piled out of the plane. Frank was going to pull and I was going to do the filming of the sleeve and the whole bit.

As we fell, I lined up above Frank and started taking pictures. As I was shooting, Frank waved me off. The last thing I wanted was Frank's chute to hit me in the face so we both would hit the ground hard. I peeled off to the side and passed Frank as he opened up his canopy.

When we hit the ground Frank came over to me madder than hell. "Goddamn it," he yelled, "what did you do that for? Now we're going to have to pack these things up and go do it again."

"Frank," I said, "you came in [signalled] to pull."

I hadn't been watching the altimeters or anything during the jump. My job was to film Frank, and I was trusting him to signal his intentions and keep the jump safe.

"The hell I did," Frank bellowed. And we continued with a big argument as we gathered up our chutes and prepared to repack them. We went up and did the jump again. This time I was sure I had filmed the chute deploying just the way we wanted it. Later on, in the air ops locker, we were watching the film after I had it developed. "What's that, Frank?" I said as that first jump flashed past on the screen.

"Damn," he said. "That sure looks like what I was doing [waving me off], doesn't it?"

"It sure does," I answered and settled back to watch the rest of the film.

Frank Moncrief had one of the longest track records for parachute jumping of anyone in UDT. As was normal for UDT, we didn't get a lot of support from the Navy when we first started jumping and especially for our free-falling. The first parachutes we had in UDT were twenty-eight-foot flats that we gathered up out of salvage.

We took those aircrewmen's chutes and modified them for better control in the air for our style of jumping. We would cut out one or two of the gores in the canopy and line the sides of the cut with tape, when we had the tape. The open sections of the canopy would let air flow out and the chute would glide forward at a much greater rate than an unmodified chute. The greater forward glide rate allowed us to steer the chutes better and be more able to make a clandestine insertion during a mission. The modified chute would also fall quite a bit faster as well.

We were already dropping at a fast rate with the weight of equipment we would carry along with using only a twenty-eight-foot canopy. The modifications would also cause the occasional chute to rip out—that is, blow out the side of the canopy. But the ripstop material the chutes were made of would only tear so far before stopping. But we had a bunch of the salvage chutes at that time and didn't care much if we lost one now and then. Of course, the chute would rip while it was being used, which would make for some tense moments for whoever was jumping it at the time. But if you turned into the wind when the canopy ripped out, you were usually fine. At least, we never lost anybody doing that.

There was one time that we were jumping that the wind did cause more than a little trouble. As we continued to jump, the wind would shift around and blow harder. Bob Gallagher had his chute laid out on a table to pack it that day and he called out, "What's the wind now?"

About twenty-five knots, would be the answer. And then Bob would modify his chute a little more, cutting a panel further to allow him to make headway even in the wind. This went on for a while with Bob modifying his chute as the wind kept rising. Finally he was packed and we were boarding for the jump. By this time the wind was up to around thirty knots, more than a bit brisk. But for a mission, you might not be able to pick the wind, and Bob wanted to see what he could do.

Even with that wind, Bob was making headway into it, so cutting out the panels did prove out the system. But then Bob hit the ground right hard that jump. Didn't bother "the Eagle" though. Gallagher was known for hitting targets other than the drop zone, such as hangars, buildings, all kinds of places.

Today, almost all parachutes are packed for sleeve deployment, but back then we had to work hard to try and convince the Navy that we had a better idea. It took years for the new gear to get to the SEALs. But we had proved out the system and the steerable chutes the only way we knew how, by going out and trying them.

The parachuting I had done back in UDT 21 was one of the reasons I helped Roy when he put together SEAL Team Two and the whole concept of SEAL operations. But just like trying to get the equipment we wanted, we had trouble getting the men we wanted as well. And the trouble we had came from the ranks of the UDT.

Roy told me to pick the enlisted men and that he would take care of choosing the officers he wanted. But when we put together the original roster of men to make up SEAL Team Two, we just couldn't get everyone we wanted. The UDTs just refused to give us who we asked for, with no small reason on their side—the men we asked for were the best and brightest. We would have cleaned out the cream of the UDT to make the SEAL Team.

UDT 21 told us flat out who we couldn't have, but we did receive the majority of the men we wanted. The COs of the Teams fought us almost to the commissioning day of SEAL Team Two as to who we could and could not have. Finally, I believe the roster list was filled out with five men from the most recent graduating class of UDTR. The class actually graduated after SEAL Team Two was commissioned, but those men are among the plankowners of the Team. [A member of the original crew of a commissioned ship is said to own a plank from her deck.]

I have no idea who picked the men from the training class or even how that whole phase finally came about. But the COs of the UDTs had finally just cut us off flat. There were quite a few men we wanted who were not able to make the original roster list, operational concerns being what they were, but they did manage to find their way over to the SEAL Team within a few years.

About thirty-seven guys made the first formation for
SEAL Team Two held on January 8, 1962, at 1300 in the
afternoon. That was where they were told what the SEALs
were going to be and what they were going to be asked
to do. The newly commissioned SEAL Team was set up
in less than luxurious quarters, the old chiefs' coffee mess
was both our quarterdeck and office, so that managed to
keep everybody's feet on the ground. After the announcement, the men were allowed to discuss among themselves
and decide if they wanted to volunteer for the new Team.
All except me, though—I already knew what the SEALs
were about and Roy had decided that I had already
volunteered.

Roy had always been like that with me. There had been
more than a few times that he told me, "Pack your gear,
we're going somewhere."

And my answer normally was, "Okay, where are we
going?"

"I'll tell you when we get there," was Roy's usual
answer.

Roy and I were together for more than a few missions
well before the SEALs were even an idea. Where he
wanted to lead, I had no trouble following when he needed
me. And the SEAL Team generally had that same attitude.

After the SEALs were commissioned, we still had meetings in Washington about what the SEALs would do, and
what they would use to get the mission done. The argu-
ments for equipment were still going on, even while Team
Two was going about getting what they needed. I went
up to D.C. as a technical advisor on that boat that we still
wanted. There was a commander in from the West Coast
Teams at that time who held a different opinion and he
and I would go at it big-time as to what we wanted and
what we needed.

The first commodore of the East Coast Teams would
preside over the meetings, while that West Coast officer
and I would practically come to blows over each other's
ideas. At these meetings, I was just a first class and the
only enlisted man in a room full of commanders and

above. But it takes a lot more than just gold braid on a sleeve to change my mind.

That West Coast commander stated that his people were interested in using a type of wire-guided torpedo for SEAL standoff operations against shipping and things like that. What we wanted on the East Coast was a particular kind of boat and special parachutes. Later on, that officer and I became good friends, but at that time, you couldn't convince anyone in that room that he and I wouldn't kill each other at the first opportunity.

During one meeting, I was standing and speaking about a reason for a certain piece of equipment. The West Coast commander stood up and said, "You shut up and sit down." But the commodore in charge of the meeting had his own way of dealing with that bit of rudeness.

"You see these?" the commodore asked as he slapped at the braids on his uniform sleeve. "That's more than these," and he slapped at that commander's wrist. "When that man speaks," the commodore went on, "he is speaking for me. So you shut up and sit down."

It always seemed that the meeting broke up on that one officer and me getting bogged down in some technical details. Finally, the commodore sent us out of the room. "You two go out and get in the elevator," the commodore said, "and you ride that elevator up and down until you both agree on what you want." We were holding the meetings in a big hotel at the time, and a sealed elevator would take care of any security problems we might have with anyone listening in. So we both went out and traveled in that elevator until we came to an agreement.

Soon enough, I found myself at Little Creek most of the time, working at the SEAL Team and deploying on occasion. But still the intermittent odd operation came up.

During a 1964 deployment to Greece with MTT [Mobile Training Team] 3-64, I received a set of sealed orders breaking me off from the MTT and sending me off on my own mission. The open part of the travel orders sent me on down to Malta. From there I wasn't sure what I would be doing. Once in Malta, I found out that I was assigned to a British Special Boat Unit. Reporting in to a foreign unit isn't always the smoothest thing you can do, and this time wasn't any different.

When I reported in to an office in Malta, this British officer asked me straight out, "What are you doing here?"

All I could do was hand this officer my sealed orders and let him do with me as they said. The colonel took my envelope, opened it, and read whatever it was the orders said. The next thing he did was look back up at me and ask another question I couldn't answer. "Well, who's going to pay you, Yank?" he said.

"I don't know sir," was all I was able to answer.

Calling a sergeant in, the colonel said, "Take him down to the mess. It looks like we have a bloody Yank in the outfit."

That was my introduction to the British SBS [Special Boat Service].

If it hadn't been for the second Lebanon crisis in 1964, I would have probably stayed with the SBS for I don't know how long. I never did find out what my orders read. What did happen was I went out with the SBS section when they deployed to Aden.

The British had a big stockpile of equipment in Aden, a British protectorate at that time. Besides acting with the National Liberation Front [NLF] that was pushing anti-British sentiment in Aden, a bunch of the local Arabs were just plain stealing from the military.

The colonel we were following sent us out to patrol the fence around the stockpile area with fairly simple orders. "If they're inside the fence or crawling through it," he said, "you just shoot them and hang the bodies on the fence. We'll come by in a few days and take the bodies away."

That's what we did, and the stealing stopped immediately. I was a part of the operation, patrolling along the fence line in a British jeep along with some SBS men. They had given me a Swedish K submachine gun, and we followed our orders, nailing Arabs inside the fence line and leaving them on the fence itself. A few days later, the bodies would be taken away.

This may sound pretty harsh to us, but the Brits were

fighting NLF guerrillas at the time, and stolen military equipment is a common guerrilla source of supply. And it wasn't like the Arabs who broke through the fence line wouldn't have shot at us if they had a chance. We just tried to never give them the chance.

Before very long, my SBS companions and myself were ordered back to Malta. Military operations continued in Aden for several years after we left, and the area was given its independence in late 1967, just as the Brits said they would do. But I was long gone before that happened.

My SBS section returned to Malta to a considerably less than cordial reception. After we had reported in to the headquarters, we went up to the club, where a big party was going on. At the party, every time one of the SBS men or myself went up to speak to somebody, they would just turn their backs and walk away from us. Just what in the hell was going on?

We learned later that while we were operating in Aden, there were all kinds of stories hitting the newspapers back in England and elsewhere. Most of the stories reported the same kind of thing, how the SBS and SAS [Special Air Service] were murdering civilians in Aden. That wasn't how I saw it. When somebody shoots at you, you can shoot back. But you don't have to let them take the first shot. What had been done was rough, but it sure got the job finished.

It seemed that many in the British military thought the same of their special forces as many of the regular Navy officers thought of the UDT and SEALs at the time—a bunch of thugs who somehow weren't ''sporting'' enough to use against the enemy. That situation still comes up now and then. But the SBS thought highly of the SEALs. And we had a lot to learn from the SBS as well. They had a lot of unusual gear to complete their missions, quite a bit of it from Germany as I noticed. Which made a lot of sense—more than a few of the SBS men I met were from Germany and didn't even speak English very well.

Of all of the SBS gear I saw while with the section, they had one piece of diving equipment that really fascinated me. The piece was a mixed-gas diving rig, German-made, that one of the operators tried to explain to me. While the man was speaking, I was looking over the rig, which was very solidly built on a good frame holding the tanks and all the plumbing securely.

The system had what looked like a thousand valves and all kinds of shiny gauges, a typical German piece of equipment in my mind. There was this one piece of tubing that was attached to the top and bottom of the rig. "What does this piece of tubing do?" I asked the man explaining the rig to me. "You've got everything here meaning something, and it is obviously not for sport. It's got to be transferring something. But what could it be transferring?"

He hemmed and hawed a bit, saying, "That does whatever the thing here . . ." And he kind of petered off. It was plain that he didn't have any idea what the answer was.

"Really," I said, and I took the tubing off first at one end, then the other. There were no holes or anything in the fittings the tubing was attached to. Nothing could be going through the tube. Maybe it was a spare part, but it sure did look pretty on that piece of equipment.

When the second Lebanon crisis looked like it was going to heat up, I received a set of orders sending me back to the U.S. Navy. I soon found myself back at sea, getting ready to transfer to another ship while underway.

This was something a bit new to me. The two ships rendezvoused at sea and sent a line over connecting the two together. Sitting in a platform swinging from the line, I was transferred from one ship to the other. That isn't exactly the best way to travel at sea, but the passage was made without incident, at least without incident for me, and I soon found myself aboard the LPA 38 Amphibious Transport ship *Chilton*.

It seems my baggage didn't quite make the transfer. All of my gear, carefully packed in parachute stowage bags, broke free and was lost in the drink. That was more than a dollar or two of equipment, counting my operational gear, parachutes, and personals, and I was less than happy but made do. About a month later, I received a message from some LSD [Landing Ship, Dock] that had picked up my bags at sea.

It seems that the parachutes I had packed inside the waterproof parachute bags had held enough air to keep everything floating for a month at sea. The only way the LSD had known the gear was mine was that they found my logbooks inside the bags, still dry and readable.

During most of the mid-1960s, between deployments I spent a good deal of time running UDTR training. When it finally came time for SEAL Team Two to deploy operational platoons to Vietnam in 1967, I waited for my rotation to come up just as everybody else did.

Though I had spent a lot of time in the field, so to speak, while in the SEALs and especially UDT 21, I only deployed once to Vietnam. I went over to Southeast Asia as the platoon chief of Sixth Platoon for its first tour late in 1967. We arrived in Vietnam very late in the summer. Enough time had passed since Team Two had been sending operational platoons to Vietnam that some of the guys who had deployed earlier in the year were returning while I was still in-country.

Bob Gallagher came back to Vietnam shortly after my platoon arrived. The Eagle had been the platoon chief of Second Platoon, the first SEAL Team Two platoon to deploy to Vietnam, in January 1967. In late October, Gallagher was back as the platoon chief of Seventh Platoon. By December, Dick Marcinko, who had been Gallagher's squad leader during their first deployment, was also back, this time as the platoon leader of Eighth Platoon.

One night, a bunch of us, Marcinko, Louie Kucinski, J. P. Tolison, Ron Rogers, and myself, went out boozing it up. We ended up at what you might call a house of ill repute, not that SEALs were known for frequenting such places. But it was just our luck to arrive shortly before the MPs decided to raid the place. Heading to the attic, all of us swung up into the rafters.

We were all about half smashed and were not about to let the MPs wreck all of our fun. Louie was reaching down from the rafter over the door, a small sap in his hand. The door was open a crack and the MPs would pass it every now and then. If one of the MPs came into the room, Louie was going to slap him upside the head and

we would all make a break for it. This did not sit well
with the officer with us.

Marcinko had only made lieutenant a short time earlier
and was a bit concerned about his further Navy career.
"Oh my God, Louie," Dick whispered. "Jesus Christ,
I've just made lieutenant and you're going to get me court-
martialed!" We did manage to get out of that situation
without Louie tapping out an MP, much to everyone's
relief.

Going to Vietnam and combat wasn't that new a thing
for me. Of course, it was a war with all of the horrors
that go along with that. But it wasn't the first time I was
ever shot at. There had been a number of men in the
SEALs who had experienced combat before Vietnam, only
not in as concentrated a dose as we got over there.

Though I probably shouldn't say it because it will be
misunderstood by many, Vietnam was a cut-and-dried war
for the SEALs, right down our alley. I loved it. Everything
the SEALs trained for was part of the combat in the jungles and swamps of Southeast Asia. The reputation of
today's SEALs was proven in Vietnam.

When we were first commissioned, there wasn't any
SEAL Team, at least not as far as the public was concerned. For the first year of our existence, the name
"SEAL Team" wasn't written anywhere that wasn't a
high-security area. You couldn't call Little Creek and ask
for the SEAL Team, not like you can today.

In my opinion, things were better that way, when the
small number of active SEALs could operate in secret. No
one would know we were coming because they wouldn't
even know we existed.

When the UDT operated with some of the early Special
Forces cadre, they were in much the same boat as us.
Those first Special Forces men didn't number much more
than three hundred. Now in the Special Forces, and in the
Teams, there are thousands of men.

But when we first got into Vietnam, the VC had no
idea who we were. And for a long time, we liked it that
way. There wasn't more than a couple of hundred SEALs
in the whole Navy during the Vietnam War. But because

the enemy never knew where we would be or how we would come at them, the actions of a few dozen SEALs could seem like hundreds.

My first impression of Vietnam was proved out during my first op: the whole damn country is wet. Other than that, I really didn't think much about the place other than it just being another jungle. What did surprise me was what the place looked like when we went into Can Tho right after we arrived. Here were all these buildings and built-up areas, a regular growing city rising up from the Mekong Delta.

The appearance of Can Tho was not what I had been expecting to greet us when we arrived in Vietnam. We had loaded up a cargo plane with everything we thought we would need to operate in Vietnam, everything and more. The pilot of the plane was one of the very few flying chief petty officers in the Navy, and he wasn't sure about what we had stuffed on board his aircraft.

"Are you sure that this is all of the weight you have aboard?" he asked as he looked over my manifest.

I assured the chief that all of my figures were correct to the pound. When we were about halfway down the runway, that chief looked back at me as if to say, "You lying bastards." But he managed to get his own back at us.

When we were approaching Can Tho, the chief told us that he was going to have to come in high and land fast because of the groundfire in the area. So here we came in and I was expecting to get into combat as soon as the plane stopped and the doors opened. Expecting sniper fire from the jungle, we moved out from the plane ready for anything, at least anything but what we saw.

All around us were Quonset huts and permanent buildings, all this good stuff. "Just what kind of a war is this going to be?" I said, mostly to myself.

At least we hadn't charged off the plane locked and loaded for combat. What did happen is one of the SEALs who greeted us came up to me and told me just how things were going to be.

"Hey, Tip," he said. "I'm glad you're here."

"Yeah, so am I," I answered.

"You see that mud puddle over there?"

"Yes," I said, puzzled.

"Well, you just throw all of your shit in there and get it wet, because that's the way it's going to be until you leave."

He was right.

But our platoon wasn't going to operate from Can Tho. Sixth Platoon was assigned to Vinh Long, where we were to relieve a West Coast SEAL Team One platoon commanded by a Lieutenant White. To get over to Vinh Long, we had to assemble a convoy. We had some Army support as far as protecting the convoy and escorting us to Vinh Long, but transportation for our gear was our problem.

We had a weapons carrier, kind of a medium truck, from SEAL Team One, which we loaded up with our equipment. But that one vehicle wasn't going to be enough for us in Vinh Long. I told the guys, "Go get a jeep and paint that sucker up and we'll take it out of here tomorrow in the convoy."

My platoon was as creative a bunch of SEALs as anyone had, and they did just as their chief suggested. The only problem was my men had stolen Captain Gray's jeep. Gray was one of the Navy officers overseeing SEAL operations from his office in Can Tho, and we would be operating with him at least once before our tour would be over. But that was something for the future and not a concern when we arrived. The guys did a good job of preparing the jeep, though. In one night, they had repainted that brand-new jeep and threw dust on it, made it look like it had been halfway through the war already, but they did make a mistake.

When I saw the jeep the next day, it looked great for what we wanted. But when the guys had painted Navy identification numbers on the body, they had gotten the first number wrong. All of the other Navy jeeps around were identified by a number starting with a 9. Our ID number started with a 3. I thought for sure that somebody would catch that before we left, but nobody did.

Now we packed up our convoy and moved on down the road. We came up to where we had to catch the ferry across one of the branches of the Mekong River with our parade of Army vehicles, our own jeep and weapons carrier, several more Army vehicles behind us, and behind all of this was a bunch of civilians who also were waiting to use the ferry.

For all of the mess and confusion, we crossed the river without incident, formed up again, and continued on to Vinh Long. No big problems on the way or after our arrival. We had a big villa we lived in while in Vinh Long, a little ways up from the water. Right next door to us was an ARVN artillery battery. That made for some noisy neighbors but worked out well for us the next year during the Tet offensive.

Vinh Long was a good base for us to operate from. Right nearby we had a PBR [Patrol Boat, River] base on the river for our transportation and support. Before operating on our own, we would do a couple of simple ops with one of the Team Two platoons that had already been in-country for a while. That would let us get a better feel for just what we could expect during the tour.

My first combat op in Vietnam was a learning experience. Even with all of the missions I had done before going to Vietnam, there was still a lot for me to learn about operating in Southeast Asia. Guiding us on the op was Fourth Platoon, who were nearing the end of their tour. Lieutenant (jg) Charles R. "Moose" Boitnott, Jr., the platoon leader of Fourth, was leading our patrol, with me following right behind. It was a night op, as most of our operations were, and pitch-black as we crawled through the jungle.

The operation was near the shore of the South China Sea in the Long Toan Secret Zone. The secret zones were heavily jungled swamp areas where the dense plant growth kept most everyone from ever entering the area. This had made the secret zones a haven for pirates and smugglers years earlier, and now the Viet Cong found it just what they wanted for their hiding areas. Since the VC were hiding there, that was where the SEALs wanted to be.

We were the first SEALs to operate in the Long Toan Zone, and the op was a simple two-day patrol to gain intelligence on the area. But a secret zone was tough to get through even for us, and the area had been bombed and shelled in an attempt to get at the VC we were now hunting.

So I was on my hands and knees following Moose through the undergrowth. His squad was taking us out on this op to show us the area and get our feet wet operationally. Moose couldn't show me much of anything right then—it was too dark to see. As I crawled forward, I was reaching up when I heard this real quiet whisper: "Jim? Jim!"

It was Moose, only he wasn't in front of me anymore, more like below me. There was this big bomb crater right in our path, and Moose had fallen into it. The soft mud didn't even make any noise when he hit so I never heard him fall into the hole. I reached down to Moose and he grabbed onto my arm and pulled himself out of the hole.

Falling into a hole wasn't the worst thing that happened to one of us on that op. We had been on the patrol for almost two days on what turned into just a plain screwed-up operation. The only decent targets we found were a couple of training areas, but the VC were gone by the time we got there. We took a little fire a couple of times and returned fire, running into probably not more than a VC squad.

We were paddling sampans through parts of the secret zone. We were in so deep that they were the best means of travel. I know Robert J. "Archie" Grayson didn't like that op one little bit. Archie was my radioman and was paddling right behind me with his radio on his back.

Finally, we were paddling towards the shore, on our way out from the interior. Nobody or anything was supposed to be moving in this secret zone. The whole area was regularly bombed or shelled, so there was no regular civilian population around, and that made it one big free-fire zone where anything would be a target. That made our patrol a little easier, because anyone we ran into would be a bad guy and we could deal with him. The trouble was, as few people as possible knew we were in the area so as to maintain operational security.

One of our large fixed-wing aircraft flew overhead while we were paddling along in our sampans. This was one of the armed observation craft outfitted with infrared viewing system. They were on the lookout for any VC moving through the area. There wasn't any VC in the area—we had been looking for them. The trouble was that *we* were moving through the area.

The plane spotted us and came in for a closer look before opening up on us with its guns. I shouted over to Archie, "Quick, get him on the radio!"

Archie was fiddling with his radio, flustered at not being able to get the pilot and not even knowing what the right frequency was for whoever was in that plane.

The plane came in closer and we knew we were in for a bad time. Then he suddenly waggled his wings at us and flew back on his way. I had been getting ready to un-ass the sampan right on the spot and take my chances in the water. The way that plane was coming at us, I knew he was just seconds away from opening up. But it was either Archie on the radio or he recognized us as not being VC, whichever. That plane flying away was one of the better sights of the war to me.

But we didn't get away from our first mission completely unscathed. Bob Stamey was with Moose's squad, and I had worked with Stamey for years. Stamey was a good man but I had a bit of a problem with him in the past. He had been in my platoon more than once, both in the SEALs and the UDT. It seemed that every time we went on an op someplace, before it was over, for some reason, Stamey would have had to come back off the op early.

When I saw Stamey before the op, I put it to him straight. "This is it, Bobby," I said. "You are going to complete this operation, the whole damn works." There wasn't any real problem—Stamey had been with Moose during his tour and had held up his end as an operator should. But a sailor has his superstitions and I have mine. Sometimes they prove true. Stamey was shot in the throat during our extraction.

We found the VC during the op, or at least they found

us, and we had to extract under fire. We were caught among the sand dunes on the beach as we were preparing to extract by an unknown number of VC. The VC had machine guns flanking us on both sides and had us in a bad crossfire. The large sand dunes gave us good cover— we could lay among them and fire across the tops of the dunes. We could hold off anyone from the position we had, but we couldn't go much of anywhere either.

The VC had heavy .51 caliber machine guns set up and they had us dead to rights. The fire was so heavy we couldn't get to our STABs [SEAL Team Assault Boats] to extract. The boats had come in to extract us when we got to the beach, but before we could get to them, the VC opened up. The heavy machine guns chopped the boats to pieces, and we ended up losing both boats when they broached on the beach. Nobody in the boats was killed but most of the crewmen were wounded.

The VC knew we were in the area but didn't know exactly where we were. I told one of the men from Moose's platoon to get a couple of the men together and move off to the beach. "You know that they know we're here," I said. "Go down to the beach and make some backtracks in the sand. Maybe we can fool them into thinking we moved out into the water."

So the guys went down to the sand and were carefully following their own tracks backwards, looking like they had entered the water and not returned. Suddenly, those two heavy machine guns opened up and knocked up a line of spray on either side of them. That was when we learned that they knew exactly where we were.

We had some Seawolves on call and that was the operation where we first learned just how much we could depend on those Navy gunships. Putting out fire to keep the VC's heads down, the gunships came right into the beach to extract us and get us the hell out of there. Even with the other gunship laying down covering fire, those VC opened up, hoping to take down a chopper and continue using us as bait. The Seawolf took a number of hits but was able to take us on board and we could finally extract.

But before we could get aboard the chopper, Stamey

took a regular rifle bullet in the throat. We were able to treat the wound and he lived through the operation, even got to go home ahead of his platoon. But that was a rough way to go home. Stamey never did complete a whole op with me.

That was Sixth Platoon's first operation in Vietnam and our introduction to the Seawolves. All through our tour, and the tours of every other SEAL platoon in Vietnam, we could always depend on the Navy Seawolves to cover us from overhead or do whatever it took to support us on an operation.

Once later when I was hit, I couldn't get a medevac chopper to come in and get me out. Archie was on the radio talking to this medevac bird that was circling overhead at five thousand feet but he couldn't get him to come down and get me. Without air cover for the hot LZ, that bird just wouldn't come in. While this was going on, two Seawolves came into the area, following the river we were next to.

The two Seawolves had overheard the radio transmissions and decided to take a hand in the situation. "Give me a perimeter and throw out a flare," one Seawolf said. "I'm coming in to pick him up."

That Seawolf did exactly what he said. As the flare burned, he came in and picked me up himself. More SEALs than just me owe a lot to the Seawolves in Vietnam.

Soon after that initial op, Sixth Platoon was operating on its own, taking the war to the VC as only the SEALs did. One of our early ops involved a body snatch with a Chieu Hoi leading us in. The Chieu Hoi program had been started by Saigon back in 1963 as an amnesty program for VC deserters. Safe-conduct-pass leaflets were dropped all over VC-held areas, and all a guerrilla had to do was turn himself in holding one and he would be well treated by the allied forces. The program worked well and brought in a number of VC, who were debriefed and gave us a lot of good intelligence. It was also a way for the VC to infiltrate their people into our units.

We used Chieu Hois to guide us on some operations.

But we never forgot that these men had been VC once and could turn turncoat again without much warning. As far as I was concerned, you could trust the man who had come over with you from the States and not another living soul. I used Chieu Hois when there was no other way to get into a target, but I never trusted them. Some of the other platoons learned to trust some Chieu Hois completely, even let them stay in the barracks with them, but my platoon was not one of those. To me, not trusting a Chieu Hoi was showing them a measure of respect. They might be a VC turncoat, but I still considered them dangerous.

The Chieu Hoi leading us on this snatch op reportedly knew the location of some high-ranking VC. He was scared of his old comrades and asked me for a weapon he could defend himself with. I didn't feel comfortable about giving this supposed ex-VC anything but handed him my .38 revolver anyway. Of course I didn't mention to him that the revolver was empty.

That Chieu Hoi stood there happy with his .38 and things were all fine and dandy for the op. Going into the area, we came up dry on the target. Nobody was there, no body to snatch. The op was a bust, so we headed back to the extraction site.

While we were waiting for the STABs to come in and take us out to the Mike boat, this one ugly sucker came bopping on down the paddy dike right near us. I mean, this was a VC whose look could stop a clock. His face was more dangerous than the weapon he was carrying. Art Hammond didn't like him at all. "Let me get him, Tip!" Art said.

"No, goddammit, Art," I answered. "This whole damned op's a washout anyway. We're going on back."

"But he's an ugly son of a bitch, Tip."

"Yeah he is that isn't he."

"Let me get him."

"Okay, if you want him, you go get him."

Art slipped up on this VC and just nailed him. He laid that VC out saying *"Lai day"*—"Lay down"—and shoving him down on the dike. The man's arms shot up and his weapon went flying. Art had his prisoner and was pretty sure he had to be somebody.

"Man," Art said, "anybody that ugly has got to be somebody. They wouldn't allow nobody lookin' like that to carry a gun."

So the op wasn't a complete bust and we were all having a good laugh as we extracted and headed back to the Mike boat. Moving on back up the river, I didn't give the prisoner much thought, and we were going to hand him over when we got back to our base. So much for what I know.

We turned the prisoner over to Army S2 for interrogation. The word came back later that the guy was a colonel in the regular North Vietnamese Army. Those boys in S2 were so happy. That prisoner was a big hit. But the only reason Art even wanted the guy was because he had been so ugly.

Mostly, we did small unit operations, ambushes and prisoner snatches, during our tour. Running up a body count wasn't the way we wanted to operate. Intelligence-gathering was our real expertise, that and hitting a specific target quickly and efficiently. But we went on one op early in our tour that was anything but small, or efficient for that matter.

Operation Crimson Tide was this big operation against Tan Dinh island. Three SEAL Team Two platoons, Fourth, Fifth, and Sixth, just about everybody we had in Vietnam at that time, were going to sweep this island with support from the South Vietnamese River Assault Group [RAG]. Lieutenant Jack F. "Blackjack" Macione was up in Ben Thuy as the OIC of Detachment Alfa. Det Alfa was in overall command of all of the SEAL Team Two direct action platoons deployed to Vietnam. Since Crimson Tide was Blackjack's idea, he was in charge of our part of the operation.

On 15 September at 0800 in the morning, we began making insertions. By the end of the day, we had all done nine insertions. As far as we could tell, the whole op was nothing but a giant hooch-burning. Depending on whose report you read, we burned forty-two hooches, blew up fifty bunkers, destroyed thirty sampans and fourteen motors, and captured three rifles and three grenades.

That was our first big op in-country, and none of us could make much sense of it. All we did for a whole day was just go up and down on this island, effectively just looting and burning. We would take a few shots now and then, but this wasn't the way the SEALs were intended to operate. The most of what we did that day was blow up bunkers all around Tan Dinh island.

This was a Macione production, and that meant it was going to be well documented. There were Navy photographers along with us taking pictures of everything, and getting in the way. We had just thrown a forty-pound demolition charge into this one huge bunker when the Navy photographer ran up to the bunker.

"Get the hell out of there!" was about all we could shout before the charge went off.

There was this big WHOOM! and the photographer went flying, him in one direction and his camera in another. He wasn't hurt, but I don't think he wanted to take any more pictures for a while.

None of us could ever figure out what the idea was behind Crimson Tide. It seemed to us to have been a publicity thing more than anything else. We took to calling it Blackjack's Folly, which I don't think sat very well with Lieutenant Macione. But it was probably the best-photographed SEAL operation of the entire war. We did do another large op in January that used two SEAL platoons, the Sixth and the Seventh. Operation Wind Song I involved a full village search by both platoons supported by a group of PBRs, RAG boats, and Seawolves. We inserted about 7:30 in the morning and swept the entire village area of Mo Cay.

At that time, I was running the entire platoon. Both of my officers had been wounded earlier and were gone. Lieutenant Fred Kochey had come over to help on ops for a while along with Lieutenant (jg) Ron Yeaw.

The Mo Cay op had been put together on somebody else's intelligence, Bob Gallagher at Seventh Platoon may have had a hand in the planning, but I know I hadn't developed it. But the Mo Cay area was a bad one, with a lot of enemy activity around. This was before the Tet offensive hit just a week later, which would have explained the activity level.

When we inserted in the morning, we quickly surrounded the village and had the area secured. During the sweep we burned or destroyed fifty bunkers, forty other structures, and found a large cache of rice, some medical supplies, and a bunch of documents. There were fifty-one males in the village who couldn't account for themselves that we took prisoner and turned over to the local authorities. Later, we learned that one of the detainees had been a VC tax collector.

But even though the Mo Cay op was a large one, it went relatively smoothly and none of our people got hurt. And we did put a stop to the VC activity in the area for a while. When we searched the opposite side of the stream next to the village, we didn't find any VC but there was a bunch of pungi pits dug in all around. The Seawolves circling overhead shot the hell out of the area around the village, which would have driven any observing VC away anyway. It was a good op and there were no more problems coming out of Mo Cay.

It would be hard to say what I remember best out of my time in Vietnam. It probably isn't the best thing to say, but I enjoyed it. Vietnam was well suited for the SEALs style of operating, and we made the best of it. We were successful and tended to show it on our time off. I didn't like getting shot up and that kind of crap, but all of that is a part of being a SEAL.

Early in November, I had been wounded, shot through the shoulder, which landed me in the hospital. The op I was hit on was a fairly simple area search, what we called a hammer and anvil. In a hammer and anvil, one unit sits in an ambush position while the other unit moves through the suspected area, driving the enemy into the killing zone of the ambush.

My squad was patrolling through the area when we spooked up a VC, just a kid really—he couldn't have been much more than twelve, I think. We had been approaching a clearing when this kid came moving along a trail with a rifle in his hands. I had the kid dead to rights and right in my sights. Telling him to *lai day,* I swore I had him captured. So I was wrong—he shot faster than me. As soon as I had *lai dayed* him, he shot me.

I followed through with my own weapon fast enough, but that kid had nailed me right in the shoulder. He was also the last VC prisoner who got a *lai day* from me. I got over any reluctance about treating a local as the enemy real fast after that. Man, woman, or child, it was the weapon they carried that concerned me.

After being hit, I was at the field hospital in Dong Tam waiting to be medevaced up to Saigon. One of the orderlies came running into the room telling me, "Hey, they just brought one of your boys in. They've got him down in the operating room right now."

This was something I wanted to check out, so I went on down and walked into the Quonset hut they had there, and here was Bob Gallagher all laid out. Bob looked like shit right then, all covered with blood from head to toe. "Goddam!" I said.

"No, no, he's all right," the doctor said quickly. "He's going to lose a finger or two, but other than that all of this is just superficial."

Gallagher was laying there and started talking real concerned. "Tip, Tip! Let me tell you," he said. "It looks like it's filed but it's not filed. Goddam Chicom! It's not filed, just remember that! Now don't grab the son of a bitch."

I had no idea what the hell Bob was talking about, so I tried to calm him down. "Now, Gallagher," I said, "you're all right—"

"No, no!" he interrupted. "Listen to me! It doesn't look like it's filed but it is!"

What Bob had been talking about was the Chicom grenade that had wounded him. The damned thing was booby-trapped with part of the safety mechanism cut away with a file. When Bob had picked it up to check it out, it went off in his hand. He was really concerned that I know about what had happened but finally calmed down. Soon after that, I was flown out to Saigon for treatment of my own wound.

They patched me up in Saigon and I spent about a week or so there. Later, I grabbed a flight back down to Ben Thuy and the field hospital there. From Ben Thuy, it was no problem to get transportation back to Vinh Long and my platoon. But while I was at the field hospital I saw Gallagher again and knew he would be fine.

After finding out where Bob was, I wandered into the place just while a nurse was there. As Bob was lying in the bed and the nurse was next to him, I could see his hand slip up under her uniform. He ran his hand right up on her ass and she didn't even flinch. What she did was reach over and slap Bob a good one. While Bob was reeling back the nurse said, "You're in good shape, mister. You're catching the same plane back to Saigon that brought this guy in," she continued, pointing at me, "so get your stuff packed."

You just didn't mess with those nurses. And I thought the SEALs were tough.

Later, Bob and I were in the latrine and I guess Bob was running late for his flight. That same nurse came right into the latrine while Bob was busy and grabbed him by the arm. While the nurse was dragging Gallagher out of the latrine, she was telling him, "You're getting on that plane!"

"Lady," Bob complained, "I've gotta go!"

"You're damned right you've gotta go," she said, still dragging him. "I've got your stuff packed and they're out there waiting on you."

And she dragged Bob off and sent him on to Saigon.

That wasn't the only time I was wounded on that tour, but it was the only time I was shot. Real early on I caught some fragment from a grenade, but that wasn't too serious. Late in the tour, I caught some shrapnel in the head on an op and they sent me back up to Saigon for another week while they picked it out of me. I did receive three Purple Hearts on that tour, which I could have done without, but I wasn't hit near as bad as some of the other men in the squad.

Right off the bat after we arrived in Vietnam, Lieutenant Hennigan was hit and had to be sent back. Just about ten days after I was shot in November, Lieutenant Marks was shot in the chest and he had to be medevaced out. That was why I had to get back to the platoon so fast from the hospital—all of our officers were gone. Even patched up, I was out operating with the platoon just a few days later.

But we didn't operate without an officer all of the time. Lieutenant Jake Rheinbolt, who was OIC of Det Alfa by then, came down from Ben Thuy to operate with us for a bit, and then Lieutenant Fred Trani came in to operate with us for a few weeks. Finally, Lieutenant Kochey came over and then Lieutenant (jg) Ron Yeaw. Both of them stayed with us off and on for the balance of our tour. So sometimes we operated with an officer in command, but the majority of the time we didn't have one.

Sometimes it was funny how an officer would react. We didn't operate with any one man for a long time, and that didn't let us get a feel for each other the way you do when you train together for a long time. There was one op with Jake Rheinbolt that stood out because of this.

We hit a VC village and had already been in a firefight with the inhabitants. Jake had done more than hold his own when it came to the fighting and operated just fine. But later, when I told him to shoot up a bunch of sampans we had captured, he hesitated. Jake had already nailed a few of the enemy, so that wasn't the problem, it was his background.

The sampans we captured had a bunch of these outboard motors on them supplied by U.S. aid, "Hands Across the Sea" and all of that. We were running like hell to get out of there when I told Jake to shoot up the engines. Jake shook his head for a minute and then said, "Oh hell," and cut loose on the motors. Jake had been an enlisted engineman before taking his commission and he just couldn't see shooting up those perfectly good engines for a moment.

Other people would come and go on operations with us during our tour. Frank Thornton was working out of Saigon and came down for a couple of ops. One mission that

Frank went with us on resulted in me being called "Doctor" for some time after the op.

We had set up for an ambush on a hooch and it was looking to be a good hit. I was going to initiate the ambush by firing first, and Frank was right next to me. There wasn't any question that we had the right place—the VC had been stacking their weapons outside the hooch in plain sight to us.

This one VC came out of the hooch carrying his weapon and coughing. Every step the man took, he hacked a bit more. As he took his weapon and laid it on the stack, he stood up coughing heavily. That was when I opened up and put one right through his chest, initiating the ambush. Frank Thornton looked over to me and said, "Dr. Tipton, you just cured the common cold."

After that op, people took to calling me Doc in the platoon. But the instruments I carried on an op wouldn't be recognized in most hospitals. Most of the time, I carried an M16, usually with an XM148 40mm grenade launcher mounted underneath the barrel. It was a new weapon for me, and I really liked the firepower it gave. But I really had to get some experience with the rig to get the proper use out of it.

On my first op armed with an XM148, I ran into the two luckiest VC in all of Vietnam. The op was a little three-man canal ambush. We had to crawl up to the ambush site about a hundred meters or so through brush and vegetation, just from the insertion point at one canal to the other where we were going to set up the ambush. Getting into place, I set up loaded with one of the new rounds of ammunition we had.

They had just come out with a new flechette round for the 40mm launchers, and I had some. The new round didn't fire round shot but a bunch of thin finned steel needles. This looked pretty neat, and I wanted to see what these suckers would do.

As we waited by the canal, along came a VC sampan being paddled along quietly. As I waited for the VC to enter the killing zone, I clicked the safety off on the XM148 and curled my finger over the trigger. As the VC centered in my sights, I raised up, pulled the trigger, and nothing.

Instead of setting up to fire, I had put the XM148 on safe. All during that crawl through the brush, my loaded and cocked launcher had been ready to fire. And the trigger on an XM148 is an exposed bar on the right side of the weapon—it could have caught on brush and gone off at any time.

My weapon wouldn't fire and start the ambush. Just as I was reaching for the other trigger to fire the M16, the VC saw me, tossed their weapons away, and shot their hands up into the air. So then we had some prisoners and took them back with us. None of the other guys on the ambush knew what had happened with my weapon, I think, but I never did see what the flechette round would do.

It was the kind of operation we were going on that determined just what weapon I would take. Generally, I carried the XM148 mounted on a full-size M16. It was a good ambush initiator and a heavy chuck of firepower in a decent-sized package. We had a Stoner light machine gun with the platoon, and that was also a good weapon for us. It took some care to keep it working, but the Stoner would put out a lot of fire for its weight and was well worth the extra time it took to clean and maintain. Though I personally liked the Stoner, I wouldn't carry it on an op.

As the platoon chief, I would usually be leading the op from the front, acting as the point man. That was my philosophy and was how I trained the officers who operated with me. That was probably why officers didn't last too long with Sixth Platoon that tour. The front was where you could see and know everything the best, but it was also where you were the most exposed.

Right behind me on patrol would be my radioman, usually Archie Greyson, and I don't think he liked that spot very well. The radio makes you a target but it also protects you. Radios saved quite a few lives in Vietnam—more than one guy came back off a patrol with his radio shot full of holes but with his back unhurt.

Stationed in Vinh Long, we didn't have much contact

with the other services in Vietnam. There was the air base nearby, but in Vinh Long itself there was just the PBR base, and we were always real tight with the PBRs. One of the PBR officers had an interesting background. He was the son of Rear Admiral James Calvert, who was assigned as the superintendent of the Naval Academy in 1968. I met Lieutenant Jim Calvert, Jr., and we hit it off fairly well together.

There was one good operation that Lieutenant Calvert took us in on with his PBRs. Calvert was taking us in with two PBRs to a tree line along a rice paddy dike. We were going to insert at the tree line and cross the paddy, setting up an ambush on the dike at the far side, about one or two klicks away. There was another tree line on the far dike, so cover wasn't going to be a problem with us. What was a problem was finding where the canal we were on ended and the paddy dike began.

We wanted to be able to cross the paddies and get to the tree line on the far side by daybreak, so we planned to insert at about 0400 hours. We slipped up to the tree line at the first paddy dike at high tide and moved in very slowly. Just softly putting away, the PBRs moved in to the trees, trying to find the shoreline of the dike itself. The bunch of us were in the bow of the PBR intending to climb off as soon as the boat grounded. The trouble was, the PBR never grounded.

We were easing in and slipping around trees. Up in the bow, I was signaling for the coxswain to keep the boat coming in. All of a sudden we broke through the tree line and found ourselves in the rice paddy itself. I wasn't about to step off the boat into unknown water if I had any choice in the matter, so I signaled for the boat to continue ahead. Now we had two PBRs just quietly moving through the middle of the rice paddy itself.

Finally, we hit the dike on the far side of the paddy and stepped off. Lieutenant Calvert was a bit concerned at that point. "My God," he said to me quietly. "What do I do?"

"I suggest you get those PBRs the hell out of here before daylight," was my answer. We set up on the tree line and waited for our target, which never showed up. Finally, we crossed back over the paddy and moved up the dike to a canal about two or three clicks north of where we inserted. We would hole up at the canal and call the boats in to pick us up. That way the PBRs wouldn't be returning to the same spot where we had started our little paddy cruise.

Before we managed to extract, we stirred up some trouble and got into a firefight with some VC. The VC were in the tree line on the far side of a paddy, and we were well covered at our own position. There was nothing we could do during the fight—the VC were just too far away. We would fire back and forth and all you could see was the bullets hitting the water at best. Finally I told the guys, "Don't waste your ammunition. We can't do anything anyway. You might as well just smoke a cigarette and relax until the pickup gets here."

Arthur "One-Lump" Williams had his sniper rifle with him and wanted to give it a try. The rifle was a bull-barrel .308-bolt action with a telescopic sight on it, just like the Marines were using for sniping in Vietnam. One-Lump had been carrying that rifle around on several of our missions hoping for a chance to use it at some kind of range. It looked like this was his chance. There was this one VC whose head we could see popping up regularly at this one spot. "I think I can get him," One-Lump said to me.

The range had to be a good thousand yards at least, maybe more. "That's one hell of a shot," I answered.

"No, I really think I can get him from here."

There was no harm in trying. We were laying behind the dike and there was nothing but paddy water between it and the VC. Behind us was a short tree line and then the canal. Nothing else could be done, so I told him to go ahead, and One-Lump settled in for his shot.

Willy was sure he could get the target, but it looked like just a little pinhead bobbing up and down to me. The VC would pop up, fire a few shots, and then duck back down. Laying his rifle across the top of the dike, Willy held his position and waited for his shot. Finally, there was this *pow!* as Willy fired.

Far across the dike, this head rose up and just kept rising. That VC did a backflip away from the dike. "You got him, Willy!" I said. "There isn't any doubt in my mind. Now that's a shot!"

That sniper rifle didn't get used much, but One-Lump liked it. And he proved it out for that one shot. Willy had liked to carry the sniper rifle for distance when he could, along with a shotgun for close-in work. If fact, when Willy was hit later in our tour, it was the shotgun he was carrying that was hit first.

We were going in on a search operation early in the morning on 18 January 1968. The intel that led to the operation indicated that there was a big medical supply cache of French medicines or maybe even a VC hospital hidden in the area, and we were going to try and locate it. The platoon had split into two squads, and I was leading the first squad in on the insertion. We were going to use the Mike boat for transportation into the area and then use our STABs for the insertion.

The Mike boat was a converted LCM Mark 6 landing craft that was heavily armed and armored. There were M60 and M2 .50-caliber machine guns all along the sides of her as well as a Mark 2 81mm mortar in the bow and a 106mm recoilless rifle on the overhead deck. The Mike was big and slow, so we used it for fire support and transportation. By tying our STABs up alongside, we could tow them along and use them as shallow-draft boats for the insertions and extractions. To keep the Mike boat from drawing too much attention, we would use the STABs to travel some miles away from her before we inserted. The combination worked well for us and we had used it throughout our tour.

Personally, I had learned to like the Mike boat and some of her crew. There was a Chief Canby operating with the boats who was one of the most experienced men on the water in Vietnam. Besides knowing the VC and their ways, Chief Canby was also one hell of a good shot. He could drop a mortar round right where we needed it, aiming from our instructions over the radio. These were the kinds of people who supported us, and they made our lives a lot easier while in Vietnam.

Going in on the cache search, we inserted about 0400 or 0500 and moved inland for a short distance and then set up to wait for daybreak. We patrolled inland for a ways after the sun came up, crossing four or five canals on the way. The op had turned into a dry hole and nothing much more than a long walk. Fred Kochey and I were looking over our maps, trying to decide exactly where we were and how to get out of there. We were a long way from the river, but there were canals all around us that led back to the water. We finally called for extraction. Moving over to the canal, we waited for the STABs to come in and take us out to the Mike boat. While we were extracting is when the VC opened up on us.

The STABs—SEAL Team Assault Boats—we had were the first ones that had been brought into the country a year before by Second Platoon. The boats were getting tired, and I felt that all of the armor they had on them just slowed them down that much more. The STABs were just too slow in getting out of a situation.

The platoon's two engineers were Art Hammond and Bull Knox. Before the op, I told the two of them, "Get that armor off of there [the outboard engines]. We don't need that stuff on there in the first place. Just get rid of it."

Of course my men followed my directions, as they always did, without question and with a snap: they ignored me and didn't do a damned thing to the boats. When we went out on the op, we did have a pair of officers with us—Fred Kochey and Ron Yeaw had both come along, Fred with me and Ron with the other squad.

When we finally decided to call a halt to our patrol, Fred and I had a small discussion about which way to go. "We'll call them [the STABs] in up the canal rather than go down the river to meet them," Fred said.

"I don't think so," I countered. "I think we ought to cut back through. Go back at an angle to the way we came, and cut through and walk out of here, we can meet them on the river."

The op was a bust, and Fred didn't want to waste any

more time on it. "No," he said, "let's call the boats up and get them in here."

All I had was a different idea about which way to go and not anything worth arguing about. We called up the boats, and the STABs came into the canal where we were waiting. As it turned out, the VC had known we were in the area and prepared an ambush for us. If we had kept going in, searching for the cache, we would have walked right into their ambush. Instead, when we called for extraction and settled into a perimeter, the VC figured what we were doing and decided to wait for a bigger target.

When the STABs pulled in to us, we didn't take more than a minute to get on board and get ready to leave. While we were in the canal being picked up, the boats had their sterns to the shore to pull out fast. When the VC opened up, they weren't shooting at us, they were trying to hit the engines at the back of the boats. Kill the engines and we would be sitting ducks for the ambush.

When the shit started hitting the fan, we were too busy to argue about who may have been right. Fred looked over to me and said, "Well, what the fuck do we do now?"

Kochey knew as well as I did that the only thing we could do was get the hell out of there, but that wasn't what I told him. "You should have asked me that about an hour earlier!" I said as we pulled out in the boats.

The armored housing covers on the outboard motors were being ripped to shreds by the incoming fire. The VC were concentrating their fire on those engines, trying to kill our way out. If my men had listened to me and removed those armored covers, I'm sure we all would have been waxed that day. But those two Mercury outboards never died, they just kept running. We were all standing in the STABs, shooting back with everything we had, while the STABs tried to build up enough speed to get us the hell out of there. That was about when Willy got hit.

A VC round struck the stock of Willy's shotgun, traveled along it, and went in under his arm and lodged in his spine. When we had gotten away from the ambush site, we called in one of the Seawolves to medevac Willy out. We didn't move more than maybe a klick before we came onto an open clearing next to the canal large enough to bring a chopper in.

Moving the boats in to the bank, we put a fast perimeter around the clearing, got One-Lump into the chopper and away, then reboarded the boats and got ourselves the hell out of there. One-Lump survived the wound while in Vietnam but died at the hospital in Portsmouth almost eight months later.

The armor covers on our STAB engines were pretty much in shreds when we got back to Vinh Long. There were seven direct hits in the engine armor and covers and one in the hull of the STAB. But by this time I had learned my lesson. "Repair those covers," I told Art and Bull, "but don't take them off of the engines." That was a direction that they followed.

Though I did occasionally have a good time off duty while in Vietnam, I didn't take any official leave or R&R while there. One time I was called up to Saigon for a meeting and managed to stay on for three days. The time in Saigon went very well. I stayed with Joe DiMartino, one of the plank-holding officers of Team Two, at his place at the Saigon BOQ [bachelor officers' quarters]. Joe D also loaned me his jeep while I was in town.

Saigon wasn't a place I was used to. There were more rules and regulations than I could get along with. Everyplace I went, I ended up adding to my collection of traffic tickets. My mile-high stack of tickets included ones for not locking the jeep properly, parking in a restricted zone, improperly parking in an unrestricted zone—just all kinds of bother you couldn't stay ahead of.

One night, there was a bunch of Aussie troopers came into this one bar where I was sitting. Another regulation had caught up with me, but I figured I was going to beat this one. I had already paid for a room upstairs above the bar. Now I was really staying at the BOQ, but since I had a room at the bar, they couldn't throw me out at midnight when the bar closed to the U.S. military.

So I was sitting quietly and drinking, just shooting the bull with a couple of people at the bar and a few of the

Aussies. Sure enough, as midnight rolled around, in came the MPs. "Out of here, Chief," they said.

"Not tonight," I said. "Here's my key. I live here."

Still things weren't going to work. "That's upstairs and not down here," the MP said. "Out of here now, Chief."

That was when the Aussies got involved. One of those Down Under fellows got up and approached the MPs, saying in a less than friendly tone, "Leave the man alone. You get out of here."

The MPs must have felt generous that night, or outnumbered, and they left, leaving me alone. "Thanks, fellas," I said. And we went on drinking, chasing the girls, and generally having a good time. All in all, the Saigon trip was a pretty nice time.

After the meeting was over and I had to go back to Can Tho, I grabbed a seat on an Air America flight. At Can Tho, I had to report to Captain Gray about the results of the Saigon meeting. The meeting at Saigon had gone a helluva lot smoother than the one with Captain Gray. When I walked into his office, he had a collection of papers on his desk. They were my Saigon traffic tickets.

"Look at this, Tipton," Gray said. "Just look at this. All of these are yours. What in the hell am I going to do with you?"

"Send me to Vietnam, Captain," I answered.

He didn't like that one bit. "I'll tell you one damn thing," Gray said. "You're not going to Saigon again!"

"I didn't want to go this time. You're the one who made me go."

"Well, I'm not going to make you go again. You get your ass back to Vinh Long and your platoon and you stay there."

"Aye, aye, sir," I said, and I left.

Actually I did end up spending more time in the Saigon area. Twice when I was hit they sent me up to the hospital in Saigon for a week. But during those trips I just stayed at the hospital and didn't go into town. Somehow, the hospital trips just weren't as much fun as that meeting trip.

For me, I didn't really have any trouble continuing to operate after being hit. I did get three Purple Hearts on that tour, but I never had any qualms about going back into the field afterwards. When I was wounded, I just wanted to get out of the hospital and back to my men. I wasn't in all that big a hurry, though. The food at the hospital was pretty good.

Three Purple Hearts might sound like a lot, but for us there were booby traps going off and shrapnel flying around all of the time. For me, I never thought about the danger itself much, and I don't think many of the other guys in the platoon did either.

One thing I took away with me from those operations was the opinion that the VC were a whole lot smarter than many people gave them credit for. Charlie was operating in the open country and swamps, hiding in the population during the day and mostly being active only at night. The SEALs were helping to take the night back from the VC, but more than a little of that credit goes to the areas and the way we operated.

I'm thankful we never had to operate under the same rules of engagement that the regular Army doggies did. Those soldiers had it rough not being able to operate freely. They patrolled areas where you had to be fired on before you could shoot back. The same papa-san you had just passed working in a rice paddy could be ambushing you that night.

For myself and my platoon, we only operated in free-fire zones. These were areas that all of the civilian population had been moved out of. The people knew where these areas were and were supposed to know enough to stay out of them. When we went into a free-fire zone, everything in there was a legitimate target and we could defend ourselves aggressively. Our operations were bad enough when we knew we could shoot anybody we ran into, but I always felt sorry for the way those doggies had to hold fire until it was practically too late.

When the Tet offensive began on 31 January 1968, we were told to evacuate our villa in Vinh Long. The VC forces were coming down the river, and the orders were to abandon our villa and the PBR base nearby and move to the Air Force base about seven miles away. Once we arrived at the base we were assigned to set up part of the base defense.

The SEALs are not normally part of a static defense. Our best actions come when we can fight the enemy on his own turf, using our speed and mobility to surprise him where he feels most safe. But the Tet offensive changed all the rules suddenly. Instead of fighting a guerrilla war, the VC were coming in as an aggressive army fighting as large units. At the base, we held our positions and had no idea what had been going on back at Vinh Long.

The VC had overrun the city, and we had to take the area back. From where we were at the air base, we could see the smoke rising from the burning town. Mortars would come in on us occasionally, but no major pitched battle took place at the airfield. A couple of days after we had arrived at the airfield, Captain Gray came flying over from Can Tho in a helicopter.

Landing at the airfield, Captain Gray came over to me and told me to get together six or seven of my men. "We're going to retake the villa," Gray said. "We only have to hold it for one day. The 9th [Infantry Division] is coming down from Binh Tuy. They'll be here tomorrow morning."

By that point, I should have known something would go wrong. We gathered up Mac—James MacLean—and all of the guys and moved out with Captain Gray in his chopper. We had ammunition and weapons hanging all over us—we looked like a cross between the Wild Bunch and a garage sale at an arsenal. I sat down in the open doorway of the chopper with Captain Gray sitting right behind me with his Swedish K submachine gun.

We circled over the city before setting down. Looking out, all I could see was ashes. The fighting had totally demolished the city of Vinh Long. As we started heading up the river, everything we could see was either burnt down or shot up. "Shit!" was the only thought going through my head right then. You could still hear sporadic bursts of gunfire going off all around us, so the fighting had yet to completely die down. Not a good place to go visiting.

We continued up the river to where our villa was. As we approached the villa, we could hear the sounds of artillery going off. There were the ARVNs still in their artillery park right next to our villa. They hadn't moved an inch during all of the fighting.

What the VC had done was travel down the river until they had come into range of the artillery. While they were still out of range, they had crossed the river and continued on down to Vinh Long, completely bypassing the ARVN artillery unit and our villa next door. There wasn't any enemy forces in sight and the ARVNs were shelling the VC positions across the river some mile and a half away.

Everything we had left was perfectly intact. The ARVNs were working around us and little kids were running up and down the street as our chopper put down right in front of our building. Captain Gray was ready to lead us into combat as he jumped out from the chopper. Trouble was, he wasn't going to do much fighting himself. As soon as Captain Gray hit the ground, the magazine fell out of his weapon.

Gray never even noticed that he was running around with an unloaded weapon. I reached down, picked the magazine up, and slipped it into my back pocket. Gray went running up to the villa like a scene from an old war movie. For myself, I just walked up to the building with my weapon on its sling. What the heck—the ARVNs were doing their fighting at long distance, and there wasn't anybody around to bother us.

You wouldn't have known that if you watched Captain Gray. To enter our villa, you had to first go up this short flight of stairs to reach the front door. Gray had his back against the wall facing the stairs as he slipped up on the building. With his Swedish K at the ready, Captain Gray would swing around and around as he swept every corner of the rooms we passed while searching the villa. We went through the whole villa that way, Captain Gray courageously leading the way as we walked along behind. Reaching the top of the stairs and having swept the last room, Captain Gray turned to me and said, "It's okay, you're secured. Now you just have to hold it through the night. The 9th will be down here tomorrow."

It wasn't that we weren't doing our job. Everybody moved through the villa and took up positions overlooking the outside area. It just was that nobody was excited about the situation. There wasn't anybody to shoot at or anybody shooting at us.

"Well, I think I'll set up here," Mac said, indicating a window. "I have a good view of the river from here with my 60 [M60 machine gun]."

"Yeah," I answered. "That's a good idea. Wherever you want to go."

That was how we looked at the situation. Captain Gray had made this big deal out of moving through the area, and it just didn't warrant that much concern. He finally went back down to his chopper and flew off. Later, I learned that Captain Gray awarded himself the Silver Star for his part in the breathtaking operation of retaking the villa. I wonder when he learned that his weapon wasn't loaded. As I watched him fly off, I still had his magazine in my back pocket.

Soon after the Tet offensive was over, Sixth Platoon left Vietnam and returned to Little Creek. Out of all of my time in the Teams, I just did that one tour in Vietnam with Sixth Platoon. After all of my years jumping, running, and everything else, there wasn't much left of my legs, and especially my knees. That was when I figured I would have to go.

The Team made me operations officer for a while, which was a desk job for me, being that I was mostly walking on canes by that time. That wasn't the best situation I would have liked to be in, but it was a damned sight better than sitting at the hospital, which is what the doctors wanted. "Hell no, we have a desk he can sit behind—we'll run him over every day for treatment or whatever" was a phrase put out by the Team for more than one SEAL on the injured list.

Before I left the Teams and the Navy, I did run one more training class at Little Creek. It was the second-to-the-last class they ever ran at the Creek. All basic SEAL training takes place in Coronado, California, now. And for my last class I had some good company. Georg Doran

was there, as was Big Daddy Sheehan, good friends, and
between us we raised a bunch of young SEALs.

I finally retired from the Navy in 1970. The mileage I
had put on myself had finally caught up with me. They
do a lot of things differently in today's Teams. The young
lions are smarter and stronger than we were, and they take
better care of themselves too. But I am very glad I made
that last long run with my final class.

SOURCES OF THE MEN

Because of the relatively small number of men in the
UDTs, filling out the ranks of the new SEAL Teams was
difficult. Not only were the parent UDTs reluctant to give
up all of their best men, but taking too many of the best
away, especially in critical ratings, would limit the support
the UDTs would be able to give the new Teams.

To answer the manpower problems, some men were
taken directly from the most recent graduating class from
UDTR. In fact, the men selected were still undergoing
training when the SEAL Teams were formed. Given that
they were on the selected list, this still makes those same
men "plankowners" of the SEAL Team. One of the many
traditions of the Navy holds that each man of the original
crew of a newly commissioned ship—and the SEAL
Teams were commissioned—owns a plank from the quarterdeck, hence the term "plankowners."

Officers for the new SEAL Teams were assigned from
the Personnel Bureau, with recommendations and sugges-
tions from the Team selectors. Each of the enlisted men
was handpicked by Lieutenant Roy Boehm. The newest
members of the SEALs had in part the hardest assignment.
Their lack of field experience in the UDTs made them the
perfect candidates to try the various military schools being
examined for use by the SEALs. This could result in one
man being sent to a number of the same type of schools
in order to evaluate them. For the best efficiency in examining a particular school, both experienced and new men
would attend a training course to give the widest possible
view of its use.

PLANKOWNERS OF SEAL TEAM TWO

Officers

Gordon Ablitt
Roy H. Boehm
John F. Callahan
Joseph DiMartino
Georg W. Doran
David H. Graveson
Tex Hager
William Painter
Dante M. (Stephensen) Shapiro
Charles C. Wiggins

Chiefs

James C. Andrews
Rudolph E. Boesch
Donald Stone*

Men

Harry M. Beal
B. Benzschawel
Pierre Birtz
Wayne Boles
Richard Brozak
William Brumuller
Charles Bump
William E. Burbank, Sr.
A. D. Clark
John W. Dearmon
James F. Finley
Samuel R. Fournier

Ronald G. Fox
William H. Goines
William T. Green
Tom Iwaszczuk
Stanley S. Janecka
Charles W. Jessie
Rex W. Johnson
Michael D. Kelly
Claudius H. Kratky
Louis A. Kucinski
James P. MacLean
Richard D. Martin*
Frederick McCarty*
Mike McKeawn
Melvin F. Melochick
Tom Murphy
Richard Nixon*
Robert W. "Pete" Peterson
John Ritter
Paul T. Schwartz*
Bobby G. Stamey
Joseph Taylor
John D. Tegg
James C. Tipton
James P. Tolison
Robert A. Tolison
Per Erik Tornblom
Jim Wallace, Jr.
James D. Watson
Leonard A. Waugh
Harry R. Williams

Assigned as Corpsman

FIRST CLASS AVIATION ELECTRICIAN

RICHARD BROZAK

(LEFT 1965)

*Dick Brozak was one of the more unusual plankowners of
SEAL Team Two. He was still in training when the Team
was formed. As one of the very newest SEALs, with no
UDT experience behind him, Brozak was used to check
out many of the training schools that later became a part
of the SEALs' required courses. Though he never went to
combat with the Team, Dick Brozak still managed to make
one very lasting impression on SEAL Team Two.*

Responsibility was something I learned young, as my parents separated at an early age. My father was a coal miner
in Pennsylvania, and my sister, brother, and myself lived
with him. Since I was the eldest and Dad had his troubles
with work and everything, I took over raising my siblings
and trying to help keep them straight. The friends I hung
around with tended to be carousers and quit school. School
was something I intended finishing, so I stuck it out. I did
well in classes that I liked and the others I didn't do as
well at, but that seems to be a pattern a lot of people
have followed.

Holding the family together didn't work out as well as
I would have liked. My sister ran away from home in her
sophomore year in high school, and that left only my little
brother and myself at home. In my later years in high
school, I started looking for what I might want to do as

an adult, with the industrial arts having a lot of appeal. I probably did more shop projects in one year than most students did in four. That was the time that I learned most of my skills were in my hands.

One of my friends was in the Marine Reserve while in high school, and that also looked like an interesting proposition. I spent a year and half in the reserve, which helped give me some military background and experience. But the Marines wasn't where I wanted to go. But before I could go anywhere I had to graduate.

When it came time to graduate, I had some problems getting my diploma. When I went to pick up my actual diploma after the graduation exercise, my English teacher was there and refused to let me have my graduation certificate. She said that I owed her a book report and couldn't have my diploma until she received it. The words I gave her right then probably couldn't have been made into a report, but I walked out and didn't look back.

A couple of my uncles were in the Navy, the Air Force, and the Army, so the military looked good as a career a few weeks after high school was over. Out of all of the services, it was the Navy that held the most appeal for me—I had always liked the water—so that was the recruiter I spoke to.

The trouble was that the Navy wanted you to have a high school diploma or equivalent. Back to school I went. The people there told me I had received my diploma, so I told them the story about my English teacher and her book report. My shop teacher heard about what was going on and took a hand in events. He was the same man who made sure that I attended graduation and supported me more than anyone else in that school. Looking in the school safe, my shop teacher found my diploma and saw to it that it made its way into my hands. Now with my diploma and the enlisted forms filled out, I was on my way into the Navy in 1958 at the ripe old age of nineteen.

My mother by that time had remarried, and her husband was in the Navy, stationed out of Charleston, South Carolina. That looked like the best place for my brother to be with me gone. So I sent him on his way, made my goodbyes, and soon arrived at Great Lakes Training Center, north of Chicago.

My experience in the Marine Reserve served me well while at Great Lakes. It wasn't long before I was appointed recruit chief petty officer, the company commander of my recruit company. At that time, I could only swim a little bit, dog-paddle really. Where I was raised, we used to swim in the rock quarries and ponds mostly, the YMCA sometimes. The Navy saw to it I learned more swimming while at boot camp, but nothing compared to what I would do later.

There were about 2,500 men in my graduating class at boot camp, and I was chosen to receive the American Spirit Honor Medal for my standing in the class. That was a big bronze medal with a blue ribbon that they gave the top man in his class. You had to get in front of everybody to receive the medal and it was handed to you by an admiral, so that became my first real taste of leadership and the recognition that could come with it.

After boot camp, I had three choices as to what I wanted to be. The first was a dental technician, the second hospital corpsman, and the third was also in the medical field as I remember. My second choice looked the best to the Navy, so I found myself still at Great Lakes at the corpsman school there.

The first few weeks of school wasn't bad, until I learned about brushing the teeth of bed patients and the pleasures of bedpans. That was not for me, and I quickly started looking for another field of training. But switching from what was called a Class A school was not easy. The only way I finally made it out of corpsman school was that I had pulled a 98 average on my placement tests and the Navy decided to give me a break.

Sent to the West Coast, I was assigned to VA-212, an aviation attack squadron at Moffett Field, California, to become either a yeoman or personnel man. Now I was a black-shoe [Regular] Navy man in an Airdale [aircraft support] outfit and a West Coast puke to boot, but I didn't know that then. It wasn't long before the squadron deployed to the Far East. Aboard the aircraft carrier USS

Lexington, we did a cruise of the Pacific, and I saw Japan and some of the islands.

When promotion time came around, I told the board that I didn't want to be a yeoman. Changing my rate allowed me to get another stripe and I became a plane captain. A plane captain is assigned to an aircraft and the pilot who flies it. You help strap the pilot in for a flight, get him out of the plane afterwards, and help with the fueling and upkeep of the aircraft.

After we returned to the States I played around at being a plane captain for a while. Again, I was asked what I wanted to be in the Navy as a career and what school I wanted to go to. By now, I had some idea of what I wanted to do. Several of my buddies were electricians, so that was what I asked for. After putting in for aviation electricians school and being accepted, I was sent to Jacksonville, Florida, for training.

After graduating AE school, I was assigned to VP-30, a patrol outfit right at Jacksonville for training aircrew members. I learned to operate all the antisubmarine warfare [ASW] gear and received my aircrewman's wings. Fully qualified now, the Navy sent me to Brunswick, Maine, and VP-23, another patrol outfit.

Now I was up in cold country, and my first deployment put us up in Newfoundland. Things were cold, but I passed my tests for promotion and made third class. Our next cruise was down to warmer climates in the Caribbean at Puerto Rico and Gitmo—Guantanamo Bay, Cuba.

It was while we were at Guantanamo Bay that our plan of the day came out with the announcement that the Navy was looking for volunteers for UDT. "What's UDT?" I asked.

"That's the Navy frogmen," was the answer.

All of a sudden, the lights went off in my head. That's what I wanted to be in the Navy. With no question, it was with the UDT that I wanted to spend my Navy career. I had known about the frogmen from the Richard Widmark movie *The Frogmen* that had come out while I was in school. For nine cents, I had seen that movie at the theater in town, and it had stuck with me. The mechanics of what the men did and the challenging aspects of being underwater just thrilled me.

Putting in through the squadron, I volunteered for UDT training. In those days, one of the officers in your unit would give you the basic physical fitness test. I had stayed in shape and had always been somewhat athletic, so passing the physical wasn't any trouble for me. Even the swimming test—it was just a hundred yards—I passed readily, so the squadron sent my paperwork forward.

Now while in Gitmo, I started training myself for what lay ahead. Bits and pieces of what I could expect came to me from my shipmates, and I wanted to be ready. The second physical test was going to be a little more challenging, so I started running around the base in the tropical heat. Push-ups and calisthenics as well as hundreds of laps in the base pool were also on my daily list now.

The second physical fitness test was a lot harder. It was the test required by Little Creek before you could report for training. But my extra training paid off, and I passed that test as well. My orders came through and I was sent up to Little Creek, Virginia, and UDTR.

It was in late January 1962 that I arrived in time for Class 27 to begin training. A winter class at Little Creek is considered by some to be the hardest version of what is already the most difficult training in the Navy. I thought I was in pretty good shape, and the first week was mostly general indoctrination and straightforward physical training. The class started with around 140 or 150 men and we lost about a hundred men as the training went on.

It was during the third week of training that the class had the most men quit. That was Hell Week. As we came up to the weekend leading to the third week, it looked like hell was going to freeze over. It was snowing and cold. Our instructors came up to the doors of the barracks and said that Hell Week had been canceled and liberty was authorized for us. This sounded like great news, and most of us decided to leave the base.

There was one of several little bars just outside of Gate One that a number of us gathered at Saturday night. We were having a good time generally partying and talking.

Our class curfew was about 11:00 p.m. and we returned to our Quonset-hut barracks way back in the corner of the base. Some of the instructors were there, but we didn't think anything of that as we climbed into our bunks.

When midnight came around, so did our instructors. All hell broke loose as the instructors were shouting at us to get with it and start moving. Finally, it dawned on us what was happening as someone said, "This is Hell Week."

Unlike some of my other classmates, I didn't drink at all when we went out on liberty. Most of the guys were pretty cautious, as I remember, and nobody got very drunk that night before we went back to the barracks. But everyone sobered up fast as that cold night air hit us.

Hell Week was cold and a rough deal all around. The swimming in the cold ocean, crawling through the almost frozen mud flats, and running the obstacle course as the snow fell all added up to one long period of pure misery. The lack of sleep was bad, but it was the cold that I found the worst of all. Even though I was from Pennsylvania, the cold was very uncomfortable.

There would be times that we passed through the water and your pants legs, from above the knees on down, would freeze solid. You would have to break the ice around your knees just so that you could walk, and walking was like wearing two cardboard tubes around your legs. This was especially bad on the O-course where you had to climb over and around, under and through all of these different obstacles.

The only thing that didn't bother me a lot was the runs. It was years later at a SEAL reunion that Eve Barrett, who was one of my instructors, remembered me as one of the "jocks" of the class. Running along just two steps behind the instructors had proven to be a great asset while at UDT training.

But just running ability alone isn't enough to get you through Hell Week. What it really takes is determination and a proper mind-set. The word "quit" just wasn't in my vocabulary. I had no idea of what Hell Week was or how it would be, but the idea of quitting just never occurred to me.

The time (Hell Week) was rough, and the work was the toughest I ever did, but I just kept going. The harder they made it for us, the harder I worked. I was in the class because UDT was what I wanted and they weren't going to make me stop unless I died or just came apart along the way. Wondering when some particular piece of misery would stop or end passed through my head more than once. But it was the other students who quit and not me.

So Solly Day was the last day of Hell Week. Named after the Japanese faced by our forefathers in World War Two, So Solly Day was where the instructors tried to recreate the noise and confusion of a beach landing during wartime. As we crawled through the sand and the mud, explosive charges were going off all around us. The crash of the explosions just went right through you, rattling your teeth and bouncing you on the ground, but you had to keep moving ahead and doing what the instructors told you.

From the top of my knees down, my pants legs were completely torn away and my exposed legs were all bloody. A corpsman came up to me and wrapped my legs with gauze, then it was on with more of So Solly Day. The Death Trap was up and running for my class. This wonderful device was a pair of ropes hung one above the other and five feet or so apart, spanning a muddy pond between two poles. Students had to cross from one pole to the other while the instructors pulled and swung the lines and set off explosions in the water and all around. Every student had to cross the pond and nobody made it all of the way.

Finally, they led us up the beach and to a roaring fire to get warm. Hell Week was over and they jogged us back to the barracks. We applauded or cheered, whatever you were capable of doing. Right then just thinking straight was real hard work. As I've heard, all Hell Week stories are just about the same. There are variations on details but the long string of misery is a tie that binds all UDTR and BUD/S [Basic Underwater Demolition/SEAL] graduates together.

After Hell Week our real technical training began. The difficulties of Hell Week help UDTR and BUD/S to weed out those individuals who don't have the intestinal fortitude to make it to the Teams before the Navy spends a great deal of money on their training. For underwater swimmer training, my class went down to Roosevelt Roads, Puerto Rico.

Sunny and warm Roosey Roads was a real change from winter at Little Creek. Our physical training remained hard, but now we also learned the stuff that made UDT work so interesting and fun sometimes. I thought I had known how to swim before entering training, but the instructors showed me just how much I had yet to learn. Even back at Little Creek we had spent hours swimming in the pool. Pool evolutions included holding a bucket with your hands and just swimming with your legs, swimming while holding a towel in each hand, and swimming the length of the pool while holding a diver's weight belt in your hands. Lastly, you had to swim a mile in the pool, and then you were awarded your swim fins.

The swim fins we used then were the big solid-rubber ones known as "duck feet." I still have mine from that time, and they are much heavier and stiffer than anything you can find today. In Puerto Rico, we swam in the ocean, around in the dry-dock area, and then in open water. Distances grew, first a half mile, and then a mile, three miles, and so on until the final swim, between Puerto Rico and Vieques Island.

Bob Gallagher was one of our instructors, and he had an interesting way of measuring distance for our graduated swims. Wetting his finger and putting it into the air, Gallagher would announce, "That looks like about a mile and a half. Everybody out." At that announcement, the transport boat would stop, we would get out, and the swim to shore would begin, even though we would be out of sight of land. I think there may have been some leeway in Gallagher's measuring system. It seemed that for every half-mile swim we covered two miles, and for every three-mile swim we covered five miles.

Bob Gallagher, or the Eagle as he was known in the Teams, was one of my instructors along with others including Bernie Waddel, John Parrish, Casey, and Mr. Wilson as our officer in charge. My memories of Gallagher include his very short hair, rough character, foul mouth, and stature. The Eagle had thin runner's legs and he was always one of the guys who would take us out on runs and try to drive us into the ground. But distance runs we could do back at Little Creek. At Roosey Roads it was the swims and the water that were really important.

The distance between Puerto Rico and Vieques Island is only ten miles as the bird flies. But it is a much longer distance when you swim it in the water. The currents and tides work against you to hold you in one place no matter how hard you try. For myself and my swim buddy, that swim took twelve and a half hours. I saw the same tree in the same place for an hour and a half. The same rock on the bottom wouldn't be passed for an hour and a half. Even with fins on, the Vieques swim proved what real distance swimming meant and what it took.

Other water training was fun and I enjoyed it. Cast and recovery involves rolling off a rubber boat tied to the side of another, larger, boat while moving at high speed, and being snatched up from the water by sticking your arm through a rubber loop snare and being pulled back aboard that same rubber boat. Though I was beaten half to death by that rubber snare, cast and recovery training is what really made me feel like a frogman.

Arthur "One-Lump" Williams was the snare man for most of our cast and recovery training. One-Lump was an Army Special Forces trooper who came over to the UDT for cross-training. Later, One-Lump left the Army and joined the Navy to be an official member of the Teams.

After finishing demolition training at Roosey Roads, we returned to Little Creek for our final exercises and graduation. But even after graduating UDTR, we still had more training to do before being assigned to a Team. Now we went down to Fort Benning, Georgia, and Army jump school. Physically, jump school was a breeze for those of us fresh out of UDTR training. The distance runs and PT the airborne did was simple compared to the miles of sand runs and hours of PT we had already completed. We were in the best physical shape of our lives, and it felt pretty good.

In spite of the physical ease of jump school, there were some aspects of training that made me apprehensive. Long before we jumped out of a plane, we had tower training that could be at heights of up to 250 feet above the ground. The low towers where we slid down a cable in a harness came first, and they were only about thirty feet off the ground. But that distance seemed plenty high for someone who had never been much off the ground before, someone like myself.

But I wasn't about to quit now, and I completed the jump training with the rest of my class. After the first couple of times jumping from the towers, the training became fun. The 250-foot tower was even invigorating, maybe a little challenging, but still fun. For some reason, the airborne instructors insisted on the UDT guys doing extra push-ups everywhere in training. While we waited in line, we did push-ups; after landing from a jump, we did push-ups. We were harassed constantly, and if it wasn't for our basic good natures, we might have had to take over the Fort Benning jump school.

My first drop off the 250-foot tower was memorable after I got over my initial apprehension. After I was released, I had looked about and it felt like I could see the whole United States from where I hung. Off in the distance was the patchwork colors of fields and forests, greens and browns and tans as far as you could see. And further away still, the haze of the horizon meeting the blue sky. And all of this was only from about two hundred feet up! I never even felt myself hit the ground on my first real parachute landing fall [PLF]. But I jumped up ready to do it again.

One of the guys in our jump stick had a lot more trouble than I did with the 250-foot tower. The wind shifted after I had dropped and one of our guys drifted over and became hung up in the tower itself. He was all right, just banged up his leg a bit. But he did have to hang there, tangled in the girders, until the instructors could climb up and get him down.

Later it was time to stand in the door on my first parachute flight. Jumping from one of the old twin-tailed Flying Boxcars, I was back in the middle of the stick. It was "Stand up, hook up, check equipment, and stand in the door." Before we could jump, the order came out that the wind was too high and the jump was canceled.

The next day, we prepared for our first jump again. The difference this time was that I was the first man in the stick. When the order came to stand in the door, I was the guy doing the standing. On my first jump, I had to stand there with my hands on the sides of the door until the jumpmaster said "Go."

Everything was moving fast, the wind rushing past tugging at me as I waited for the order. Most of the time, they say your first jump will be a night jump, you'll parachute in the dark. It won't be that the jump will actually be made at night, you'll just have your eyes closed for the whole thing. I can't really say if I did or did not do the jump with my eyes closed. I do remember looking up at the opening shock and seeing the full canopy. But I did not close my eyes while standing in the door. That ground looked a far distance away, and I was concerned that all of my equipment worked correctly. But I did the jump and everything was fine.

Hitting the ground, I rolled to a stop and was thinking, Wow, that was great! Then things became busy as the other guys started to land and I had to roll up my chute and continue the training. The rest of the jumps were nothing special, and I completed them without incident. But that first one is something that sticks in my memory to this day.

From jump school it was on to dive school in Key West, Florida. Here again, we were in great physical condition and the PT and runs were nothing to us. The underwater training was great, and I really learned a lot. In the mixed-gas course, rolling the bottles to help mix the gas prior to a dive stands out. In those days, when you calculated out your gas mix, you would fill the bottles—tanks—under supervision and then roll the bottles around the floor to ensure an even mix. Also diving on a wreck at eighty or 120 feet was a high point in the training.

My first time deep underwater was also my first real look underwater. Equalizing my ears against the pressure was something I had to learn, but that wasn't any problem. Looking up, I could see the surface of the water shining, rippling from the waves passing. Of course, with the systems we were using, there weren't any bubbles being released to betray our position. So everything was calm.

Scuba diving was different. Releasing the bubbles as you breathed the air was noisy. We had big aluminum bottles that were filled to three thousand pounds pressure so we could stay down a long time. On some of the deeper, longer dives, we did decompression stops to allow the nitrogen dissolved in our blood to escape through our lungs safely.

We may have been the last class to use the LCPRs, Landing Craft, Personnel, Reconnaissance. These were the wooden Higgins boats that the UDTs had been using since World War Two. The boats had a small bow ramp you could enter the water by and were real convenient to use. But the last LCPR had been built at the end of World War Two and the ones we had were showing their age.

The dives in general were interesting, especially closer in to shore where you could see things on the bottom and watch lobsters move about. On our first night dive, the thing that stood out most to me at first was the fluorescence of the water. The glowing of the water every time you moved looked like a comet tail following your hand. By this time, I was so at ease underwater that the dive itself was just another job to do. I never did run into anything underwater that might have bothered me, so I just continued on.

Finally, we were done with all of our basic training. Out of the huge number of men who began back in January, in May of 1962, something over forty-five enlisted men and officers graduated UDTR and entered the Teams. Most of the guys were assigned to the two local UDTs, UDT 21 and UDT 22. For myself and several others, we found ourselves assigned to some kind of new unit called the SEALs.

But it was some time before we arrived at our new assignment. While we were still in training, we all expected to be assigned to either UDT 21 or 22 after graduation. After the graduation ceremony itself on a Friday at Little Creek, most of the class received their orders and reported to UDT 21 or 22. By the end of the day, there were five of us left who hadn't received any orders at all.

The guy who gave out the orders had just come in the barracks and started calling out names. "So and so," he said, "report Monday to UDT 21." As the individuals called came up and picked up a copy of their orders, another name would be called and the actions repeated. Finally, everyone's name had been called but the five of us, Jim Wallace, Pierre Birtz, Melvin Melochick, myself, and one of the officers, Ensign William Painter.

"What about us?" we asked.

"We don't have any orders for you. Maybe they just didn't go through yet or have been misplaced. Just stay available until they come through."

This wasn't any real reason for concern. We had gotten to where we were supposed to be, we had graduated UDTR, and the Navy has lost paperwork before and probably will again. But on Monday, when everyone else had reported to their new assignments, still no paperwork had come in for us yet. To move things along, we decided to go over to UDTs 21 and 22 to see if our orders were there by mistake.

We were all just as green as grass. None of us had any idea about who to ask, where at the Teams to go, or anything. When we finally found the personnel who were in charge of such things, we got the same answer at both Teams. "We don't have any orders for you guys," was what we were told. "You might as well go back to the barracks and stay there until someone tells you something."

These were directions we could follow, but they didn't sit very well. Monday went by, and then Tuesday, Wednesday, all week went by. Apparently we were lost in the system. Every day we would go over to the Teams, and every day they wouldn't have any orders for us. It was an easy time. We just hung out in the barracks and Mr. Painter was over in the BOQ, but we were starting to become concerned about what was in store for us.

After a week had gone by, some guy just came into the barracks and told us, "Okay, you guys report to the SEAL Team."

What in the world was a SEAL Team? The SEALs were a top-secret organization and were only a few months old at that time. None of us had ever heard of them. "Where are they?" we asked.

"Right across the grinder [exercise yard] from the chow hall. Those buildings down there, that's the SEAL Team."

That was how we learned of the SEAL Teams. After we arrived at the Team, things followed a pretty normal chain of events as they would have at the UDTs. First we were checked in, assigned our operating gear and a locker to put it in. Then we were introduced to the other guys in the Team. Then we were assigned to a department for our everyday work.

For myself, I was assigned to work with Claudius "Kraut" Kratky. Kratky did work with the radios and intelligence as well as cartography. Since I had some mechanical drawing and cartography experience, drawing underwater gradients earlier in training, as well as my mechanical ability, which helped with the cameras we used in Intelligence, it seemed like a good department for me to be in.

It wasn't very long before I did make it over to UDT 21. The draftsman running the UDT 21 chart shop was William "Fat Rat" Sutherland, and I was introduced to him as a man who would help me learn to draw up the underwater beach charts that were so much a part of both UDT and SEAL operations. Fat Rat and I did some projects together, and the department's work soon settled into a routine.

But I still hadn't found out just who the SEALs were and what they did that was different from the UDTs. No one explained things to me, and I was too new to know who or even how to ask. Besides, I wasn't given the time to wonder about what was going on. Almost immediately after settling in at the SEAL Team, I was sent off to schools.

As far as catching any ribbing from the guys in the Team for being so new, that just didn't happen. There was no "new guy" harassment that I can recall. You had passed training and were assigned to the SEALs; that made you one of the guys immediately. Outside of good-natured fun on birthdays and whatever, and the occasional practical joke, you were just accepted. Possibly it was due to the fact that SEAL Team Two was only a few months old and everyone was still new. That and we were all so busy that no one had time to give me any grief.

There was a lot of talk about Bob Gallagher coming over to the SEAL Team. Gallagher had been one of my instructors, so I knew who he was, but that was about all. Apparently, he was on deployment at first and otherwise floating around at UDT. What was taking so long was that the UDT didn't want to let him go. But finally, Gallagher showed up at SEAL Team Two. He had a lot of buddies already in Team Two who were very glad to see him when he finally did arrive.

Immediately, Gallagher fell right into working at the Team. Being an old-timer, Gallagher already had an assignment and duties to perform. He was off and running, not like those of us who had come into the Team directly from UDTR. For us, the first two years at Team Two were spent going and coming from one service school to another.

It wasn't long after my arriving at what would be my home in the Navy, I found myself back with the Army. The first service school I was sent to was HALO [high altitude, low opening] school at Fort Benning, where I was taught free-fall parachuting.

My class was only the second group from SEAL Team Two to go to HALO school. The first group had gone to the school soon after the SEALs were commissioned to check it out for possible use by the Team. The decision was then made to add the HALO school to the regular SEAL training curriculum.

Since the SEALs were so new, the Navy wanted to learn just what our capabilities could be. This was something we also wanted to know ourselves. As parachuting was going to be a primary means of infiltrating a target area, we also needed to know which planes we could use to take us into a drop. All of these questions resulted in my HALO class jumping from almost anything that could fly and you could fit in a man with a parachute on his back.

The regular HALO training jumped from different Army and Air Force aircraft. In addition to those, we also jumped from all types of Navy aircraft; the P2-V Neptune antisubmarine craft that I was already familiar with, the S2-D Tracker, the A3-B Skywarrior twin-engine jet, and all kinds of helicopters were only a few that I remember. These aircraft each had their own peculiarities and we had to learn them in order to jump from them safely.

The ones that were the most challenging and thrilled me the most were the P2-V Neptune and the A3-B Sky-warrior. The P2-V only had one way a jumper could leave the craft while in flight. Back in the tail section of the Neptune was a square scuttle hole, about two feet wide by three feet long, that you could open in flight. To jump, you sat on the edge of the open hole, pulled your head down tight, and tumbled through the hole. If you didn't pull yourself in tight enough while leaning down through the hole, your parachute pack could hit the far edge of the hole and hang you up for a minute.

The A3-B Skywarrior was a lot of fun and almost as challenging as the Neptune. The pilot and copilot in the A3-B sit side by side to each other. Between the two seats was a chute that led out the bottom of the aircraft. To jump, you would sit between the pilot and copilot, slide down the chute, and be gone.

The HALO jumps were a lot different from the static line jumps we had made in regular jump school. Well before we jumped, we had to learn all of the different kinds of maneuvers you could do while falling through the air. To practice and learn these kinds of moves, you would lay down on a narrow table with your arms and legs hanging free. You'd lift and hold your arms and legs as well as arch your back in the proper position to remain stable while falling. By turning to one side or the other and moving your arms and legs, you also learned how to turn or control and get out of a spin or tumble.

Table work can be difficult for some—you have to hold your arms and legs up for such a long time. But for those of us from the Teams, the physical part of training wasn't very hard at all. The nomenclature and classroom work were relatively easy for me at least. Free-falling on your first jump could hold a little apprehension, but you quickly got over that and realized that you were coming as close to flying as a human is able.

As you develop skills while free-falling, they drop you out of the plane at higher and higher altitudes. At least one jump at the school is to be made at 21,000 feet, almost four miles up. The high altitude gives you well over a minute of free-falling and you can work all of the techniques they teach at the HALO school. Of course, the higher you go, the longer your free fall.

There were dangers involved with HALO jumps that were unique to the altitudes we were working at. Most of the jumps we made were at such high altitudes the air pressure was so low that you couldn't get enough oxygen to keep from passing out. To eliminate this problem, we would use a large oxygen tank in the plane while preparing to jump and switch to a smaller personal oxygen bottle on the jump itself.

The proper use of oxygen while the plane was depressurized and on the jump itself was part of the training that we received at HALO school. Working with breathing mixtures was nothing new to us—we had more than a little experience with that while in dive training. But even the most experienced UDT or SEAL can still get into trouble.

On one jump, Jim Finley was going to be the first man out in the stick. There was the four or six of us in the stick as well as the pilot and copilot on board the aircraft. Seats for the jumpers lined the walls of the plane, and there was a chute in the floor for exiting. The seats faced the chute—if you stood up and took a step, you would fall right through the opening. The chute itself led aft from up between the pilots' seats. Finley was sitting on the deck, facing aft and hanging his legs down the chute. One man was behind Finley, sitting between the pilots' seats, and would be the next man out of the plane. The rest of us would tumble into the chute, landing on our backs and sliding down the chute on our parachute packs. Once we had left the plane, we would then orient ourselves and join up on the free fall.

For some reason, Jim Finley went off oxygen. It may have been he just made a mistake or that his equipment failed for some reason. But whatever it was, Finley went into convulsions from oxygen deprivation.

We had to grab Finley and hold him down while he was thrashing about. If he had managed to fall through the hatch, Jim probably would have never regained consciousness before hitting the ground.

Besides the obvious problem with trying to control someone having convulsions in the crowded confines of an aircraft, we had a little more to contend with. Jim Finley is not a little man to begin with, and we were all in very good physical condition. This made hanging on to Finley to keep him from hurting himself, or us, a lot more work than it may have been with someone else. But the guys controlled Finley and got oxygen running back to him again without much incident.

One of the weird things about oxygen deprivation is that after you regain consciousness, you go right back to what you were doing without even noticing that anything took place. After we finally had him settled down, it took us a minute to convince Finley as to just what had happened. After everything was over, Jim was just as surprised about what had happened as the rest of us.

Jumping from high-speed military aircraft has an interesting situation that you experience right after you leave the plane. You actually have to slow down before you can fall. These planes are moving fast, and you're going right along with them. When you exit, you're still moving at the same speed as the plane for a short distance. Zipping along at like 250 knots [about 287 miles per hour], you remain level and relative to the plane. Then after only a second or two, the plane snaps away, leaving you to your free fall. Then you become stabilized and oriented and move on to the target.

Man, can you see a long way off into the distance on a HALO jump! I had been impressed with just going up on the 250-foot tower back at jump school. Going out on a HALO jump was like reentry from orbit in comparison to the tower. You could see dozens of miles in all directions. The horizon was even a little curved on the higher jumps. Way out in the distance, you could see the target, a tiny white cross, on the ground in the drop zone. On the free fall, you would practice how to track and maneuver, literally gliding across the sky just by moving your arms and legs.

Some of the guys from the Team who were at the school with me were already very experienced with free-falling and had been skydivers for years. Bill Goines, Stan Janecka, and Frank Moncrief had hundreds of free falls between them. In addition to what our Army instructors showed us, the guys from the Teams also taught us a lot. We would do little maneuvers and play around on a jump, like touch hands, do somersaults, fly figure eights, and generally add to the learning process.

At the school, one of the many safety rules they had was that we were not allowed to jump through clouds. Passing through a cloud obscures your vision of the target area and can cause you to come down far from the LZ along with having other dangers. For our highest jump at HALO school we had Navy pilots flying us in one of the jets and we passed close by a cloud bank.

"Looks like we won't make this jump," somebody said. "There's clouds."

This was going to be our highest jump on record at the school, and the thought of having to delay it was disappointing. But looking out the window, sure enough, all you could see was clouds.

"Look out the other window," somebody said.

Out the window on the other side of the jet was nothing but blue sky. The jet went into a hard right turn and we climbed into the clear sky for our jump. The school had put a limit on high-altitude jumps to not over something like 23,000 feet, but one of the guys in our stick bargained with the pilot to move us to a higher altitude.

The jet was moving so fast that we could climb ten thousand feet in only a few seconds. That was the argument that was put forward to the pilots, and it worked. In moments we were at 34,000 feet, over six miles up, and we quickly exited the plane.

The fall itself was great. Jumping from that altitude, we could safely fall for something like two minutes and fifteen seconds. All during that long drop, you could see for miles and move all over the sky. Tracking from one point to another just involved moving your arms a bit and you would scoot through the air.

At the Teams during an operation, we would use a HALO drop to exit a plane well above normal detection or antiaircraft range and use our free-fall techniques to hit a landing zone miles from our exit point. But while learning at the HALO school, the serious nature of what we were learning sometimes just took a backseat to the exhilaration and sheer fun of the free fall. Our high-altitude jump was one of those.

Of course, our jump logs do not show us exiting the plane at 34,000 feet. Because of the "paperwork" limit put on your highest jump at the school, we logged the jump as only 23,000 feet. Soon after the record jump, we returned to Little Creek. But we kept up our jump qualifications, and a number of the guys had a local skydiving club where you could continue using the free-fall techniques from HALO school while just having a good time.

After HALO school, I went to a number of smaller schools and signed up for some that I never managed to attend. Most of SEAL Team Two went down to Fort Bragg and attended kitchen demolitions school, where you learned how to make all kinds of destructive devices from household materials. Though I had completed the paperwork for kitchen demolitions, the time for me to go to the school never managed to be available.

There were other demolitions that I learned while at the SEAL Team that were considerably different from those they taught us in UDTR. Though I was never fully qualified to use it, I was one of the SEALs familiarized with the SADAM or Small Atomic Demolition Munition, a backpack A-bomb.

All I was really taught about the SADAM involved familiarization with what the device did and how we would use it. Though they did bring a training device into the classroom, I was never exposed to the real bomb. A number of students from the class were later given advanced training where they learned how to arm the weapon and emplace it. Mostly for us, we were shown what it was and how we would carry it around. It should have been more impressive than it was, but for me at the time it was just another class.

Radio school was the next training school for me. We already had SEALs in the Team who could run the radios and communicate a number of different ways using voice or code. Jack Rowell was one of the guys from the Team at radio school. Jack knew Morse code very well, could type quickly and accurately, and could run any of the radios we might use. Though Jack tried to teach radio skills to the rest of us, it always seemed that we ended up turning the cranks on the generator while Jack did the radio work.

Probably one of the most rigorous, and certainly one of the most uncomfortable, schools I went to was the arctic survival course that was taught up in Canada. Sam Fournier, John Dearmon, and myself went up to Edmonton, Alberta, right in the middle of western Canada, arriving in the late fall of 1963.

The arctic survival school was run by the Canadian military for their own pilots and crewmembers. With the huge area of northern Canada that was covered with ice and snow the instructors at the school had a great deal of knowledge about just what it took to survive in such a naturally hostile environment. The actual school was located west of Edmonton at Jasper Lake in what is now Jasper National Park.

There were about twenty-five students in the class, including the three of us from SEAL Team Two. During the first three days of the course we lived in a twenty-by-twenty-foot-square hut with four-foot-high walls and a parachute-canopy roof. For those three days we were each issued a ration package holding three Canadian C rations. The ration pack was to last us the whole three days, one meal a day. That was intended to get us used to a survival situation right from the beginning of the course.

After only a few days of our arrival at the survival school, we found ourselves in less comfortable living conditions. For myself, I found the school to be a learning experience but not a real challenge. The challenge of the training would have been even less if the instructors had allowed those of us from SEAL Team Two to stay together. Instead of working with our Teammates, we found ourselves assigned to a group of seven or so Royal Canadian officers and men.

After we were assigned to groups, we were sent out to face the real survival situation. The weather was deteriorating. It started cold with a little snow around, but soon it started snowing for real. With no weapons but a pocket-knife and no food, we learned to live off the land. If you were smart enough, you had saved some of the three ration packs to take with you on the course. If not, you became hungry fast.

For myself, I had only saved a few small items from the ration packs, some small candy packets of gumdrops and things of that nature. All we had to do was survive, and the instructors gave us the information we needed to do it.

But not everything you need in order to survive in the wild can be taught. A certain mind-set has to be learned quickly if you didn't bring it with you. For those of us from the Team, we already knew how to keep going through almost anything without giving a thought to quitting. For some of those Canadian officers, that was something they had yet to learn.

We had been given a piece of parachute cloth among other materials. The instructors showed us how to build a little lean-to for shelter where you had to do little more than chop and stack small trees. As far as the rest of the course went, the rules were simple. You were supposed to survive in the wild, and you could eat as much food as you could find or kill. There wasn't an enemy to evade, just nature to contend with. And Mother Nature can be a very cranky lady to deal with.

During that course, game was more than a bit scarce. I didn't see so much as a bird. But just in case there was something around that we couldn't see, the instructors showed us how to make snares and deadfalls to trap what game there was.

We had been paired up to run the course, and I had a small Canadian I had been teamed with. Using a backstop, we had built a fire facing our lean-to to keep us warm. And staying warm became a problem. During some of the nights, it became cold, very cold. The instructors told us that it had gotten to seventy degrees below zero, far colder than anything I had felt while back home in Pennsylvania.

From what I had learned in the Teams, traveling light is the way to move best through any terrain. Back when the school first issued clothing and equipment for the course, I refused most of the mountain of gear that was piled in front of me. The guy issuing the gear told me flat out that I would need everything that they were giving me. Even though I had said no, the instructors had seen to it that I accepted everything that was issued to me. And when the temperature dropped, I was wearing every piece of clothing I had been given.

When the cold hit, the thermal underwear, extra clothes, socks, boots, and mitts went on. Everything I had was wrapped around me, and I would have taken more if it was available. The cold was intense and the area very quiet. Everything was frozen and would break at a touch.

That was the first time I ever snuggled up to a guy to keep warm. We had an air mattress to sleep on, insulating us from the cold ground. And when your air mattress got cold, you had better get up and knock the ice crystals off of it that had formed or you would just get colder and colder. In the mukluk boots we had been given was a nylon mesh screen. When you felt your feet getting cold, you had to immediately stop, take out that screen, and knock the ice crystals off of it. The cold would cause the sweat from your feet to freeze on the mesh.

The instructors told us that you had to clean off the mesh as soon as your feet started to feel cold. If you didn't do what they said, within three to five minutes of the cold feeling, you were in danger of getting frostbite on your feet.

We chopped trees down to make firewood with the small hatchet they had issued us. Cutting wood normally wouldn't be a problem, but that is also when you're well-fed and warm. It took me forty-five minutes to cut down a three-inch tree. The reason was simple and probably comical to watch. In five swings, you would hit the tree probably once, fall down four times, get up and look for the tree again, and then give it another swing. Between the cold and lack of food, your equilibrium was just about gone, and on top of that, the tree would be frozen rock-hard.

Moving through the area, I had found some berries on a bush near a stream that tasted pretty good. It wasn't until years later that I learned the berries had been rose hips and were a great source of vitamins, especially vitamin C. But besides gathering all of the berries I could find, a meal was very hard to come by.

On the last day of the course, the survival game was played out with you being "found" by a search aircraft. You were supposed to signal the plane with a mirror, and then they would drop a parachute with a small container of groceries. The bag didn't hold much more than a few onions, potatoes, and some bread, but that was more than welcome. Of course, our parachute decided to make us work for our package.

Our supply drop landed in a tree, and not one of the smaller ones but one of the great big trees. This is when I really learned that most of the Canadians didn't have the mental attitude necessary for survival. Instead of doing something, the guys I was with just stood around or gave up entirely.

While the other guys were asking, "What are we going to do? How are we going to get that?" I had my answer ready: "I don't know about you guys, but I'm going to get some groceries."

Finding a small piece of line or rope, I went up to the tree, put my arms around it slinging the rope between them, and started climbing the tree. I could barely get my arms around the tree even with the rope and had to climb up about sixty or seventy feet. Grabbing up the little parachute and freeing it, I threw it down to the guys on the ground. That was when I learned the rest of my survival lesson.

Those guys were on that bag like vultures when it hit the ground. I was lucky anything was left by the time I got to the ground, but there hadn't been that much to start with. With the few potatoes and onions in the bag, we made up a little stew and managed to have a hot meal.

For everything I went through in that school, it wasn't any of the training that stands out the most in my mind. It was November 22 and I was walking down the road, wrapped up like a mummy against the cold. A group of instructors drove up to me, which wasn't very unusual, since they kept a reasonable eye on us while we were out in the field. But what they had to say wasn't usual at all. The instructors told me that my President had been shot.

That was how we found out about President Kennedy's assassination. Though I wasn't with them I assume the instructors went to the other areas and told my Teammates what had happened. Everything was just kind of numb after that. Wasn't long before we graduated and were sent back to Little Creek. That was when we learned that the entire Team had been put on alert in case the assassination had been part of a plot to overthrow the government. But there wasn't any plot that anyone found, no coup took place, and things finally calmed down. But the world and the Team were never exactly the same after that.

Judo and instructor school was next for me, at Stead Air Force Base. Hand-to-hand combat was something that was considered a necessary skill at SEAL Team Two, and judo was the martial art decided on during our earliest years. By the time the Vietnam commitment came around, judo school was dropped from the classes you had to attend in order to be qualified to operate. Today, other martial arts are taught in the Teams.

Probably the most physically and mentally challenging course I had to take, next to UDTR, was the Marine E&E (escape and evasion) course taught at Pickle Meadows in California. Officially, the course is given at the U.S. Marine Corps Cold Weather Training Facility at Bridgeport, California, just twelve miles or so north-northeast of Yosemite National Park. But to just about everyone in the service, that notorious school was known as Pickle Meadows. UDTR was hard, and I had been hurt during the course, but that was only raw skin and sores. Pickle Meadows sent me home with broken ribs.

The Marine school had you learn survival techniques and then use them out in the open, much like what I had already done in the Canadian arctic survival school. But the Marines also exposed you to what it was like to evade an enemy force intent on capturing you. And when they did capture you, you got a taste of what life might be like in a POW camp.

Ron Fox, Tom Murphy, and Gordy Ablitt were with me from Team Two for the course. The three of us were out in the field, surviving separately from the other students in the class. There was a large tree that had fallen over that must have been five or six feet in diameter. The bark was coming loose from the tree trunk, so we peeled it off and stacked it around the trunk, making a kind of lean-to shelter.

For food, we foraged off the land, fishing in the small streams and whatever. Food could be found in small quantities—four- and five-inch fish will feed you but they don't make much of a meal. There were deer and antelope around, but they were much too far away for us to get, even with the homemade bows and arrows some of the guys had turned out. We spotted a large chunk of meat ambling by in the form of a porcupine, but he climbed up a tree before any of us could catch him. We spotted the spiny little critter up in the tree and determined to have him for lunch.

This time, I had something of a weapon to use on the course that extended my reach a bit. I had carved up a piece of wood earlier and, with the use of some rubber surgical tubing, made myself a serviceable slingshot. Using old .45 pistol bullets as ammunition, I was a pretty good shot with my slingshot and opened up on that porcupine, hoping to nail him and knock him out of the tree.

Those quills on a porcupine are hard as well as being sharp. All my slingshot did was bounce pellets off that porky. Nothing we could do would bring that porcupine out of the tree. Finally, I just went up the tree after him. For some reason, I kept ending up climbing trees in survival school when going after the groceries. But this "bag" wasn't going to be tossed from the tree by my grabbing him. After I managed to knock the porcupine from the tree with a stick, the guys on the ground made short work of him with a stick or two of their own.

Skinning out that porky, we had meat in a reasonable amount now. In our scrounging around, we had found where someone had buried some C rations, and the salt and pepper packets hadn't deteriorated. Some old stovepipe made a burner and a rusty can served as a pot. Along with our condiments, we found wild onions, wild dandelions, and already had our fish. With those ingredients, we must have cooked up about five gallons of soup. And with the single tea bag we had, I think we brewed up about five gallons of what may have passed for tea, if you didn't know what tea was supposed to be like.

Some of the parts of the porcupine, like the liver and other delicacies, we buried in the snow for later use. Ron Fox swore that he was never going to eat that stuff, but three days later hunger had managed to change his mind. As for the porcupine itself, they taste just like the pine bark that they live on. Turpentine-flavored meat, yum.

Later in the course, we were captured by the enemy and found ourselves in the prisoner of war camp. The POW camp at Pickle Meadows was more than a little realistic.

In UDTR, one of the things that could help you keep going was the knowledge that the instructors weren't out to actually kill you. At the Pickle Meadows camp, you weren't sure about that fact almost from the start.

The guards stripped our clothes from us and put us into metal sheds. Taking us from the sheds one or two at a time, the guards would interrogate us. Simple questions would be asked, such as what your name was, but you weren't supposed to answer at all. My memories of that time don't include much recollection of what happened to the other "prisoners." Mostly, my mind was concerned with keeping itself stable mentally and just getting through the ordeal without breaking.

All we had on was our skivvy shorts, and it was cold. There was snow on the ground, and a small moving stream of water went through the camp. A dam had built up a small pond, not much more than a puddle really, inside the camp. The guards threw me down by the pond and questioned me enthusiastically. When I continued to refuse to tell the guards what they wanted to know, they stood on my head and held it under the water.

The water wasn't able to force me to tell the guards what they wanted to know. Now they started kicking me in the ribs, and that was when several of my ribs were broken.

From my little interrogation session, I remember being hauled up and dragged back to a little wooden box. This wasn't as comfortable as the bare metal shed I had been in earlier, this was a small box without the room to lie down or stand up in. All I could do was sort of crouch there crammed in the box with my knees in my face, feeling the cold and hearing all kinds of noises around me.

While I was entertaining myself by wiggling my toes and elbows and moving my eyelids—there wasn't room for anything else—the guards remembered me and brought me out to play again. More questions were asked along the lines of what was my name and rank. But just that one period of being kicked around and shoved in the box was the worst that happened to me. The guards also had the other prisoners to interrogate.

One of the guys with us from SEAL Team Two was J. C. Tipton. Along with the pond and the box, one of the other little interrogation techniques the guards had was two fifty-five-gallon oil drums welded end to end and buried in the ground. Filled up with water, the drums were known as the tank.

With his arms and legs secured, Tipton was lowered into the tank headfirst. Tip wasn't about to break, and the guards had some experience with SEALs by this time. They left Tipton in that tank for so long that he damn near drowned. They finally dragged him up from the tank with his lungs filling with water. They worked on Tip for a while and got him breathing again, but I learned later that it may have been a close thing whether or not he was going to make it.

When I had heard about what the instructors had done to Tip it shook me up pretty badly. Other prisoners had been put in the tank, but most of those were in right side up. Those guys could grab the grating over the top of the tank and just push their nose out of the water. The guards would step on their fingers and drive them back into the water, but at least they could breathe now and then. Tip was put into the tank upside down. He never had a chance to breathe. The guards just waited until the bubbles stopped. Maybe they didn't realize how long a SEAL could hold his breath or they just misjudged the time. But that was a near thing and it could have been any one of us, including me.

One thing that I took away from that school, besides a couple of healing ribs, was a new hardness and determination. No one who ever took me prisoner would get anything from me. I had learned that you had to stay sharp. The only way to beat these guys would be to outfox or outmaneuver them. And that sort of thing would hold true anywhere in the world.

Captors would have had to kill me before I would have given anything out to them. Some of the guys from the Team who went to Pickle Meadows decided that they would never be captured, whether it would be to save their last grenade for themselves or whatever.

That idea seems pretty easy to just talk about but much harder to do in reality. But in the Teams in those days, it was even more special to be a SEAL than it is even now. Your adrenaline was pumping all of the time and everyone was gung-ho to get the job done no matter what it took. Each guy was his own person, whether he was a wild man who was always on the go or a quiet individual who would just keep going no matter what. Everyone did their job and worked together, backing one another up all of the time.

We worked so hard and long together that the Team became one big unit. Everyone thought the same thing together. When you were going up against a problem, the other guys who were with you would be thinking in the same mode that you were. This was totally different from anything else I had ever experienced, and the mutual support could let you face major obstacles and overcome them. You knew that if you were taken out of the race, your Teammates would keep going and complete the mission.

This attitude was what helped the guys from the Teams get through situations and schools like Pickle Meadows. Though it was very hard, the E&E school at Pickle Meadows was a good training experience. It exposed you to something that you would hopefully never experience for real, and it taught you what your limitations were. Sometimes even a SEAL has to be reminded that he is only flesh and blood.

Our training in UDTR, especially Hell Week, was a snap in comparison to some of what we experienced at E&E school. Hell Week had been a grind that tore at you, but you could see what was at the end of it and it taught you a lot about yourself. E&E school was different, it reminded you that you were mortal and that everyone had a breaking point. It was just what you were willing to do to keep from reaching that breaking point that you had to accept. And Hell Week had given each of us the determination to make it through anything, and that is what helped you get through E&E school.

There were other people taking the course along with us who weren't from the Teams. Some of the Air Force,

Navy, and Marine pilots didn't have the internal support that we had from being in the Teams. Even though some of those guys broke right away, I at least didn't have any contempt for them. Some of those guys broke almost immediately. It was amazing what the mind could do to you without anyone even touching you. A few of those men broke down almost into tears as they surrendered everything to the instructors. Those same people were consoled and led right away from the camp, just practically coming in one door and going out the other.

It would have been easy to lose track of reality in that POW camp and forget where and who you were. The light food and exposure of the evasion and survival phase made you more susceptible to what the guards were doing, and that was part of the training. Myself, I managed not to ever lose track of where I was and what I was doing. Even that time in the box, I knew what was going on around me from the sounds I could hear and what I could decipher.

That camp got to the point where it seemed you weren't in the United States anymore. Your mind would play tricks on you where you wondered if these guys were real or not. Was the camp just another military game or the real thing? It took concentration to remember that what we were experiencing was a school and that the instructors were there to teach us something about ourselves and how to survive what we could possibly expect to run into someday. And that was the most sobering thought of all.

For myself, I was never really in the Teams in the sense that most of the guys mean. After graduating UDTR, I hadn't gone into the UDT but went straight from training into the SEALs. SEAL Team Two was separate from the UDTs and we operated in a different environment with a different mission profile. This didn't make us any better than the UDTs, just different.

Without the experience of being in the UDTs, I never really had a mentor or "sea daddy" in the Teams. There were a number of men I looked up to in the SEALs, but during those busy early years, I didn't really develop any close relationship with anyone. There were friends of mine in the SEALs who I palled around with during our off-duty time. But I had never been a drinker and didn't take partying to the level of an art form like some of my Teammates did. During training classes away from Little Creek, any SEALs at the course would automatically try to team up together as I did. But I never did have any of the lifelong friendships come up that some of the other SEALs did over the years.

Individual SEALs stood out to me, such as Per Eric "Swede" Tornblum, who always struck me as different from the other guys. Another unusual SEAL was Bill Green, who struck me as being a bit drifty, as we would say in the Team. Today, I think I might just call Bill a space cadet. But he was qualified to operate and I would work with him automatically, just as I would with any other Teammate.

Other SEALs stood out for other reasons. Rudy Boesch, the chief of SEAL Team Two, always had impressed me. Always involved in the operations of the Team, Rudy seemed to be the most gung-ho and hardest-pushing man in the SEALs. I wasn't as close to Rudy as were some of the other guys who had come over from UDT with him. But Rudy always treated everyone fairly and equally.

The individuals who were in the SEALs were a wide and varied bunch. There were quiet ones and loud ones. But we were all Teammates together and would support each other no matter what. It was a relief, though, that some of the schools we attended weren't the gut-wrenching learning experiences that Pickle Meadows had been. Some of the training was just plain fun or had definite applications to life outside the Teams.

Along with Jim Watson, Swede Tornblum, Rudy Boesch, myself, and several other guys from Team Two, we all went to the Kiekhaefer Mercury Service Training Center to receive instruction in maintaining Mercury outboard motors. SEAL Team Two was developing a SEAL Team Assault Boat [STAB] from a Powercat Trimaran hull that mounted twin hundred-horsepower Mercury outboards. Since the boats would be uniquely ours, it was decided that we should be able to maintain the motors as well as the boats inside the Team itself. This school was a fun one, where we wore civilian clothes and were in a comfortable atmosphere. Also, working on an outboard motor would be handy in the civilian world as well as the Teams.

Sailboat school, taught at the U.S. Naval Academy in Annapolis, Maryland, was probably one of the most fun and truly old-Navy schools I ever attended. We had a good time in Annapolis, learning how to run with the wind on all kinds of small craft. Even when we ran aground, it wasn't too bad and was a good learning experience. Several of us learned that ''3 FT'' on an inland water chart meant three feet and not three fathoms [eighteen feet]. This difference is really important when the skeg on the bottom of your sailboat draws three feet of water.

Running aground just meant we lowered the sail, raised the skeg, got out of the boat, and pushed it into deeper water. There may have been a ghost or two of the old deep-water sailors who looked down at us with a bit of disapproval, but we learned from our mistakes. We became real sailors at that school. Just as men had done for centuries, we harnessed the wind to move us where we wanted to go. Or at least close to where we wanted to go most of the time.

For the five of us new guys who had come into the SEALs right out of training, we weren't able to relax and have quite as good a time at the schools as the older guys who had come into the SEALs from UDT. It wasn't that we didn't have our fun or that the older guys excluded us. It was more that we just didn't fit into the Team as well during its early years. The older guys were able to joke and carry on with each other, relaxing more and being at ease in the schools. At least for me, I was never able to fit into that picture as well.

The older operators had stories and experiences they could share with each other from their time in UDT. That sort of thing really helped draw the Team together. We were all Teammates, of course, we could listen to the bull sessions and enjoy the sea stories as much as anyone. We just didn't have much in the way of our own experiences to share yet. But each of us managed to make his mark at SEAL Team Two in one way or another.

Physical activity was always a big part of the Team's daily activities, and some of us kept things active even beyond the daily PT and runs. Melvin Melochick liked running on his spare time, and Jim Finley was into boxing, so he ran a lot to stay in shape. I just liked distance running, so the group of us would run every day, no matter what deployment or school we might be on. For myself, I ran about fifteen to seventeen miles per day with an average speed of five minutes per mile.

Besides the running, we also had a lot of sports we could get involved in. UDT at Little Creek was good with intramural sports, and tag, or touch, football was the most popular sport in the Teams. There were other sports, and I enjoyed soccer quite a bit. But we were competitive in all sports.

Trying out for the football team, I soon learned that there was a certain amount of favoritism as to who got to play. I was the "greenie," the new guy in the Teams, so I spent a lot of time on the bench during my first year. During the next season, I managed to play a few times, but still not a lot of time on the field. The third year, it was looking good for me to play with the team. In the first practice of the season, during the first play, I had my foot stepped on and broken. So much for my football career in the Teams.

The doctors put my foot in casts, but they didn't last long. Between PT and running every day, I put a lot of wear on those casts. In spite of the cast, I was still running every day, so about every third day, I would go over to the base hospital and have a new cast put on. Doing the runs with my cast on was tough, but it was also real good exercise.

What we all learned in training was that you didn't let things get to you. No matter what happened, you didn't quit. Little things were not allowed to hamper you. You learned to cope. If you were hurt, you kept going to the best of your ability.

That was why I still stayed interested in football and

got back on the team as soon as I could. By this time, I was one of the guys and would play along with the best of them. That year we won every game we played, went into the Atlantic Fleet playoffs, and were finally beaten once by another Navy team. Except for that one team, we tended to have pretty one-sided games. Scores of fifty-two to nothing, sixty-four to nothing, forty-eight to nothing were not uncommon for us. We were a tough team. Our touches tended to be a lot more like tackles.

Volleyball was also popular, and I played on Bob Gallagher's team. Again, we went into the fleet competitions in volleyball just as we had with football and a number of other sports. Track and field was also done as a base competition. Dashes, broad jumps, mile runs, and other events were something that I was good at and enjoyed. But training, deployments, and the different places you went to in the Teams was what really appealed to me more than anything else.

One of the places we had gone to a number of times for training and qualifications was St. Thomas, one of the Virgin Islands just east of Puerto Rico in the Caribbean. At St. Thomas, we would do more advanced underwater training and develop new equipment and techniques. Since we usually went down to St. Thomas during the winter months, it was also a good time and something of a vacation from the cold and wind of Little Creek.

In March of 1963, SEAL Team Two went down to St. Thomas on what was my first trip there. At least this training wouldn't be another cold-weather-survival course. This was a trip I had been looking forward to. All of the older guys had St. Thomas stories they had been telling, and now was a chance for me to develop a few of my own.

Partying at St. Thomas started when the first guy hit the beach. The uniform of the day was your swimming gear, tan swimming trunks and a T-shirt. That was how we fell in for the morning formation. At the formation, muster was called, and then we fell out for the morning run. Off we went, running around, down around the airport, and back to our starting point. The main town on St. Thomas is Charlotte Amalie, and we would go in there often. Swimming was the big Team operation while at St. Thomas, and we spent a lot of time in the clear, warm waters of the Caribbean.

There was one weekend in St. Thomas that stood out for all of the wrong reasons. SEAL Team Two wasn't the only Team down on the island training during the winter months of 1963. The UDTs had come down from Little Creek, and we were all using the island facilities both for training and our off-duty time. Guys from both Teams would often go down to the beach on Magens Bay for swimming and relaxing in the sun.

This one day, 20 April 1963, some of us were out in the water on just a fun dive. There wasn't anything particular about the dive itself that stands out, but when we surfaced, there was a great deal of commotion on the beach and all around us. We got the word from one of the people in a boat nearby that a UDT man had been attacked by a shark.

This was something that was very unusual and of more than a little concern to us. Nobody out on the water had any more information for us, but we soon got the story after we got back on shore. The story that was making the rounds was a fairly simple one, which usually means it's the truth.

Lieutenant John Walter Gibson from UDT 21 was out on a date with his girlfriend and they were both just having an easy time on the beach at Magens Bay. While his lady was laying down on the beach, Gibson was in the water having a swim. There was a floating platform out in the water and Gibson may have been swimming out toward the platform when the shark hit. Whatever his plans were, Gibson was in deep enough water that he couldn't touch bottom. The shark moved in on Gibson, and he may have tried to fend the attack off with his hand.

One thing that we're taught in the Teams is that a shark will normally leave you alone. If a shark gets curious enough, it may approach you underwater and things would start getting tense. If you smack a shark on the nose, they will almost always run away and you can just continue on with what you were doing. At least that's the theory, and enough divers have punched a shark over the years to prove the system works, most of the time.

Gibson may have been trying to use the punch routine with the shark that came up on him. If he did, it didn't work, and the shark bit off Gibson's left hand, high up on the wrist.

The shark came in again and attacked Gibson again, this time on the leg. When Gibson started yelling about the attack, he got the attention of his girlfriend, who came into the water to try and help him. While the lady was pulling on Gibson's arm, trying to get him in to shore, the shark attacked and bit off a large chunk of Gibson's leg.

Gibson finally was free of the shark and managed to get in to shore with his lady's help. But his wounds were far too serious, and before he could get any real medical attention, Lieutenant Gibson bled to death.

Immediately after the incident, the Team put together a crew to catch the shark. It didn't matter that Gibson was in UDT 21 and we were in the SEALs, we were all brothers and Teammates, and we were going to deal with something that had cost us one of our own. The question was, what were we going to do? Gathering up some big fishhooks, bait, and some fifty-five-gallon drums, we planned to string up a set line across the mouth of Magens Bay.

If the shark was still around, we might have a good chance of catching it. And we had gone into action within hours of the attack, so the shark was likely to still be in the bay. We laid out our set lines and things became a matter of waiting.

The barrels stayed up all night, and the next day we went out to see what we might have caught. Luck had been with us, and there was a shark hanging from one of the lines. Attaching our catch to the side of our boat, we brought the shark in to the UDT pier.

There wasn't much question that we had the right animal. We dragged the shark up onto the lower platform of the pier and somebody cut him open. Inside the shark was Gibson's ankle and hand. Not much more proof was necessary.

Somebody contacted one of the big museums back in

the States, and I believe that the Smithsonian Institution sent a scientist down to gather up the shark. What everyone wanted to know was how come this one shark decided to attack a swimmer. Later, we learned that the shark had been an older one and probably sick and hungry, which was why it attacked a swimmer. Shark attacks were pretty rare, and that was the only one I ever heard of happening to anyone in the Teams.

Years later, a picture and letter caught up with me from the governor of St. Thomas. The letter thanked me as one of the people from UDT 21 and 22 who hunted down the shark that attacked Gibson. The SEALs were still very classified then, so there was no mention of SEAL Team Two personnel in the letter. The letter was a nice touch, but outside of the loss of one of our own, there was very little lasting effect from the attack on the Teams.

Working in the water was something that we did every day. In the thousands of hours spent by the UDTs and SEALs in the water, this was the only shark attack on record. All of us received danger pay for the additional hazards that our duties exposed us to. Sharks were just something that came with the package. For myself, the action never fazed me.

On a lot of swims, we would run into schools of barracuda and sharks. You just accepted their existence as part of the environment. There was no "being afraid" to be concerned with. You kept an eye on whatever was around during a swim, and if it kept its distance, you just forgot about it. On some swims, I can remember seeing barracuda just off the tips of my fins behind me. Barracudas are a curious fish and are constantly opening their mouths. And a 'cuda is a fast fish with a really well-armed set of jaws. But none ever threatened us.

One time, during training at St. Thomas, I had some trouble with a shark. We had been working on lockouts from the submarine *Sealion*. Coming up to the surface, we were going to meet with our safety boats and climb aboard some rubber rafts that were waiting for us. Once on the rafts, the *Sealion* would snare a line between the rafts with its periscope and we would swim down and lock back in.

As we approached the surface, off in the distance we could see a group of sharks coming in.

Underwater, sharks will sometimes suddenly just appear, fading in from the blue-gray haze of the water and mostly fading out just as fast. This time, the shark didn't just fade away. First there was one shark, then another and another, finally a whole school of sharks were in the waters around us.

The sharks were keeping their distance, but for myself and some of the other guys, we were starting to get concerned. We reached our rafts without incident, but the sharks had started to become more aggressive. As the sharks were circling us, we climbed out into the rubber rafts and the safety boats nearby. Effectively, that pack of sharks chased us out of the water. I don't know how close the sharks got to us. As soon as the word was passed, I was out of the water and so were a number of the other guys. There wasn't any close encounter or direct contact with the sharks, but that situation was one to make your heart beat a little faster.

There was one guy in the UDTs who really had a thing for sharks. Scott Slaughter in UDT 21 hunted sharks on his own time whenever he had a chance. With his bang-stick, which would fire a 12-gauge shotgun shell when pushed against a target, Slaughter would free-dive, no scuba gear, as deep as 110 feet to kill sharks.

But for the most part, St. Thomas had proved itself to be everything the guys had said it was and more. On the weekends, your time was pretty much your own as long as there wasn't something planned on the training schedule. During my liberty time, I palled around with Arthur "One-Lump" Williams. One-Lump and I both liked to look around the island, especially in the waters offshore. We went out on a lot of sport dives, hunting for coral and artifacts. When one was available, we would check out a boat and move further offshore for our dives.

There was one weekend that One-Lump and I decided to check out the waters around the old submarine pier in front of the Grand Boco Hotel, a large building facing the bay. The pier extended out into Charlotte Amalie Bay, and the area had been featured in the Richard Widmark movie *The Frogmen* with a "Japanese sub base" drawn into the shoreline with special effects. We used the pier regularly for our boats, and when we weren't there, small cruise ships would tie up to the same location.

One-Lump and I were swimming off the dock out towards the channel that led to open water. On the bottom around the dock itself, we had found odds and ends, spoons, cups, and bottles, from either the ships or things that had just been dropped in the water over the years. Our big find was out from the dock in the direction of the channel.

About thirty or forty yards off the corner of the pier, on the side that faced our bachelor officers' quarters, I was swimming along and found a big anchor on the bottom. This was something a little bigger than a cup or spoon, and I swam back to where One-Lump was still diving around the dock.

"Hey, Lump," I said, "I just saw an anchor out there," and I waved my arm out off the end of the dock.

We got out on the dock and gathered up a rope that we could stretch between us. With our scuba gear on, we swam back out towards where I had seen the anchor, following along the bottom with the rope stretched between us. The idea was that the rope would snag on anything that was sticking up from the bottom. Most of the time, it isn't raising what you've found underwater that's the problem, it's finding the darn thing in the first place. I had spotted the anchor while just swimming along. Now we had to locate it again for recovery.

It wasn't long before the line had snagged on something. We had been using a good long piece of parachute cord, probably twenty or thirty feet of line, to drag the bottom. When the line stopped moving, I gave it a good pull to make sure it had hit something solid. Pulling myself back along the line, I found where it had hung up on the anchor, and One-Lump was already there.

Underwater, this thing looked monstrous. There was a length of anchor chain still attached and partially buried in the sand, and the forged links of the chain were each

a foot in length and ten inches wide. The anchor itself
was the type called an Admiralty or fishermen's anchor,
a lot like the one on the SEAL trident but with a bar stock
across the top of the shank with a ball at both ends and
with one end of the stock bent ninety degrees outward.
This was the kind of anchor found on the old multimasted
clipper ships and could have been in the water for over a
hundred years.

Magnification from the water aside, this anchor was big.
It must have been close to ten or twelve feet long and the
stock at the top of the anchor ten feet wide. The central
shank was something like ten inches thick and the flukes
at the end of the arms were like two-by-three-foot trian-
gles. This thing had to weigh several tons and could be
worth a lot of money.

One-Lump and I surfaced and talked about what we
were going to do next. The first thing we had to do was
mark the anchor and then see about recovering it. We had
an old inflatable rubber swim bladder from a demolition
pack that we tied off to the anchor with the parachute cord
we had used to find it.

Swimming back to the pier, we tried to decide what to
do next. This was kind of exciting, but it wasn't going to
do us any good out in the water.

"What are we going to do?" I asked One-Lump.

"We're going to drag it in."

"And then what?"

"We're going to sell it for junk."

So now we had sort of a plan. We were going to raise
that anchor and sell it for scrap metal at the very least
and make ourselves a little money. How we were going
to get it anywhere that we could sell it was another question. The anchor was so big that our floating it up would
have been pretty hard, to say the least. On the concrete
pier was a rubber-tired movable crane on like a truck body.
As I remember, we went back to the barracks to see who
could help us or if anyone knew who owned the crane.
Swede Tornblum said he could operate a crane, so he
came down to the pier to give us a hand.

There wasn't enough cable on the crane to reach the

anchor, and dragging that cable under the water to the anchor wasn't going to be a picnic either. Finally, we tied a rope to the end of the cable and One-Lump and I swam the rope out to the anchor. Tying on the rope, we signaled the crane to try and pull the anchor in.

Now we didn't know what was going to happen. Either the crane was going to pull the anchor in, or it was going to pull the crane off the end of the pier. In addition, the anchor could turn, which is what it was built to do anyway, and the flukes could dig into the seafloor, making it even harder to raise. Luck must have been with us, because the crane was able to pull the anchor close enough to the pier for us to lift it vertically.

There had been a few tight minutes there when the crane started to slip on its tires before the anchor began to move. Lump and I were in the water, so we couldn't tell when the audience started to gather. But when we climbed up onto the pier, there were people from the hotel and the town, just a bunch of locals looking at our catch.

And our catch was kind of impressive. Even with the water running off of it and it being all slimy, that anchor was a serious chunk of iron. We hosed off the mud and slime and moved the anchor off the pier and outside the old warehouse, our barracks chow hall.

Our first thought was to try and sell the anchor down in St. Thomas. Popular opinion had it that we would get more money for the anchor back in the States, so we decided to try and take it back with us. While these decisions were being made, we also spent time, as all good sailors do, chipping rust and painting up the anchor a bit.

When it finally came time for the Team to leave St. Thomas, One-Lump and I approached our Team officer and asked for permission to take the anchor back with us. We were given permission to negotiate with the transport ship's captain to get our anchor loaded aboard. The captain didn't have any trouble with our request, and the anchor was loaded aboard along with the Team's Conex boxes that were holding our equipment.

The anchor went back with the ship, but I went back to Little Creek aboard the APSS 315 *Sealion*, a World

War Two Balao-class diesel-electric submarine that had been converted to an underwater transport boat. A couple of the guys from the Team went back with our gear on the surface transport and said they would take care of our anchor for us.

The *Sealion* got back to Little Creek well after the transport ship had arrived. But our anchor had been off-loaded along with the rest of the gear and moved over to the Team headquarters. I was sent off for another school and so didn't get back to work on selling our prize for some time.

When I was back at the Team, the anchor was still where we had left it. We had been going to chip the rest of the rust off the anchor and generally clean it up better than the rush job we had done down in St. Thomas. Rudy Boesch had gotten involved by this time. He wanted us to clean up the anchor and make the area shipshape, not just leave this rusting chunk of iron laying about. While I was gone, somebody had gotten the Seabees to come over to the area and sandblast the anchor so the nastiest part of the job was over by the time I returned.

The anchor just sat there in the dirt outside the Team headquarters for quite a while. We had painted the anchor black and the attached ten feet or so of anchor chain white. To keep it from settling into the dirt, we raised the anchor up and set it on its side on wooden blocks. By this time, we had grown attached to the anchor as kind of a Team trophy and decided to keep it. Neither One-Lump nor I ever did look for a buyer for it.

To make more of a permanent installation, a concrete pad was poured and the anchor sunk into the pad, securing her in place. As SEAL Team Two moved its headquarters around the base at Little Creek, the anchor was picked up and moved right along with the Team's gear. That old chunk of iron really did become something of a mascot for SEAL Team Two.

After a while, it was decided to set the anchor upright and sink its nose into concrete. The anchor was lifted straight up and the chain wrapped once around the shank in a large curve, the links welded together, and the tag end welded to one of the flukes. Sinking the nose a couple of feet into a concrete block left the two big triangular flukes exposed and held the anchor securely upright. Eventually, the anchor was painted blue with the SEAL Team Two patch painted on a sign and hung from the arm of the stock with the bent end.

Besides just going to schools and other training, I was sent out on some of the deployments SEAL Team Two conducted in the early 1960s. In June 1964, I was part of Mobile Training Team [MTT] 3-64 that was going to teach some members of the Greek Army Raiding Force how to operate underwater and parachute-jump. Georg Doran was our officer in charge and the team was made up of only five more men: Fred McCarty, Swede Tornblum, Ron Fox, Frank Moncrief, and myself.

The trip itself was exciting for me, my first real training mission outside of the United States. The Navy had made accommodation for us to live in a hotel in a little town just outside of the Greek shipyard where the Greek Army had their base. As part of the operation, I was going to act as the radioman for the MTT. "Kraut" Kratky was back at Little Creek, and I was going to try and contact him over the radio on a regular schedule.

The long wire antenna I had strung for the Angry-109 [AN/GRC-109 radio] just never seemed to work right. Kratky was running the base station back at the Creek and I would try and get in contact with him, but our commo didn't seem to ever work right on that deployment and we never did get through to the States. Some of the guys became tired of the Angry-9 with its hand-cranked generator fairly quickly. But at that time we were trying to learn what would work for us in the field and what wouldn't, and the Angry-9 didn't.

In general, we each had a job to do as part of the MTT and we cooperated with each other in completing the overall mission. Scuba diving and demolitions were two of the subjects the Greeks wanted instruction in, and all of us were qualified to teach that. As I remember, there weren't any assigned instructors per se—each of us would teach whatever class came up as needed.

The hotel the Navy was putting us up in was a fairly interesting situation all by itself. The rooms in the Hotel Fantazio were real small, and the turnover of the other guests seemed to take place fairly quickly. Not to put too fine a point on it, the Hotel Fantazio was nothing more than a little whorehouse for all of the transients working at the shipyard. All night long, people would move in and out of the rooms. The people who had the roughest time of it were the two maids who ran the hotel laundry service. Day and night, those two ladies washed clothes, mostly sheets it seemed.

Even for Navy men, this was a bit much. It wasn't long before we had enough of the Hotel Fantazio, and we looked around the village for what other accommodations might be available. We ended up renting a fully furnished house with multiple bedrooms. Each man in the MTT ended up with his own bedroom. The total rent came up to something like $450 a month as I remember, and each man put in his share. That was where we lived for the three months of the deployment.

Each day, we would go to the Army base and give our classes. For us, the instruction was nothing out of the ordinary. We would use the Greek boats when needed for swims, set up demolitions, and in general work pretty well with our Greek NATO allies.

Some of the work we did was just fun for us. Frank Moncrief and I put on a demonstration water-landing parachute jump for some high-ranking Greek officers. For us, this was a standard part of our mission profile, and the Greek officers seemed well satisfied that we were teaching their men how to do the same operations.

Not all of our time was spent teaching the Greeks. We had a jeep assigned to us and I went back and forth to the U.S. embassy nearly every day to maintain contact and collect orders. The Greek countryside was always an interesting view, and the traveling was part of what I had joined the Navy for in the first place.

There was some excitement that came up while we were in Greece, but we didn't hear of it until we were back in the States. Cyprus is an island in the eastern Mediterranean that the Greeks and the Turks have been arguing over for years. While our MTT was in Greece, the old argument heated up again. As our OIC, Georg Doran was probably kept informed about what was going on, but none of us in the MTT knew a thing until after we returned to the States. There wasn't any politics involved with our mission from our point of view. We just taught the Greeks what we had been told to and when the mission was completed, packed up our gear and returned home.

After we had gotten back to Little Creek, we not only learned about the Cyprus troubles, but we also learned about MTT 2-64. That MTT was also from SEAL Team Two, and they had been assigned to teach another NATO force generally the same thing we had been teaching the Greeks. The only thing was that MTT 2-64 was in Turkey teaching their UDT how to operate. Chances are that some of the students from both MTTs may have met each other while on Cyprus and sort of compared notes.

There was something else that happened while on the Greek deployment. Just like so many other sailors before me, I latched onto a Greek girl while with MTT 3-64. Looking back on the situation, perhaps that girl latched onto me instead. But she was a lovely lady and I was sure I was in love.

To marry a foreign national at that time, you had to have the permission of your commanding officer. The boss of SEAL Team Two then was Commander Tarbox, so it wasn't long after returning from Greece that I was facing him in his office. Marrying a foreigner was frowned on back then, so I also wanted Commander Tarbox's opinion on what I should do.

The situation was one that a lot more people than me have found themselves in. I suppose it was what you might call puppy love, to put a nicer face on it. But Commander Tarbox did good and talked me through the situation, so that particular marriage never took place.

By the next year, I had more decisions to make about the balance of my life. Early in 1965, I was one of the SEALs tagged to go with Commander Robert J. Fay and a couple of other guys from SEAL Team Two to do some liaison work in Vietnam. We didn't have any platoons deployed in Southeast Asia at that time, but some of the guys had gone on other deployments to Vietnam, and it was obvious to us that the war was going to heat up before very long.

When I first heard of my going to Vietnam, I was pretty excited about the idea. This was the chance for another adventure of the kind that you could only have in the SEALs. The bunch of us who were tagged for the deployment were looking forward to the operation. Being that I worked in the cartography shop, I had the opportunity to have some business cards made up for those of us on the deployment. Our humor was a bit rough in those days, and the cards read "Buddha's Delight Gasoline," referring to the Buddhist priests who were setting fire to themselves publicly as a protest to the escalating war.

But before we could leave on the deployment in April, I received new orders sending me off to another school. Because of those orders, I never did see duty in Vietnam.

On 28 October 1965, Commander Fay was killed in Vietnam while acting as an advisor to the Military Assistance Command–Vietnam, Special Operations Group [MAC-V SOG]. He became the first casualty from the Teams to lose his life in Southeast Asia. According to the official reports, Commander Fay was killed during a Viet Cong mortar attack on Da Nang. Later, the main SOG base at Da Nang was named Camp Fay in his honor.

My ETS [End of Time in Service] date was coming up that summer. A chance for me to go to college had developed, and I had the GI Bill to pay for it. I had always liked working with animals and hoped to be able to get into veterinary school, so I decided to leave the Team. Even with my planning to leave, the SEALs were still sending me to schools. Three months before I left, I was sent to language school to study Spanish with a concentration in Portuguese and the Cuban dialect. The physical end of things wasn't ignored either.

Three of us from the Teams went on a forty-eight-mile

marathon run around Little Creek, Dam Neck, and Virginia Beach. That was only three days before I was leaving the Navy. Everybody in the Team was glad for me and the chance I had in school. There wasn't any real pressure to stay in the Team after my decision had been made, though no one was happy to see me go.

After I left the Navy, I lived near Fort Walton Beach, close to Eglin Air Force Base in Florida. SEAL Team Two was sending guys down to Hurlburt Field at Eglin for training, and the guys would come over and visit. We had a house right on the beach, so more than one party was held and a few kegs of beer were tapped at my place. We had a good time, and those parties continued for a number of years.

Once you have been in the Teams, you never completely leave. Personally, I don't have the same stories to share as some of the guys do about their years in Vietnam, so there is a difference between us. But there is a brotherhood among us who shared the experiences of training and life in the Teams, and I will always remain a SEAL at heart and am proud to have been given the chance to be a plankowner of SEAL Team Two.

Over the years, I've regretted, or just feel awkward, about not having gone to Vietnam with the SEALs when Team Two started deploying direct-action platoons. It wasn't that I wanted to be a fighting, gung-ho, kill-them-all SEAL. But I do wish I had shared the camaraderie of the Teams in combat. Also, there is a regret that I never tested myself in that ultimate arena. That is something that I toy with mentally on occasion, whether or not my training and personal mind-set would have been up to the task. I'm fairly sure it would have been, but the question will always remain.

In the Team then we were all operators who were still in the green stages of being SEALs. All of us were learning, testing new equipment and techniques to see what would and wouldn't work for us. Putting all of that together and testing it in combat was one opportunity that I missed.

THE FIRST MISSIONS AND FIRST COMBAT

One of the first orders of business in the new SEAL
Teams was to decide which military, and some civilian,
schools offered skills that the SEALs would need in order
to operate effectively. While a large number of the men
in the fledgling SEAL Teams were undergoing training
evaluating these schools, there were still a number of missions to perform. Details on some of the early operations
of the SEALs remain classified and cannot be described
in this work. But a number of other missions have been
declassified.

Like the Army Special Forces (Green Berets or "blan-
ket heads," as some SEALs jokingly referred to their col-
leagues), the Navy SEALs were expected to be able to
train foreign forces in the skills the SEALs had in demolitions, working in the water, and guerrilla warfare. Some
of the very first field missions conducted by the men of
the Teams, within days of their commissioning, involved
training foreign troops.

Mobile Training Teams, or MTTs, were sent from the
Teams to many allied nations to instruct select members
of their forces. In many cases, the SEALs were training a
cadre of local servicemen who would later open their own
school and further train their countrymen. Officers from
SEAL Team One were in Vietnam in January 1962, and
further MTTs went into Southeast Asia some months later
to begin training what were called indigenous (local)
forces. Some of these later MTTs were made up of men
from both SEAL Team One and SEAL Team Two.

But it wasn't just in Southeast Asia that SEAL training
was being conducted by MTTs. NATO allies also received
SEAL detachments. Though direct combat by any of the
SEALs in the MTT detachments was discouraged, individuals were suspected of being involved with "field problems" on occasion. The first real combat involvement for
the SEALs did not take place in Vietnam but happened a
few years before direct-action platoons were to be sent to
Southeast Asia.

In 1965, a war took place in the Dominican Republic, which shares the West Indian island of Hispaniola with Haiti. A short time after the United States committed military units to the conflict, detachments from the SEALs found themselves on Hispaniola. Working both undercover and partially in the open, the men of the Teams had their first taste of combat against the Dominican rebels. Almost thirty years later, SEALs would return to Hispaniola, this time to operate on the west side of the island in Haiti.

LIEUTENANT

GEORG DORAN

U.S.N. (RET.)

When SEAL Team Two was first commissioned, there were assignments for sixty men—ten officers and fifty enlisted men—according to the commissioning orders. Assigned as the officers were two lieutenants, several lieutenants (junior grade), and a few ensigns. Georg Doran was one of those new ensigns to come over from UDT 21 to first lead the men of SEAL Team Two.

I'm an old Iowan who finished school at Tempe, Arizona, in 1948 and went directly from school into the Navy. It was when I was maybe nine years old or so that I first decided that I would be a sailor, just like my father had been. That's kind of an odd thing coming from someone who grew up in the Midwest states. But when you spend seven days a week on the farm, looking at little more than the animals, you want to get away from that stuff. In the Navy, I figured I would never have to feed, chase down, or corral another farm animal. And that was something that appealed to me in no small way.

It was my reading of my dad's old Bluejacket's manual when I was a boy that made me decide on the Navy as a life. That basic Navy manual told all about working in the Navy and operating aboard ship, the traditions of the service and everything. That looked like an adventure I would like. One thing I am is stubborn. Even though my mind was set young, it stayed set that way.

Working on the water was something I figured I would like. I already liked swimming. During my four years in high school, I worked part-time as a lifeguard at the YMCA and had even taught swimming as part of my job.

Once in the Navy, the job I asked for as my first choice was engineman. My second choice was cook, since campfire cooking was, and still is, a hobby with me. The Navy needed more enginemen than cooks, so I spent my first hitch keeping the ships moving.

Not all of the ships I worked on were at sea. I spent a year at Great Lakes, north of Chicago, working on what we called the cornbelt fleet. I loved that duty, but while doing it, saw something that changed my life forever.

It was while I was in Chicago that I saw a flier the Navy had posted on joining the UDT. I had read about the frogmen in the Navy earlier, and these were the guys that I wanted to join up with. I shipped over [reenlisted] for another six years in order to get to UDTR training, passed my tests, and reported in to Little Creek, Virginia, to take my place with Class 17. As it turned out, I had arrived at the place that would be my home in the Navy for the next eighteen years.

One hundred and twenty-five of us started training in the winter of 1957. Nine enlisted and five officers finished, as I remember. My classmates included Bob Gallagher, Gene Tinnin, Bill Goines, and more than a few others who made their marks in the Teams. Bill Goines was my swim buddy for much of my time in training, and UDTR training put us all into very good shape indeed.

Training was a long time ago, but I still remember it well and individual parts are still sharp memories. Probably the most permanent thing my class did was make the Officers Beach down at Roosevelt Roads in Puerto Rico. There were all these old World War Two buildings down on the point at Roosey Roads that the Navy wanted destroyed. The old barracks, sheds, and buildings were on the side of a hill overlooking the water and had deteriorated to the point where they were just junk.

As part of our UDTR training in explosives, we wired all of those old buildings and the surrounding area for destruction. And when we blew the charges, the destruction was pretty well complete. Not only did we get rid of all the old structures, the whole side of the hill was blown away and the area leveled. Rudy Boesch still has pictures of what was left after the blast, not much more than some pipes sticking up from the concrete rubble. In true frogman fashion, we loaded that target area with tons of high explosives. And off the point where there were coral heads blocking access, we loaded those up too.

When we set that charge off the whole area was cleared out, including the water. Now that spot is the Officers Beach down at Roosey Roads, thanks to UDTR Class 17.

All of us in the class thought that blast was pretty neat. But our instructors didn't let our fun get out of hand. And we had some of the legendary instructors. Rudy Boesch, Jim Cook, and Everett Barrett were the primary instructors for my class, and they don't come much better than them.

Long before we got down to Puerto Rico and Roosey Roads, the class had been whittled down to a manageable size. Most of our quitters dropped out during the first weeks, especially when it came time for Hell Week. Personally, I thought Hell Week was pretty interesting. We had different things to do every day. Tiring, but different. I got through the whole thing in part because I was just too dumb to quit, that and I can do without sleep better than some.

What really got me through Hell Week was the strong desire to become a frogman. That was what I had made my mind up to be, and there wasn't any way those instructors were going to make me quit. Not that they didn't try. No sleep, heavy exercise, and the evolutions and obstacles all knocked me down as much as the next man. But I wanted to be a frogman more than anything else, and I just couldn't see quitting.

But the funny thing was, the hardest part of training for me wasn't Hell Week. The thing that sticks out the most in my mind was the forced march that was part of our graduation exercise. We marched on the concrete roads from Little Creek down to Camp Pendleton, some fourteen miles or more away. And during the march we carried everything with us but the kitchen sink and our rubber boats. Our packs weighed about seventy-five or eighty pounds apiece, and the roadways were more than a little rough on our feet.

The path of the march took us right out on Shore Drive, across what was then a wooden drawbridge over Lynn-haven Inlet and across another wooden bridge over Long Creek, and on down to Camp Pendleton. Or at least that was the way we were supposed to go.

Our problem was that the leader of our group got lost on the way to the camp. Instead of going around the front of the Oceana Naval Air Station, our leader forgot the split in London Bridge Road and we ended up behind the instal-lation. We figured out real quick that we were in the wrong place. The only trouble was that the air station was be-tween us and where we wanted to go.

We had already been marching for miles and we didn't want to walk way in the hell out of our way to go around the air station, end up south of Camp Pendleton, and then walk back north to get to where we were supposed to be. So being good frogmen, we climbed the back fence and started to cross the station itself. Only trouble was, we didn't have permission to be on the air station grounds. We found that out real quick when the shore patrol came running out in jeeps to nail us for trespassing.

There wasn't any real problem with the shore patrol, and we soon found ourselves back on the march. We had already been marching all day, and this was for a forced march that was supposed to be finished during the morn-ing. A Public Works driver in a school bus spotted us and took pity on our bedraggled bunch. He put us on the bus and hauled us out to Camp Pendleton. For a march that was only supposed to take half a day, it was dark by the time we finally arrived at our destination.

When we returned from our final exercise on Friday, we graduated from UDTR the next day. There were more than a few sore feet and blisters in that graduating class. I lost several toenails from all that marching in boots with a heavy pack on concrete roads. But that seemed a small price to pay, a dumb one but a small one, to graduate and become a Navy frogman.

After graduation, I was assigned to UDT 21, where I stayed until SEAL Team Two was commissioned on January 2, 1962, backdated on the commissioning orders from our first formation on January 8. But before the SEALs were even commissioned, I was one of the men working behind the scenes to help create the Team.

While I was at UDT 21, I had worked hard as an engineman, keeping our boats and outboards running in the engineering department. While there I worked under the sharp eyes of Frank Scollise and Bernie Waddell. Later, I qualified to go to officer candidate school and receive my commission.

Running the engineering shop at UDT 21 was Chief Robert Sheehan, and everybody looked up to Sheehan, especially anyone who had worked for him at one time or another. Sheehan was known as Daddy Warbucks, and those of us in the engineering shop were Daddy Warbucks's Little Orphan Annies. Besides Frank Scollise, Bernie Waddell, and myself, Pat Patterson and quite a few others worked for Sheehan over the years, and that was a time few of us will ever forget.

Out of all the guys I met in the Teams, probably the one who stands out the most was Frank Scollise. It wasn't that Frank was a sea daddy to me or anything like that, it was just that he seemed to be the most likable guy in any of the Teams. When I first met Frank was in the engineering department at UDT 21, and we worked closely together as fellow enlisted men for years.

In 1959, our engineering department at UDT 21 was doing the experimental work on all of the LCSR [Landing Craft, Swimmer Reconnaissance] turbine boats BuShips [Bureau of Ships] was developing for the Navy and the Teams. When UDT 21 went down to St. Thomas for winter training, we took the turbine boats along with us for testing. The whole bunch of us, Scollise, myself, Daddy Warbucks, Patterson, and a couple of other guys, were all working on these new boats. The turbine boats were neat, but they just weren't dependable enough for us, or anyone else in the Navy for that matter. The turbines would just heat up too badly and have to be shut down. So the turbine boats didn't work out for us while at St. Thomas. But other things sure did.

St. Patrick's Day was going to pass while we were all down in St. Thomas training. Patterson and I realized this well before we left on the trip, and, bringing Frank Scollise along with us on the plan, we prepared accordingly to celebrate in proper frogman style. We bought turbans and some other supplies with us to St. Thomas just for St. Patrick's Day. When the day came, Pat, Frank, and I broke out our gear, which included a half gallon of green food coloring. Working with the dye, we both colored ourselves completely, and I do mean completely, green. With the skin color properly Irish for the occasion, we wrapped sheets around ourselves, put on our turbans, and went out for the day as the three wise guys, Baloney, Salami, and Cheese.

Frank always had a sense of humor and could be a lot of fun to be around. While walking through St. Thomas in our green getups, we went into this one bar where there was a beautiful woman dressed to kill in one of these light white linen outfits. Frank just went right up to the woman and gave her a big hug, green dye and all. He stepped away and the woman was covered all over in green. "Madam," Frank said to her, "have you ever seen a genuine Irish shillelagh?"

"Why no," she answered, puzzled, "I don't believe I ever have."

Frank then picked up the front of his sheet and laid himself out right there in front of her, all covered in green dye.

"Oh my," was all she said, but she said it several times—"Oh my, oh my!"

I've still got a picture of us, Pat Patterson, Frank Scollise, and myself down in St. Thomas as the three wise guys. Later, Frank transferred over to SEAL Team Two from UDT 21. And Frank had the proper skills to be a good SEAL. He could rob and steal with the best of them, a good-hearted guy and a great cumshaw artist. And he could even cook reasonably well while out on deployment, even if he didn't use a clean sock to hold the grounds when he made coffee. Without a doubt, Frank Scollise was probably the biggest character I know of ever produced from the UDT.

Before I left UDT 21, I decided to go ahead and try for a commission as an officer and a gentleman. It came as no surprise to some, and some probably still don't believe it, when my paperwork came back approved. Now I was going to be an officer in the Teams, and there was a new kind of Team coming up.

Well before my commissioning date, I had been working with Roy Boehm, who was the primary force behind the creation of the SEAL Teams. Not that we could call the new unit the SEALs, or anything else for that matter. The whole idea was classified top secret at the time and we were not allowed to discuss it outside of a secured area. Roy was the head honcho and in charge of all the men who would become the new SEAL Team, picking and choosing among the men of the UDTs, and I was acting as kind of an intern ensign.

Before the SEALs' commissioning date, I had to leave Little Creek to attend OCS and receive my actual commission. With my papers in hand and official new ensign's insignia on my uniform, I had reported back in to UDT 21 in time to make the first formation of SEAL Team Two on January 8, 1962.

For the guys who got into the Team, the SEALs were the greatest thing that ever was. But for the guys who were not chosen and remained with UDT 21, I felt that there was a little jealousy against the men of the new Team. It seemed to me that the selection process Roy Boehm had put together picked out the very best men to prove out the SEAL idea and that the men who were left behind felt a little let down that they were not chosen.

As for me, I have no idea why I was chosen to be one of the very few officers in the new Team. All I know is that I received a commission and my first orders read, "Report to SEAL Team Two." It was a small handful of men who made up the Team that first day. Not all of the men who were part of the initial commissioning crew were even available to make that first formation. That has made a little question over the years as to just who was a plankowner of SEAL Team Two. The official Navy commissioning list holds fifty-five names—ten officers, three chief petty officers, and forty-two enlisted men. All of those men are plankowners, even if some of them didn't show up for days or even weeks.

The mission of the SEALs was kind of an open secret in the UDTs well before the Team became a reality. The year before [1961], men had been recruited by the intelligence services from the UDTs to go to Vietnam in civilian clothes with all of their expenses paid. These men were trained and outfitted for undercover duty. They even received an allowance for new civilian outfits. This sounded like a good way to see some action, and get some new gear in the bargain to boot. So I volunteered to go as well.

There was a group of the volunteers training at UDT 21 on the side, in addition to their regular duties. These men were drawing money and equipment, the whole nine yards, and were ready to go. And I wanted to be one of them, even before I had received my commission. But I was turned down for the operation. All I was told was that I couldn't go because I was going to receive a commission. The real reason I think was that I was on the short list to man the new SEAL Team. And the Vietnam mission would have been a great deal, because they never had to go!

The mission was canceled and all the volunteers returned to their regular duties at UDT 21. But they never had to give back any of the money or clothes they had been issued.

But during the first days at the SEAL Team, I had little time to wonder about what it would have been like to go to Vietnam as a special "civilian" advisor/instructor. Things were more than busy as we tried to get the new Team in shape to operate. I found myself right back in engineering, just the place I had left back in UDT 21. Only this time I was the engineering officer. Big deal—I was right there getting my hands dirty with everyone else as we tried to build the department up from nothing.

Our first big project in engineering started in the summer of 1962, and it was to build up and test our new Powercat trimarans. These were civilian boats that had been shipped in along with brand-new Mercury hundred-horsepower outboards that we hung on the transoms, two to a boat. With the new motors in place, we proceeded to test the trimarans and wring them out completely. The boats were later heavily modified, armored, and armed, and saw good duty in the waterways of Vietnam as the first SEAL Team Assault Boats. But I didn't get to work on the new boats much that first SEAL summer. What I did do was beat them to Vietnam.

In April of 1962, a group of SEALs from Teams One and Two under the command of Lieutenant (jg) Philip Holtz from Team One reported to Vietnam as Mobile Training Team 10-62. The MTT was going to begin training a group of Vietnamese Coastal Force personnel in reconnaissance, sabotage, and guerrilla warfare. These Vietnamese would then be the instructors for additional classes of South Vietnamese Biet Hai commandos [Junk Force Commando Platoons]. In MTT 10-62 were two men from SEAL Team Two, William "Billy" Burbank and Leonard "Lenny" Waugh. They were the first enlisted men from SEAL Team Two to go to Vietnam.

SEAL Team Two supplied the bulk of the men for the relief unit that was going to replace MTT 10-62 in Vietnam, and I was the officer tagged to go. None of us thought much of anything about where we were going, Vietnam was just a name then, and none of us knew enough to really have much of an opinion about the place. Not that we would have said anything if we did. We were all a bunch of hard-charging young bucks, eager to show what we could do, both to the Navy, the SEALs, and ourselves for that matter. We had no real idea about what we might run into over there except that we would be doing our job and training our South Vietnamese allies.

We left for Southeast Asia in September as MTT 4-63. There were nine of us from Team Two, myself as the ensign in charge, Louis "Hoss" Kucinski, Paul Schwartz, J. P. Tolison, R. A. Tolison, Fred McCarty, Charlie Bump, A. D. Clark, and Bill Goines. To travel to Vietnam, we all rode a civilian flight and wore civilian clothes. In my pocket, I had a set of orders signed by the Chief of Naval Operations himself that could get us anything we wanted without much question. Not a bad position to be in for an ensign who hadn't held his commission for a year yet.

But the detachment was not under my direct command. Instead we were under the direction of a SEAL Team One officer, Lieutenant (jg) A. C. Routh. Our training program in Vietnam was going to be coordinated through a Vietnamese Navy officer, a Lieutenant (jg) Ninh. The program we had planned would be along the lines laid out by MTT 10-62, only we would be emphasizing land navigation, guerrilla warfare, ambush and counterambush, and raiding techniques.

We flew out of Norfolk on to San Francisco, where we lost our civilian plane and were instead put on a MAC flight for the Philippines and onwards to Saigon and Vietnam. That was a very long flight across the Pacific, ourselves and the three or four tons of gear we brought along. We had everything we owned along with us, including the new AR-15 rifle.

Those AR-15s were the very first ones of their kind in the Navy and only the second batch to arrive in Vietnam. As far as our using the weapons went, they were still classified as secret and very few people even knew we had them. I don't remember how many rounds of ammunition we brought with us for those AR-15s, but we shot it all up in training. After that, those new rifles were little more than expensive clubs, since at that time there wasn't a round of 5.56mm ammunition to be had in Vietnam. Some change from five years later when there would be literally millions of rounds in-country.

We had our rifles locked up in a steel box along with some other new equipment we were experimenting with, such as the metascope, an infrared night vision device. For all that the SEALs would use night vision equipment later on, things like the starlight scopes and night vision goggles, that metascope was just not worth the trouble to us. In the wet environment the SEALs operated in, the darn thing just kept shorting out and refusing to work. Mostly we just left it in the box we stored our rifles in.

But before all this happened to us, we had to set up and start working with our Biet Hai commandos. I had been to Japan while in the Regular Navy and didn't feel much culture shock on arriving in Vietnam. The only real thing I noticed was that the women dressed so differently from the Japanese. But operating now was going to be very different from my first trip to the Orient.

Two of the men who came with us but were not part of our MTT separated from us and went into what we called the "pipeline" then. They were going to operate with the CIA with what would later become part of the Phoenix program. At least I believe that was what they were going to do. They never did tell us, and we were to have very little contact with them while they were in-country.

What we were going to do was teach the Vietnamese, and that was something I was good at. During my whole career, and even my time before the Navy, I had always been a teacher of one kind or another. Even now, I'm still instructing for the Navy. I have always gotten a lot of satisfaction from teaching, and that first MTT in Vietnam was no exception.

The West Coast SEALs had run the first class of Biet Hai commandos through the facilities at Da Nang, and our MTT was going to run the second class of about sixty-five men and help further establish the training school. My opinion of the students we had was that they were good at what they did, and they were very motivated to remain good at their training.

Our students' motivation was easy for me to see. These Vietnamese could rob, cheat, steal, and pillage with a free hand. Nobody in the South Vietnamese forces was about to stop them. The whole area was an open book to these guys, and they lived well because of it. This might have shocked some of the people back home in the States, but this wasn't the United States we were in. Actions like this were a way of life in Vietnam at that time, and we weren't about to change things.

To give you an idea of how we lived, we received a calf every second week that we were in training for extra meat for the students. And our students would lead that calf down and butcher it every time one would show up. They did have to buy their own firewood on the local economy, but that was something I could take a hand in.

"You guys are not going to be buying anything," I said through an interpreter. "Saturday morning, our PT is going to be gathering firewood on Monkey Mountain." And that's what I listed in their training program so that the guys wouldn't have to spend their money. What I did was institute Log PT in Vietnam. Every Saturday, our students would be up on nearby Monkey Mountain, gathering logs, along with the occasional monkey for the pot, and bringing the results back to our base. These men didn't get paid much and that is also what led to the way of life in the area anyway.

The Vietnamese we worked with were pretty good, and the results of our training were satisfactory. Of all the Vietnamese forces that were out there at the time, our men were probably the elite of South Vietnam. At least my opinion is that. The Biet Hai I would compare to our UDTs. The later LDNNs [Lien Doc Nguoi Nhia units, Vietnamese SEALs] received more training, especially in the years that followed as we brought in more equipment and expanded the training curriculum. Looking back, I had a better view of this than most in part because I would later be running the whole LDNN school in 1970.

But during that first training tour, we didn't really see much in the way of action in engaging the enemy. We shot up the ammunition to our AR-15s on the target range and not in combat. What we tried to do was indoctrinate our students in a wide range of weapons. Anything we could get ahold of was something we could teach to our students. And we could get ahold of a lot.

We went down to the Army Green Berets armory in Da Nang and were able to draw any weapon they had along with ammunition. Some of the guys with me would pull out all kinds of weird stuff as they found it. For myself, a little .30-caliber carbine was all I felt I needed.

We didn't see much of anything in the way of shoot-'em-up action during our field exercises with our students. In late 1962, there wasn't much in the way of real combat going on in South Vietnam anywhere. There would be the occasional sniper out in the boondocks who might pop a round or two off at us. But no damage was done while I was there, and you can't just tear off chasing one man in the jungle anyway.

And we did take the class out on field problems quite often. Night problems were something we did commonly as well. And when we went out, live ammunition was issued when we felt the situation warranted it. But most of our ammunition was spent in range firing. But though we SEALs could draw anything we wanted from our armories for training purposes, our students had to make do with what their government issued them.

The average Vietnamese is of much smaller physical stature than we are, and an M1 Garand or M1918A2 BAR is really a handful for them. They much preferred carbines and submachine guns and especially our AR-15s, but what they had were Garands and BARs, so they just made do with what they had. Not that our supply problems didn't exist for us as well.

We begged, borrowed, or just plain stole anything and everything we could get that we thought would support our training program. Later, these problems would get less and less, but we were still establishing ourselves, and very few people had any idea who the SEALs even were at that time.

At that time in Vietnam, there were very few bases at all with American forces. Saigon had the most Americans in it. Otherwise, we were few and far between. There was no rivalry between the services at all in Vietnam at that time. For the few of us who were around, we had to stick together. There was some animosity between our Biet Hai students and the regular Vietnamese Army and Navy people. There were some real fights, but that was between them and we didn't get involved. Besides, some of the rivalry wasn't much different than the games we Navy men had been playing with the Marines since our service began.

MTT 4-63 spent six months in Vietnam, returning to Little Creek in March of 1963. By that time, our Biet Hai students were able to run the training at Da Nang themselves for the upcoming classes. Back at the Creek, I went from being the engineering officer to air ops. Later in the chain of command, I took over being the operations officer for SEAL Team Two. It wasn't until 1970 that I would return to Vietnam for another tour of duty.

That first trip to Vietnam had been interesting, but we hadn't been in any real danger at any time during it. Certainly not anything like what the SEALs faced only four years later when we started deploying combat platoons to Vietnam. But before then, we still had quite a few jobs to do in the SEALs.

In 1964, it was time to leave Little Creek as part of another MTT. Only this time we would be going east rather than west. The Royal Hellenic Navy of Greece had requested SEAL training for three of its officers, nine petty officers, and forty enlisted men. As lieutenant (jg), I was put in charge of MTT 3-64. In June, myself and the five men who made up MTT 3-64 left for Greece to train their forces in UDT operations, basic airborne, and scuba techniques.

We were training the Greek Army Raiding Force while at the same time, Blackjack Macione had MTT 2-64 in Turkey assisting the Turkish UDT in running the first all-Turkish Underwater Demolition Team class. That was when the little problem in Cyprus kicked up between Turkey and Greece.

It wasn't long before I was answering questions to the Greek officers as to just why we had a training MTT in Turkey. "Just why have you got people in Turkey training them?" the Greek officers bellowed at me.

"Why, because they're a NATO force just like you," I answered sweetly. And I was sure that Blackjack was answering the same questions that the Turks were asking him. "You're a NATO force," I said. "We're not teaching you to fight each other."

The hell we weren't. My group lost two guys during their graduation problem, which was to go to Cyprus and raise hell. Even before then, I know that some of my Greeks were slipping into Cyprus and cutting throats. Though I don't know for sure, it's pretty likely that some of Blackjack's Turkish students were doing the same thing.

What we were doing was teaching the Army Raiding Force of Greece, their equivalent of the Army Special Forces. The unit knew nothing about diving and clandestine underwater work. We taught them diving, submarine ops, and were heavy into demolition training. Blackjack was overseeing the Turks training their own people. What we were doing was giving an advanced course of training to the Greeks.

Though we went over to Greece thinking we were going to be teaching their UDT, what we did instead was meet one hell of an army unit. Captain Zack, my Greek counterpart, had taken his people and done all of the mountain-climbing sequences for the movie *The Guns of Navarone*. These guys were good in general and great in the mountains. They just weren't accustomed to operating in the water.

We taught water jumps and how to go in and out of submarines. They were so inexperienced in some of these techniques that the skipper of the Greek sub didn't think it could even be done.

We went aboard the submarine and I briefed the captain about training in lock-in, lock-out techniques. This was a standard diesel-electric sub with a forward and aft escape trunk. But this captain swore you couldn't use the trunk except in an emergency. I explained in detail the technique and exactly what we would do.

"You mean we can do that?" he asked me.

"Why certainly, Captain," I answered. "It's a standard procedure in our Teams."

The Greek UDTs, and they did have some, weren't advanced enough to do the lock-in, lock-out techniques. Those Greek UDT men were little more than playboys who liked showing off for the women on the beach. At least that was the opinion I developed during my short time in Greece.

But this submarine captain was interested in the possibilities of our techniques. "I'll think about it," he said to me. "Come back tomorrow."

The next day, I came back and sat down in the submarine's wardroom with the captain. "You know," he said to me, "that system works."

"What do you mean, it works?" I asked.

"I sank this bastard by the pier right here and tried it myself," he answered. "I went out and came right back in. It works and I love it!"

That captain had put the sub on the bottom in sixty feet of water and used the escape trunk to leave and board the sub. All without gear and diving about thirty feet down to the deck. From that time on in Greece, anytime we wanted to try something from a submarine, that captain wanted to try it.

All the techniques we showed the captain just gave him that much more of a reason to operate with his submarine. They even used the technique with that sub and my class to infiltrate Cyprus. That was the situation where two of the class didn't come back. We don't know what happened on Cyprus, only that two of the students were lost. I was not involved with the operation, but I was told later that part of what went on involved the Greeks slipping into a barracks and cutting throats.

I had been invited to go on the operation with the class. But the higher-ups in the Navy and the CIA, who were running our MTT, said I couldn't go. That was sort of the class's graduation exercise, and a more dangerous or tougher one I can't think of.

The only really bad thing that happened in Greece involved the Greek UDT. We were invited to take part in a UDT field exercise while in Greece, and we jumped at the chance to work with our Greek brothers.

These weren't any brother UDT men. For the exercise, the Greek UDT men showed up in civilian clothes with tennis paddle ball rackets, volleyballs, and nets. And we were supposed to be operating in a tactical environment and living in the woods? These guys were going on a vacation.

"What in the world are you guys going to do?" I asked the Greek UDT officer.

"Well," he said, "we're going to have some fun, go down to the village, drink beer . . ."

We got to the position we were supposed to operate from and I just told him, "So long. We'll meet you here in five days." Then we went back with the army and did our thing. Never saw those Greek UDTs again.

Working with the MTTs was fun for the most part. It wasn't combat, but the job was good and we did well in training our allies. SEAL and UDT duties were always dangerous—that was why we received extra pay—but combat didn't come along very often prior to Vietnam. What was probably the most puckering situation I was in took place two years after returning from Vietnam with MTT 4-63. And that situation took place when SEAL Team Two deployed men down to the Dominican Republic during the crisis in 1965.

In April, there was a military coup in the Dominican Republic, and in the confusion that followed, rebels tried to return Juan Bosch to power. All of this was happening on the island of Hispaniola between Cuba and Puerto Rico in the Caribbean. The Dominican Republic shares Hispaniola with Haiti, Haiti holding about one-third of the western side of the island and the Dominican Republic taking the eastern two-thirds.

Most of what was going on in the Dominican Republic didn't concern us at Little Creek very much. But when the rebel fighting continued and grew heavier, the U.S. State Department decided that the Navy would evacuate the 2,500 U.S. civilians who were on the island. Four hundred Marines were landed to take care of the evacuation and they were reinforced by twelve hundred more Marines a few days later. Washington thought the Communists were going to take over the rebel movement, Cuba wasn't that far away, and President Johnson sent in the larger Marine force to prevent that takeover from happening. Now was when the Navy decided to send the SEALs in.

Lieutenant Tom Tarbox was the skipper of Team Two when the decision was made to deploy to the Dominican Republic. Three platoons ended up being deployed from SEAL Team Two, with the first detachment, Third Platoon, leaving the Creek at the end of April. My promotion to lieutenant (jg) had come in the year before and I was already the platoon leader of Third and so was in command of that first detachment of five enlisted men. We were ordered on board the USS *La Salle* on 30 April.

Besides myself, in the detachment were Bob Gallagher, Jack Rowell, Frank Moncrief, Scotty McClean, and one additional man. The *La Salle* was an LPD [Amphibious Transport Dock] acting as the flagship for Admiral John S. McCain, Jr., who was in overall command of the operation. UDT-22 had sent down a detachment made up of their Fourth Platoon to operate with the Navy and Marine forces, charting the beaches and preparing an area for evacuating the U.S. civilian population by ship.

The Marines were going to land and establish an "international safety zone" for the population, the UDTs were going to do their job in supporting the amphibious operations, and we were going to work with the Army Special Forces in routing out the rebels themselves.

When we arrived in the Dominican Republic, my platoon was sent ashore. Once on dry land, the SEAL detachment was to take its orders from the U.S. Army command on the island. Soon after arriving on the island, I received orders for myself and another man from the platoon to report to the Army's 7th Special Forces Detachment headquarters while the rest of the platoon was to stand by in town.

While the rest of the men set up a camp near what was the city dump, I told Bob Gallagher, who was my platoon chief, "Hey, look, I've got to have one man come with me. Gimme somebody." Since all of the SEALs were volunteers already, Bob just pointed out Jack Rowell as my "volunteer" for the operation.

The Special Forces sent a jeep down to get Jack and

me and we reported to the headquarters the SF troopers had set up for themselves. No tent in the city dump for these guys. Through their agency connections, the SF had set up their headquarters in this big villa. We reported in and they sent us up to what we called the "whisper room," a secure area where classified material could be discussed in a room that had been swept for listening devices.

While in the whisper room, Jack and I had to get rid of all of our identification. We were given civilian clothes and passports, set on board a helicopter, and sent north. No weapons, new IDs, and cover stories. Jack and I were now tourists, students from George Washington University in Washington, D.C., now in the Dominican Republic to study marine hydrology.

We flew up to Samana Bay, on the northeastern tip of the island, and contacted a Special Forces A-Team that was set up in a real dump of a hotel. The Special Forces radioman had antennas strung up all over the place, and they were sending and receiving messages constantly. All of this was supposed to be undercover and real hush-hush so that nobody could figure out that we were operating in the area. That was why Jack and I were given false identification, cover stories, and were wearing civilian clothes. With all of that, why we were traveling in a big green Army helicopter is beyond me.

What the situation was is that there had been "suspicious small boat traffic" in the area of Samana Bay and it was suspected that the rebels were using caves in the bay to cache weapons and supplies. The fighting down south on the island in the big town was getting real and people were being killed. The Army wanted to know where the weapons were coming from, and it was thought that the Communists might be bringing hardware in from the north.

Jack Rowell, myself, and an Army Special Forces sergeant had the mission to survey the entire bay of Samana, cave by cave, while posing as tourists on a fishing trip. Since we would be undercover, there shouldn't be any reason to spook the local rebels into moving any caches before we could discover them or spot evidence of movement in the area. The plan was a little shaky, but at least the Special Forces sergeant, a redheaded Irishman called Red oddly enough, could speak Spanish well.

The first thing we did was go down to the Catholic church nearby, where the local father just happened to have a motorboat available. So we ended up with the motorboat along with a fifty-five-gallon drum of gasoline. This sixteen-foot motorboat had been there a long time and the engine had seen better days. With that drum of gasoline sitting in the middle of the boat she would only hold about six people at the most.

To carry on with our cover, we went down to the local dime store and bought ourselves a fishing pole, a real cheap rod and reel, along with some hooks. Oh yeah, we were going fishing, all right.

Along with our fishing-trip excuse, we were introduced around the town as two students from George Washington University. We had sold the story to the chief of police of the town and a number of townspeople that we were surveying the shoreline of the bay for the possibility of tour ships coming into the area. The locals just ate this up, and we enlarged the story as necessary. With the Army sergeant translating, it was explained to the local mayor, police chief, and others how we would "have to build a big pier here and dredge out the water there."

Part of the story that was given out was that the two of us, Jack and I, had been hired by this company to come in and see just where in the area we could make a tourist stop. Red was our interpreter, that explained his presence, and we were trying to see what had to be done to the waterfront to allow the ships to come in.

The locals could see the possibility of dollar bills coming into the economy, so we were given pretty much open access to move about as we liked. So for two days, we moved up and down the coastline of Samana Bay, examining caves and looking for signs of rebels.

We found lots of signs of activity, but whether it was made by rebels or not, we couldn't tell. This one cave we found was well used indeed. People had been coming into the cave for years—you could see where campfires had been, and initials were scrawled on the cave walls with charcoal. There was even some remains of what had been an old railroad in the area. The tracks were long gone, but there was still an old trestle and other things about showing where the railroad had been. The causeway was broken down, but you could see where ships had come in to tie up while material was brought in on this little railway from some mine or other up in the hills.

The story about the mine had been learned by Red while he investigated the area. Locals were all around as well, and there was no way we could tell whose side they were on. The rebels were running hot and heavy in the big city, another detachment of SEALs had been flown down from Little Creek, but there wasn't anything we could see going on in Samana Bay. And we had the time to look around and worry about the rebels because our boat broke down.

We had surveyed the shoreline of Samana Bay and decided it was time to head back and report in. We hadn't found any sign of weapons caches or rebels in the caves we examined, and we had looked into dozens of them. It was probably the vibrations of that old motor over time that finally worked the screws out that had been holding the recoil starter onto the engine. But when the last screw fell out, the starter popped off the engine, falling over the side and into the water.

We may be mighty frogmen, but that water was deep and the starter lost. So, as you would expect, it wasn't long before that old motor coughed and died, with no way to restart it. We had to paddle the boat on to this large cave we had already examined, the one with the railroad, and find a place to spend the night.

We hit the cave without much trouble and spent the night under cover. But that was one long and puckering night. Just because we hadn't found any sign of rebels in the area didn't necessarily mean they weren't there. And that was a thought that went through all our heads that night. It wasn't like we could do much of anything if an armed party of rebels came along. We didn't have any weapons at all between us. Any kind of weapon would have immediately blown our cover to anyone who might have been watching. All through that night, it didn't take much of a noise to make us all sit up and take notice.

The next morning dawned with no rebels in sight, and that was one early wakeup I didn't have any trouble with at all. My experience as an engineman helped me as I tinkered with that motor trying to find a way to get it started. Finally, I managed to get a line wrapped around the flywheel and turned the engine over. Even then, that old motor didn't want to start, and we wrapped and pulled and wrapped and pulled on that line, finally getting the old girl to light off.

That was one happy group in that boat, cruising along on the six-hour ride back to the city. When we finally got back, that Catholic priest came running down to the water to meet us, calling out, "Oh, I thought I had lost you guys."

We had told the priest that we would be back before dark when we left with his boat the day before. And it was well into the new day before he finally saw us again. Everyone had been worried that something had happened to us, including us.

Once everyone was assured that we were all right, the priest had some men take the motor off the boat and back up to the church. They put that old wooden boat on some logs, pulled the plug on it, and drained out all the water that had come aboard. It had been a leaky old boat and we had been bailing it out as we cruised along. That had been one hell of a fishing trip, and we didn't even manage to catch any fish.

Getting back to the city, I had to write up a field report on the operation. Along with my other comments was one where I recommended that they buy the father a brand-new motor because of his cooperation and concern about us. Besides, if anyone ever had to go into those caves again, they would want a better motor than the one we had. I never did find out if that priest received his new motor.

Even though we hadn't found any signs of the rebels or their supply caches, the operation had been considered a success. Because of the covert nature of the operation and the fact that we had been operating unarmed effectively behind enemy lines without support, Jack Rowell and I received decorations for the operation. Jack Rowell received a Navy Commendation Medal and I was awarded a Bronze Star. That made us the first men of SEAL Team Two to get any medals for a combat action.

Of course, we didn't know anything about any medals when we did our job in Samana Bay. All we wanted was to get back to the rest of our platoon. By now a second detachment had arrived from SEAL Team Two, and they were set up right alongside Gallagher and the others still near the city dump. Lieutenant Kochey had flown down from the Creek on 16 May along with two other officers and ten more enlisted men. That gave us three effective platoons in the Dominican Republic during the hottest part of the fighting.

And the platoons had seen some action in the streets of the big city. Rebels had been fighting in the streets, and the SEALs were operating right alongside the Marines in controlling the area and trying to put a stop to the fighting. Before very long, the town had been fully secured from the rebels. But that didn't mean the fighting was over.

A mission came up where four of us from the platoons had to drive down to the Dominican UDT headquarters to retrieve some papers. The only trouble was that the UDT men, who we had trained in the first place, were on the rebels' side of the fighting. Whoops!

Now we had to go down to the UDT headquarters, which was in town, down in this little valley on the oceanfront. They had a nice setup down there, a walled compound with parapets that you could move along and look out over the wall. In the center of the compound was a big swimming pool, drained of water during the fighting, and the rear of the compound wall opened out onto the beach. It would have been a great place to visit, except for the rebel snipers overlooking the road leading to the place.

In this grain tower across the way were rebel snipers, and they were shooting at anything that moved along the road. Now, we wanted to get to the headquarters to retrieve the charts that had been left behind. The Army had already been to the UDT headquarters and they had stripped out all of the weapons, diving gear, and materials that might have been of use to the rebels. But the Army guys had left behind the paperwork, including the detailed charts that had been made by the UDTs.

Those charts showed every harbor and sand strip on the whole island. We wanted those charts and we intended to have them. Sitting on top of the hill overlooking the valley, we were out of range of the snipers. When everyone was set, the four of us lit off down that road in an open Army jeep.

This time, we were all armed with our AR-15s, and when we were ready, that driver just floored the gas pedal on that jeep. It was a nice straight tree-lined road to the headquarters compound, only we didn't drive straight. Weaving along the road, moving from side to side, we threw off the aim of the few snipers who popped off a round at us.

There was a wall around the compound that protected us once we were through the gate. Inside the headquarters, I found the charts, and they made a very nice armful. Stuffing our booty in a bag, we now had to figure on leaving the compound. There were some Special Forces troopers still in the compound from when the Army had taken away all the equipment. With the snipers being so active, those troopers were staying behind the cover of the compound walls for the time being. But we had to get those charts back.

When we got back to the gates, the troopers opened them up for us. Now the driver revved up the engine in that jeep until we figured it was time to go. We shot back out the gate just as steadily as we had come in. We heard a few rounds get fired, but none of them came close enough to bother us. For ourselves, we didn't fire back. We just hung on to the jeep and shot back as fast as we could, again weaving all over the road.

Things started winding down soon after that. The Army would come down to where we were and take some of the platoons to man roadblocks around the town. The area had turned into our first free-fire zone, and we were to shoot anything that moved. That was where some of the guys first saw what an AR-15 would do to a human body, and what those early ones would do didn't leave much left behind.

Roadblock duty was what the other two platoons did mostly while Jack and I were spelunking in the caves. Finally, things settled down to a point where it was decided to send us back to the creek. On 28 May, all the platoons pulled out and we returned to Little Creek. SEAL Team Two had suffered no casualties and we had seen our first taste of combat.

There wasn't going to be any more action in combat for me for a number of years. In early 1967, SEAL Team Two started sending direct-action platoons to Vietnam. SEAL Team One had already been sending their platoons to Vietnam the year before. But none of this was going to affect me for a while yet. For two years, starting in 1967, I was transferred to the UDTR training unit in Little Creek.

Now I was helping prepare the new SEALs and UDT operators to join the ranks of the Teams. At that time, we were running classes both in Little Creek, Virginia, and Coronado, California. By the late 1960s, plans were made to close the Little Creek school and consolidate all basic training in Coronado.

When I started at the school, the course was called UDTR, for Underwater Demolition Team Replacement training. By the time I left, the name had been changed to what it is now, BUD/S, for Basic Underwater Demolition/SEAL training.

By any name, it was still the toughest school in the Navy and probably the whole U.S. military. All of the men at the school, from the enlisted instructors to the officers, did their best to maintain the high quality of the graduates of training. These were men we might have to operate with in combat someday, and they were going to be just as tough and competent as we were.

Not that there was not a lot of pressure from outsiders for us to change training. Our methods appeared harsh to anyone just observing them, and in fact they were harsh. "Oh, how can you do that to that man!" would be a comment we heard more than once from unqualified observers meddling in military affairs. The popularity of the services was falling in some of the public's eye and there were more than enough politicians and busybodies to try and take advantage of that. These nonquals would insist that they knew better about how to train and weed out men for the Teams than the instructors who had been successful at it for years.

It was true that we had a lot of men quit, and maybe some of them would have gone on to be good operators in the Teams. But training techniques have improved since then, so injuries and bad exercises are less likely, and the quality of the graduates has stayed high.

There was a commander who later caused me more than a little trouble who was one of these people who knew what we were doing better than we did. This officer was the ship's stores department head, and he came down to the training area and watched what we were doing. No matter how we transported the students, whether it be in a weapons carrier, six-by truck, or other transport, the students always rode in the back of the vehicle, officers and enlisted together. It was the instructors who rode in the front of the vehicle.

This officer came down and saw this and it didn't sit with him at all. What he wanted was the student officers to ride in the front of the vehicle. The instructors could ride in the back with the rest of the enlisted men. With no uncertain terms, we told this commander that how we did things was no concern of his and we would carry on the way we knew best.

That didn't sit very well with this one officer. He caused us so much trouble that we had to go to the captain of the school to get this idiot off our backs and to get him to leave the program alone.

Normally, people who complained about the program from the outside were kept from those of us doing the training by the chain of command. The only trouble with this commander was that he was in the chain of command, so he was a lot harder to get rid of. Finally, he was told to leave us alone and to let us get on with the program. But that man did not like the way he had been treated and knew I was the one responsible for having him dealt with. That commander swore he would get me, and I suppose he finally did.

That commander was a tin-can [destroyer] sailor who had been passed over for captain and was bitter about his position. He got his nose into everything and caused trouble wherever he could to demonstrate his own importance. That commander saw to it that my fitness report from my time at the school was written in just the right language to basically sink my Navy career.

By wording the comments in a fitness report just right, things can be set up so that there isn't anything you can rebut effectively. In order to be picked up for promotion, you have to be in the top percentage of your job. And a bad, or even just neutral, fitness report will keep you from that top percentage.

Once you get a bad fitness report in your file jacket, it will follow you forever. I was passed over for lieutenant commander on my next promotion board and the time after that as well. By 1974, I was going to be passed over for the third time, and that was it. I received a letter from the Bureau of the Navy inviting me to leave the service, and so I was out. The only thing I could do was staff work, and for a guy who was used to being in the field with his men, that will kill you. I spent a year assigned to SpecWar staff as the material maintenance officer and did little more than walk around the waterfront with a clipboard in my hand.

But there were a lot more good men I knew than individuals like that commander. There were guys in the Teams who I really looked up to, and the first among these was probably Robert Sheehan. Sheehan had started as an enlisted man and was a machinist mate chief in the UDT before receiving his commission, and he finally retired as a lieutenant commander. Bob and I had quite a runaround for a while back in UDT 21.

One day I was a first class and he was a chief with me

working under him. Then I received my commission and now I was an ensign with Chief Sheehan underneath me. Six months later, Sheehan had received his commission and was now a lieutenant (jg) and I was still an ensign.

It seemed that Bob Sheehan and I worked together for years in one way or the other. There isn't much question in my mind that I looked up more to him than he ever did to me. If I had a sea daddy, it was Bob Sheehan. And that title fits better than most, since Sheehan's nickname in the Teams was Daddy Warbucks.

And giving Big Daddy Warbucks a commission didn't take the old chief out of the sailor. Sheehan was thrown off the naval air station and almost court-martialed as a lieutenant (jg) after he socked some pilot square in the jaw. That smart-ass pilot mouthed off to the wrong frogman, and Sheehan just cold-cocked him right there and then. And was promptly escorted off the base in a paddy wagon.

As for the SEALs, the man who was probably my sea daddy the most was Roy Boehm. Roy didn't spend a lot of time at the Team after we were commissioned. But the time he did spend there left a deep and lasting impression.

Roy did whatever it took to get the SEALs up and on line in as little time as possible. There was a real chance we might see action in Cuba in 1962, so Roy used his powers freely to get us what we needed in order to operate. The first AR-15s in the Navy were those Roy bought for us without going through official channels. Though the AR-15 was a brand-new kind of weapon to us, they were not the most unusual things that Roy bought.

For quick-kill practice, we had regular kids' BB guns in our armory. With a BB gun and some safety glasses, you can quickly learn and practice the point-and-shoot kind of firing that we called quick-kill back then. Besides the sawed-off shotguns and other toys in the SEAL armory, we also had some crossbows to use as a silent weapon.

A crossbow would seem like an odd kind of weapon to have available, given the silencers developed for firearms just in World War Two. But some evidence had come out of Vietnam that crossbows were still around. Back around 1961 or '62, a helicopter had come back to its base with three bamboo crossbow arrows stuck in the aluminum skin. We figured that if the Viet Cong could use a crossbow, then we could too.

Just like the AR-15s, Roy went out and bought crossbows from some sporting goods outfit and then we had them. Our crossbows were wooden-stocked models with black bows and they fired a fourteen-inch arrow, or bolt, which is the proper term, a good long way. They would have been a beautiful silent weapon for sentry removal and the like, but we didn't get to keep them.

Somewhere up in the supply chain, they reviewed all the open purchases that Roy made. Boehm was in more than a little hot water for buying those AR-15s, but the crossbows just were not going to stay. Someone in charge decided that the crossbow was against the Geneva Convention for use in modern war. That was all it took, and those crossbows were pulled out of our armory and done away with.

But we still had our AR-15s, and we were more than happy with them. It wasn't until the Army picked up the weapon later that the problems started with it. The Army had a forward bolt assist put on what they now called the M16A1, and then they changed the ammunition, since they needed it in much larger amounts. We never had any trouble with our weapons, and we sure didn't need a way to jam a round into a dirty chamber with a forward bolt assist, because we took care of our weapons.

Though the new ammunition the Army had made caused some of the trouble, those soldiers just didn't clean their weapons and take care of them like they needed. We swam with our rifles and brought them up into the surf zone and fired them. That kind of operating puts a dent in the problem the Army had with getting water in the narrow barrel of the AR-15. The little round that the AR-15 fired had impressed us with what it could do, and we had no trouble with the weapon.

That AR-15 was fired every way we could think of at all kinds of targets before we decided we could trust it.

In and out of the surf zone, on the beach, through the sand and the swamps, and that weapon kept working for us. And we fired it on every kind of target we could come up with as well. I suppose it just might be possible that some Team AR-15s could have even been accidentally fired at some deer at Camp Pickett and other places, but I would have no direct knowledge of that.

We started getting heavier weapons within a few years. Some of them were so new that we even helped in their development. When Honeywell was designing their 40mm hand-cranked grenade launcher, we tested the prototypes right on the beach at Little Creek around mid-1965. The weapon was interesting enough, but we had to belt up the ammunition ourselves, and the first belts were these sewn fabric ones with large loops for the grenades.

The Honeywell weapon, eventually called the Mark 18 rapid-fire grenade launcher, was the shoebox-sized weapon that we fit these belts into and turned a crank to operate. It was a lot like the old Gatling gun, only it fired the same 40mm grenades as our M79 grenade launchers. We experimented with all kinds of belt feeds for the darn thing, fabric belts and then plastic ones, even a machine that made up belts with the grenades loaded between two rolls of sticky tape. The Honeywell, as everyone took to calling it, worked fairly well in Vietnam from what I was told, and it was only one of a number of weapons that we used that all fired the 40mm grenades.

We had the single-shot M79 that looked like a big fat shotgun. But what everyone really liked was when the engineers put a grenade launcher underneath the barrel of an M16. That over/under weapon really became popular with the Teams, especially later when the improved [M203] model came out. The way you could use the M79 in combat was a lot like flushing birds when hunting. When that little 40mm grenade went off, those Viet Cong "birds" sometimes broke cover. Now with the 40mm sitting under an M16, when the "birds" took off, you still had that M16 to take them down with.

But well before I was going to leave the Navy, I still had duty to pull in Vietnam. After my time as one of the

training officers at UDTR, my rotation came up and I was
slated to return to Vietnam. It was in August 1969 that
Bob Sheehan relieved me at UDTR and I reported in at
SEAL Team Two to prepare for my deployment. Just like
everyone else, I had to take a certain amount of predeployment training, and part of mine included language training
and SERE [Survival, Evasion, Resistance, and Escape]
school down at Fort Bragg.

It was while I was at Fort Bragg that my orders were
changed. Now I was pulled from the school at Bragg and
sent to UDT 21 as their operations officer. I spent a year
at UDT 21 before I was again listed to go back to Vietnam. Only now my deployment would be considered a
permanent change of station and I would be the senior
naval advisor to the South Vietnamese LDNN school at
Da Nang.

In 1970 I was sent out to California, where I again
attended SERE and language school, only this time I was
allowed to finish the courses. Now I returned to Vietnam
for the first time since 1963. My assignment was as the
officer in charge of the LDNN school, where I would
remain for a year. I was one of the few American SEALs
who were assigned to the LDNN school, but I was not
short of SEAL company.

All during the year, groups of SEALs from both Teams
would come to the school at Da Nang to help with the
training, augmenting my people, and to use the camp for
in-country R&R. That was the first and last time I had
any real trouble with the West Coast SEALs. I didn't know
how the guys from Team One were operating in Vietnam,
but I didn't like how they acted when off-duty at the
LDNN camp.

It finally got to the point where I called down to Saigon
and told them, ''Don't you send any more of those people
up here. They're disrupting training and acting like a
bunch of animals, and I don't want them around.'' It
wasn't that I didn't like blowing off steam just like any
of the other guys in the Teams, but those SEALs from
Team One were just too much.

The East Coast guys who came up had a good time and

went back to their detachments better off for their time in Da Nang. But the West Coast guys would just spend their time drinking and fighting, and the fighting was among themselves when nobody else was around.

So my request just about put a lid on R&R at the LDNN school. Guys from Team Two would sometimes hop a flight and fly into Da Nang, spend a couple of days, and return to their units. But those SEALs from Team One just were not welcome anymore, and I have no trouble saying it.

It seemed to me that the West Coast SEALs were a different breed of people from those of us in the East Coast. And I had spent my first four years in the Navy stationed on the West Coast, so I had some knowledge about the situation. The West Coast Teams just didn't have the camaraderie and togetherness that marked the East Coast Teams. With all of the SEAL basic training being on the West Coast now, things are changing in the Teams and there isn't as much of an East Coast–West Coast rivalry today. But California still has a different atmosphere than anywhere else. Look at the Navy Tailhook scandal and you can see how the majority of those officers investigated were from the West Coast.

But my time at the LDNN school was busy with more than just the SEALs coming in for R&R. One training class after another went through, and we graduated about 150 students a year. And our attrition rate was very low.

That low attrition had nothing to do with the quality of my training cadre. The students were not allowed to quit. The LDNN school was voluntary for the South Vietnamese, but you couldn't volunteer to quit like you could at BUD/S or UDTR. The only way to leave LDNN school was to get killed, break a leg, or otherwise get seriously incapacitated.

We had a three-month school with about a month between classes. For myself, I ran three classes through the school while there. For the most part, the Vietnamese instructors were pretty good. I only had trouble with one of the VNs really—of course, he was the chief at the school.

I confronted that chief about stealing and almost was shot for my trouble.

The LDNN compound was separate from the Navy base at Da Nang. The senior officers' quarters on the base itself had four color TV sets in the quarters. While I was there, one of those TVs turned up missing. The set showed up again, in the chief's quarters down in the LDNN compound, and I knew where it had come from.

To start with, I confronted the chief about where that TV set had come from in private. But he took the discussion outside, where the situation quickly grew out of hand. The chief drew his sidearm on me and was prepared to kill me on the spot over that damned TV.

It was another Vietnamese SEAL who came up and started talking to that chief, while I was looking down the barrel of his .45. It wasn't the most SEAL-like thing to do, but I backed down and said, "Okay, I don't know anything about the TV set." That was not the kind of situation you can win, and the LDNNs stuck up for one another and the chief just might have been able to get away with shooting me and blaming it on someone else.

It wasn't that all of the LDNNs were bad at all. In fact, I stuck up for one myself when he was in a bad situation. This man was in the last class that I was in charge of and was a good student. This young kid was very dark for a Vietnamese, almost black, and the VNs are a hell of a lot more biased towards anyone who looks different than we are in this country.

This student got in trouble while in this local village. Americans were not authorized to go into the village, but I could—I had a pass that let me go anywhere that I wanted to. The Vietnamese Army military police—we called them the "white mice"—had my student prisoner. The white mice brought the student down to the naval base because he was a sailor.

I never did learn what that young man had done up in the village. What I did know was that the white mice were going to hold him at the naval base overnight and send him down to Saigon the next day. When he arrived in Saigon, it wouldn't be very long before my man was shot for whatever he had done. Vietnamese military justice tended to be pretty fast and rough.

My counterpart on the VN side told me something unusual about ARVN military justice. It seemed that if anyone who is a prisoner of the white mice manages to escape, he's free. An unusual situation but one I wasn't going to argue with.

At the base, the white mice were going to imprison my man overnight in a steel Conex box. When they uncuffed him and opened the door to put him in the box, he ran, right down to my camp.

All during his run, the MPs were shooting at their escaping prisoner. The kid came tearing into my camp, right past the armed LDNN guards at the gate. Nobody comes into my camp unless I know who he is. The gate guards let the student through, but the white mice had to stay on the outside until I came down to allow them in.

That student ran through the gate and right up to my office, crying out, "Lieutenant, Lieutenant," in Vietnamese. He managed to gasp out that the white mice were going to lock him up. I already knew what the situation was and wasn't about to let one of my men be turned over to these white mice fellows.

My office had both a front and a back door. "Go out the back door and make it," I said to the gasping student. "*Di-di-mau* [Run]." He tore out the back while I went out the front and down to the gate.

This Vietnamese MP had his sidearm out and was in no mood to talk by the time I got there. "I want my prisoner!" he said as he leveled his .45 at my head. When his pistol came up, my gate guards took off inside the compound.

"Whoa!" I answered him, while staring down the barrel of his pistol. "What prisoner? I know nothing about any prisoner." It was time for me to play dumb, and I had been in the hooch anyway.

"You have my prisoner in your camp," he said, "and I want him."

"Come on in," I said. "Follow me." And I led him into the camp. While I was showing the man around my hooch and he could see for himself that there was no one there, the rest of my Vietnamese had been gathering outside my door. There was a hole in the barbed wire behind my back door so that you could get to the latrine and that was where our wayward student had slipped away.

After that MP went back out my door, the rest of my LDNNs, who had been gathered up by the gate guards, escorted him back out the gate. My sailors told that MP to get out of there and not to come back. Those men had broken open the armory and each one of them was loaded for bear.

Those LDNNs had pulled out the machine guns, the hand grenades, everything that was available. And they locked and loaded right where that MP could see just what he was facing. All of the battle gear was broken out and my people manned the bunkers set up on our perimeter. There was a standoff all night long between my people and the army right outside our gate.

This was enough for me, and I left the Vietnamese to work things out for themselves. Besides, if things came to a shootout, I didn't want to get nailed for blowing away a South Vietnamese no matter what the provocation. I went up to the officers' club up at the naval headquarters and spent some time at the bar. "When you guys have figured this thing out, let me know," I said as I went out the gate.

The ARVN white mice finally gave up on what they considered a bad situation. There was no love lost between the Army of the Republic of Vietnam and the Navy. Especially not between the white mice and the LDNN. I don't know whatever finally happened to that kid, but I hope he made it. I was told later that he did get free of the white mice and that he would be supported by any LDNN unit he could get to.

But that was the last class I had. Vietnamization was growing and American support of the LDNN program was over. In 1971, I left Vietnam, and I don't know if there were any more LDNN classes run through that camp.

Returning to Little Creek, I was given a staff job over at Special Warfare Group Two. When I first arrived at staff, I was made the training coordinator for the group. What I did was coordinate the training evolutions for all of the Teams, SEAL and UDT, between the Navy and the other services. If flight services were needed, I would get them laid on. For an airdrop, I would get the LZs and air clearances made. All of the Teams' requests for training support went across my desk at one time or another during my staff tour.

One of the operations I had to coordinate was a night sneak attack on an anchored boat in the water off Little Creek. It was February and cold, and the weather got worse. The target ship was an AKA [Amphibious Cargo Ship] at anchor near the mouth of the Chesapeake Bay Bridge-Tunnel. For safety during a training attack, the systems on the target ship are shut completely down so that no swimmer would be caught up in a seawater intake and possibly killed.

So the target ship was shut down, and then the weather turned bad. A storm came up and the snow started coming down. It was snowing so badly that you couldn't see fifty yards in any direction. I canceled the exercise and then called the target ship from the command tower. What I told the ship was that the exercise was not going to happen and that I was not going to put my swimmers in the water given the bad conditions. If anything went wrong, we would have a hell of a time getting to a man in trouble.

Somebody on board that AKA wasn't smart enough to warm up the boilers again and get all the systems on line. The unpowered ship broke loose in the storm and went right through the side of the bridge. That was the end of communications with the Eastern Shore for two months. The ship was stuck in the bridge wall for twelve hours alone until the Navy could send ships to move it out.

That accident shut down communications with the Eastern Shore, eastern Maryland, and Delaware for some two months while the bridge was repaired. That also cut off Highway 13 connecting the city with the eastern peninsula of Chesapeake Bay. All told, the situation did not endear the Navy with the locals, and I was the officer in charge of that little fiasco.

Finally, in 1974, my time in the Navy was up. The bad fitrep I had received caught up to me and I was passed over for promotion for the last time. After a long time in the Teams, I was now a civilian. I've done a lot of things over the years, but nothing can compare with my time in the Teams, both good and bad.

I missed the Teams, so I joined a bagpipe band. Now I'm having one hell of a good time with the pageantry, parades, and camaraderie. Just love those bagpipes!

THE PERSONAL COSTS

At best a Navy career is hard on a personal relationship, especially a marriage. Long periods spent at sea, away from a family, can put tremendous pressure on the individuals involved. In the Teams there is the additional problem involved with security. A SEAL can be called away on very short notice for extended periods without much in the way of information to his family about where he may be going, how long he will be gone, or what hazards he may face.

It is no small wonder that divorce is the most common end for a SEAL family. Relatively few SEAL marriages survive for a number of years, fewer still for an entire career and beyond. And if children are involved, the situation is much worse for all concerned.

Thoughts of family problems can affect a SEAL, just as they can any other man, and cause his judgment to slip and personality to change. Though the changes may be subtle to the individual concerned, they can be glaringly obvious to his Teammates. Changes like this are bad at the best of times and can be deadly given the working environment in Naval Special Warfare. Even an experienced, veteran operator can quickly find himself separated from his Teammates, who no longer wish to go on missions with him.

It is difficult for an individual to even recognize the wall he may build up between himself and his Teammates, and even harder to tear it down. This can happen to the best of men and the bravest of operations. It is one of the unseen costs of a SEAL career.

FIRST CLASS RADIOMAN

JACK ROWELL

U.S.N. (RET.)

One of the men who came into the SEALs within a few months of their commissioning, Jack Rowell soon built himself a reputation as an operator and crack radioman. Working in some of the earliest combat actions performed by SEAL Team Two, Jack received awards and earned the respect of his Teammates. After returning from a tour in Vietnam, where he again distinguished himself, Jack found himself facing problems at home that his extensive training hadn't prepared him for.

Originally, I'm from Concord, New Hampshire, and was raised in the northern part of New Hampshire. My father died when I was only five years old and I was raised by my two uncles and aunts. One of my uncles was a lumberjack and the other a farmer, so I was exposed to the woods and rural life, hunting and fishing, from a very early age. Hunting deer and being in the woods are probably my most cherished memories of growing up.

Working on a farm is hard, but you learn how to enjoy the good things quickly. Fishing was something that I enjoyed a great deal back then, ice fishing in the winter and open water in the summer. Much of my summertime was spent with the water, either hanging a line into it or swimming around in it. Those activities are what helped me develop a love for the water that affected how my life would go as an adult.

In 1958, I joined the Navy, but that wasn't my first experience in the military. Originally, I had joined the Air Force back in 1953, right after the Korean conflict had ended. Everything centered around the Army draft back then. Either you enlisted in one of the other services or you took your chances on being drafted into the Army. Instead of two years as a draftee in the Army, I enlisted in the Air Force even though that meant a four-year enlistment.

After an uneventful time in the Air Force, I left the service entirely to try my hand as a college student. Junior college didn't work out for me, so in February 1958, I reentered the service by enlisting in the Navy. For boot camp, I reported to the Great Lakes Training Center north of Chicago along with several hundred other trainees.

Boot camp was uneventful and went by easily enough, especially for someone who was prior service as I had been. After boot camp, I reported to Bainbridge, Maryland, for my Class A radio school. During training as a radioman, I demonstrated a good rate of speed in operating a Morse code key on a CW [carrier wave] radio. As my training continued, my speed increased to where I could send or receive thirty-five to forty words a minute in international Morse code. Using Morse code at a decent rate of speed wasn't a common skill and was a valuable one in the military.

After I graduated radio school, the Navy assigned me to duties in Naples, Italy. Since I was fairly competent at using Morse code, you would think that the Navy would put me in a place where that skill would be put to use. If that is what you believe, you haven't spent much time in the military. In Naples, I spent two years using a teletype machine, which I detested.

But there is always some good that can be found in almost anything. While in Naples, I met Dick Marcinko, who was also working as an enlisted Navy radioman. Dick and I managed to get tangled up together, partying and generally raising hell throughout Naples. Both Dick's and my enlistments were running out at about the same time, and Marcinko had some very firm ideas as to how his future Navy career was going to go.

"Jack," Dick said to me, "you're crazy as hell. You ought to put in for UDT training. That's what I'm going to do. They don't care about what you may have done in the past, you just go out there and go balls to the wall and do what they tell you to do."

This had a certain amount of appeal to me. "Dick," I answered, "I'd love to be a frogman. But how in the hell do I get out of here?"

Radio duty, even teletype operation such as I was doing, had a high priority in the Navy. Once you were in an assignment, they weren't going to let you go easily. But Marcinko suggested a direct approach to that problem, which was how he attacked most questions.

Dick went over and talked to the executive officer of our command, and the next day I was called into the XO's office and asked if I wanted to put in for UDT training. I don't know how Dick did it, but I was now in line to get into the UDT. Now I had to get a bit more exercise than I received sitting at a teletype machine. Working out paid off, and I passed my qualifications and was accepted for UDTR training.

Marcinko left Naples and went to Little Creek to enter training with Class 26. For myself, my preparations for UDTR hadn't gone as smoothly as they could have. Because I'd managed to break my ankle, I had to delay going to Little Creek until the next class. While Dick was off somewhere doing his own training, I started off with Class 27, but that wasn't the class I graduated with.

I managed to hurt my leg again, and the instructors held me over for the next class, so I ended up graduating UDTR with Class 28 in January 1963. It may have been interesting to have remained with Class 27—they graduated forty-seven people in the class, twenty-one of whom were officers. That meant that Class 27 graduated almost one officer for each of the twenty-six enlisted men who graduated. Class 28 only graduated nine officers along with thirty enlisted men. But one of Class 28's officers went on to make quite a name for himself in Navy Special Warfare. Lieutenant (jg) Irving LeMoyne was standing along with me on the cold January morning back in 1963. Irv would later become one of the first SEALs to reach flag rank as an admiral.

Class 28 started out with around 144 students and we graduated thirty-seven. Since I did Hell Week with Class 28, that was the one I graduated, I consider that to be my official class. But my old classmates from 27 still invite me to their reunion party in the summer, and besides, we all served as Teammates together.

But before I could be a Teammate, I had to pass training. I injured my leg on the second or third day of Hell Week with Class 27, but since I was showing a good enough attitude, the instructors rolled me back to Class 28. Hell Week itself is something that's really just there as a big blur during training. But that week is the time that will show whether or not you have the undefinable "it" that will get you through training and into the Teams. For all of its physical demands, Hell Week is a test of your mental state more than anything else. If you don't have it, the "fire in the gut" as they say today, you just aren't going to make it.

All I wanted to do in the Navy was to be a frogman. To get into the UDTs, I had to get through training, and that was what I set my mind to. There were several things that were real trouble for me during Hell Week, but they don't stand out to me now. What does stand out is that last day of the week when "Thank God it's Friday" takes on a whole new meaning. It's that Friday, when they secure you from Hell Week, that you know that you have accomplished something that few men will ever face, let alone get through.

The worst day of Hell Week is generally considered to be the very first day. That's when the shock of what is being done to you hits the hardest. Getting through that first day is the big hurdle to many of us. Once that day is behind you, you can concentrate on just getting through the next day. You never look forward to Friday, you just tell yourself that yesterday is behind you and face getting through the next day, hour, minute, or evolution.

Hearing the phrase "Class 28, secure from Hell Week" is kind of a shock when it finally happens. You look around in kind of a stunned disbelief, not only that Hell Week is over, but at who's left standing there. There isn't really any great feeling or light that hits you. After that long week you're beat down into the ground and just damn glad that it's over.

Even though Hell Week is considered the "maker or breaker" of training, there is still a long way to go before graduation day. You've been put into a mold by the ordeal of Hell Week where you know that you can do anything, but there are still a lot of skills to be mastered and physical obstacles to be overcome. There is still the attitude of just getting through the day in front of you. Whether it's a ten-mile swim or a ten-mile run, or even just a day of demolitions on Vieques Island, the only easy day in training is yesterday, and that's because it's over.

Everybody in my class had to go to a circus at night, whether you'd screwed up or not. A circus is a severe set of PT, exercises that you continue to do until you can barely move, just something to induce a little more pain in a trainee's body. Earlier, a circus was awarded to a boat crew or group of individuals who the instructors felt weren't putting out enough, or had the bad luck of coming in last during an evolution or problem. But even after Hell Week, a circus just became an everyday part of UDTR training.

There were certain instructors who knew that if there was a certain way that they could reach a guy, they would pick at that problem for that individual. For myself, I was more than a little hotheaded back then, I could never quit at anything, and that was what had helped me get through Hell Week. But if the instructors saw that there was something that would piss you off, they would really get on you. The more you would get fired up, the more the instructors would pile it on. Finally, a circus would be awarded for everyone. And after a circus, you were just too tired to be mad at anyone. Anger just took up too much energy, and whatever it was that would get you mad in the first place just didn't seem important anymore. You just wanted the day to end so you could go crawl into your rack and get ready for the next day's work.

But there was a time to play as well, even during training. In the evening, we would share a beer or two after the day's work had been done, and the instructors would be right there alongside you. There was never any crossover between the instructors and the trainees—there was a definite protocol that had to be followed. It wasn't until after you had graduated training and gotten into a Team that you really learned about the camaraderie in the UDTs. But you began to have a taste of it even while still in training, and that was a very good thing.

Swimming was something that I had always been good at, even before training. And while in UDTR, I had the good fortune to be paired up with real great swim buddies, even though everyone was a good swimmer by that time. But just getting into the water, especially at night, and going out on a long swim was still a trial. The instructors were constantly trying to increase your endurance, so even though I was very comfortable in the water, those long-distance swims were a bitch. And down in Puerto Rico, there was THE SWIM, which stood out for everybody.

THE SWIM can only mean one thing to men who went through UDTR on the East Coast, and that is the long-distance swim between Puerto Rico and Vieques Island. The distance between the islands is only about seven miles on the map, but the currents and tides make it a lot longer than that to a swimmer in the water. And you must complete the Vieques swim to graduate UDTR.

There just isn't anything to it. You enter the water in the morning and start stroking. The instructors remain with you all of the way, staying alongside in boats keeping an eye on the swimmers for safety and the waters for sharks. But it isn't anything in the water that will really stop you on the Vieques swim, it's just the swim itself.

The biggest problem in the water for many of the trainees, myself included, is fin burn. Fin burn is where the rubber strap that goes around your ankle and holds your fin on just wears through the skin, leaving a large open wound. Salt water helps keep any infection from setting into the flesh around your ankle, but it also burns in the open wound.

Fin burn was a problem for me, and you would get it the worst on the Vieques swim. But there was no question of turning back on the swim, even if you could. By the time of the Vieques swim, you had already been through too much to even have a thought of quitting.

You couldn't dwell on your misery—that would break you down faster than anything. You had to forget about the fin burn, the distance you had come, the distance you had to go. Everything had to be put out of your mind except the determination to make that next stroke, and the next after that, and to just keep on swimming. Eventually, the swim was over, but you would have made it not doing the swim as a whole, but by doing it one stroke at a time.

And even the best swimmers didn't just jump out of the water at the end of the day. I don't remember clearly, but I believe we had swimmers in the water until well after dark. Running aground on the beach at Vieques Island, you gradually realized that the long swim was over and you slowly left the water. Some guys didn't even leave the water on their own power, they had to be lifted from the waves by either their exhausted classmates or the instructors. But each one of us finished that long, punishing swim.

Scott Slaughter was someone I had swum with a lot, and he was very at home in the water. Slaughter made himself a name as "the Sharkman" later in his career in UDT because of his skill and determination in hunting sharks while free diving without scuba gear. Richard J. "Hook" Tuure of Class 27 was also one hell of a swimmer. But my number one swim buddy in training was David G. "Little Fat Rat" Sutherland, whose brother, Bill "Fat Rat" Sutherland, was already in the Teams and was even a UDTR instructor. For a little guy, Little Fat Rat could seriously kick ass in the water.

And it proved to be a good thing to be able to swim well and have a good swim buddy. There is a saying in the Teams that it pays to be a winner, and that expression was proved to me in a very practical way after some swims. The hot-water plant back in our barracks was a pretty old one and had seen better days. With the size of our class, if you came in late from a swim, all you could get was cold water. For myself, I'm proud to say that I had very few if any cold showers coming in from a swim while in UDTR.

Training remained hard, even after Hell Week, but it became much more of a day-by-day thing. Now you knew what was going to be coming at you, where as during Hell Week, you didn't know what would happen next. As the training went on, it became more interesting and you could enjoy some aspects of it. It was the settings of some of the training that could throw you now.

Some evolutions took place in the heat of Puerto Rico, while others were in the middle of the night. Sometimes the instructors would play their little mind games with you, and other times it was the training itself that could get you spooked if you gave it a chance. Near the end of our UDTR training we were in Key West, Florida, for underwater swimmers' school. For myself, the spookiest thing I experienced in training took place during a night swim while down at Key West.

While at Key West, you go through your first night swim underwater. The situation seems funny to me now, but it wasn't particularly amusing back then, even though probably every frogman who graduated training went through something like it. During the evolution, you would swim as a pair of swim buddies along a set course, one man reading a compass and the other keeping a lookout for obstacles ahead.

The man with the compass had it strapped to his left wrist, and he would extend his right arm and grab his right biceps with his left hand. This posture would put the compass in front of the swimmers' face mask, and his extended right arm would help keep you moving in a straight line. From whatever distance out you were, two, four klicks or more, you would take a sighting on the beach and then swim in. This system was simple, accurate, and worked well for us back then.

On my first night swim, my swim buddy was on my left side and I had the compass. Moving along in the dark water, we could see faintly, but I was concentrating on the compass and maintaining a steady swim line. I knew my buddy was on my left, so I never expected to feel anything on my right side. Something came up on my right side, pushed against me, and rubbed all the way up my right side. It was after I looked to my swim buddy at my left that I thought: Oh, shit!

Right then and there, I knew Jaws had me, and this was years before that movie came out. I did not look to the right, I just kept on swimming. But I knew that the biggest shark in the world was keeping pace with me and just sizing me up as a snack. As I remember, that was one of the faster swims we did down in Key West. After my little meeting, I did pick up the pace just a bit.

Generally, if there was a full moon or any kind of light, you could still see fairly well underwater. We didn't carry any kind of light with us during training in Key West, but you could still see everything. The underwater world at Key West is a beautiful sight, as there is plenty of light, even at night. Later, when I was in the Teams and we trained in Chesapeake Bay, the situation was a lot different.

In the waters of the Chesapeake Bay, it was like walking in the woods in the middle of a moonless night—you couldn't see anything. As your hand passed through the water, you would disturb microscopic plankton and other critters who would put off a faint glow of phosphorescence. Little glowing bubbles would swirl behind your passing hand, and that would be all you could see.

In the Chesapeake, you wouldn't even be sure of where you were in the water until you went down and hit the bottom. On a sneak attack, everyone would take a compass sight on the target and then usually go on down to the bottom and crab in, crawl above the mud, to the target ship. The bay wasn't that deep, and we could stay within the safety limits of the breathing gear we were using without much trouble.

That kind of diving didn't have much enjoyment connected with it. Most of us just considered it a pain in the ass but part of the job we had to do. For myself, I never liked those night sneak attacks in the Chesapeake, and I don't remember that anyone else liked them either.

Even in the dark, you would know when you were coming up on the target ship. Say we would be attacking an LST [Landing Ship, Tank]. As you came closer to the target, you would start hearing the noises of the ship's machinery. The closer you came in the darkness, the louder the sounds became. If you were a rookie, you would be sure that at any moment, you would be sucked up through a seawater intake and ground up inside the ship that just had to be only an arm's reach away.

But sound travels further and sharper underwater than it does in the air. The ship you swore was only a few feet away was some distance farther. Prior to approaching the ship you could surface and take another final compass sight. On a dark night, the chances were that nobody would see you against the black water. A lot of guys would come up and take a quick peek at maybe a hundred yards out. The crews on the ships would know that we were coming and would be shining searchlights and flashlights into the water, but they never saw us coming.

Finally coming up to the ship, you might be able to see it faintly in the darkness as a blacker portion of the water where the sounds are loudest. Much like when I worked point in Vietnam later, you would crouch down low and look up against the skyline and would see shadows silhouetted against the faint light. That same trick worked underwater looking against the surface.

Feeling your way along the hull, you would plant your limpet mines and move away back to shore. After some missions had passed, the nervousness cut back. But those first few night swimmer attacks in the Chesapeake could make you wonder just why you were in the Teams in the first place. Of course, there would also be a realization that two people, yourself and your swim buddy, had just effectively sunk several thousand tons of ship. That kind of thought would also make you see just how important the job of the UDT and SEALs could be during wartime.

Once you have gotten over the nervousness of your first few training missions, you're kind of out of the play mode and think of the operation as real. And that was the object of training—to duplicate the real wartime operation and meet the problems in a safer environment. But you always knew you were just playing at attacking the ship, no matter how real the exercise would be. And there would still be a good feeling after the attack was over, you felt you had done your job.

Even though we all did our jobs and teamwork was the only way to operate for us, the Teams in those days were still very competitive amongst ourselves. Questions would be put up against the other swimmer pairs, such as "How close did you place your limpet mines to the keel? How long did the swim take you?" These kinds of things would rate you against your buddies in an unofficial, but no less important for that, competition.

Even on the runs we did in training and later in the Teams, where you were in the pack mattered. At least it did until you became an old guy and slowed down on the runs a bit. The "winner's" philosophy in the Teams came in part with the accomplishment of completing UDTR, and the pride in that was developed way back when, well before my time.

The last part of UDTR training involved going to both underwater swimmers' school and jump school. After we had completed our training at Little Creek, the class was shipped down to Fort Benning, Georgia, to attend three weeks of Army airborne school. It was after airborne school that we continued on down to Key West, Florida, and attended underwater swimmers' school. After graduation, we would go aboard our Teams as fully qualified jumpers and divers.

The physical end of airborne training was nothing to us after weeks of UDTR training. The PT that the Army would run to build up the airborne students' muscles wasn't much more than a warm-up for us. That was more than a little frustrating to the Army instructors. When the

Army NCOs would drop one of us for push-ups, all of the UDTR students would drop and do the push-ups right alongside their Teammate.

The Army students would be dropping out all over the place during PT, while we would just keep moving along. We didn't mean for our actions to be so frustrating for the Army instructors, it just worked out that way. At the jump clubs on post, we helped reinforce our relationships with the Army Special Forces who were also using the facilities at Fort Benning. So we would get along with the Army, it was just the average airborne student wasn't up to our level of physical fitness.

Airborne school wasn't a unique experience as far as the way we excelled at our training. There wasn't a single school any of us attended during my time in the Teams that the SEALs or UDT students didn't come out at the head of the class. The level of competence we expected of each other was high, and we regularly met or exceeded that expectation.

It wasn't that all of our training was easy. Some of the schools were real ball-busters. The escape and evasion school many of us attended at Pickle Meadows, California, was so hard and rough on the students that it was finally closed after a congressional investigation. Some of the training involved a lot of physical exertion, other classes were straightforward academic studying. For myself, it was the book learning that came hard sometimes. For the physical end of training, the ballsy part, I was always right up there at the front of the line.

So when it came time to make our first parachute jump at airborne school, I was the first man in the stick and standing in the door. There isn't a lot from that first jump that I remember except for being the first in line, standing in the door, looking straight ahead, and being absolutely petrified.

But I was a UDT trainee, a great big hairy frogman, and I would have taken on King Kong hand to hand if I had been told to. But that didn't mean I had to look down at the ground on my first jump. To this day, I don't believe anyone in the stick, from the smallest student to the jumpmaster who smacked me on the ass to go out the door, knew that this big frogman was shitting his pants at the thought of stepping out the door of that perfectly good airplane.

The other major memory I have of my first jump was, after leaving the plane, looking up at a big, inflated, parachute canopy. My, that was a lovely sight. The instructors on the ground were yelling up instructions for us to slip right or slip left, whatever it took for each of us to get on target. And then I touched the earth and regained my composure a little bit. It was time again to be the tough frogman who looked just a bit better than everybody else. That was particularly hard right then because I had done a very bad PLF [parachute landing fall] and had hit flat on my ass in the dirt.

Later, while in the Teams, I came to like parachuting considerably more than during those first jumps at Benning. In the SEALs, free-fall parachuting was intended to be a major method of infiltrating a unit into an area, so we all became free-fall-qualified. HALO [high altitude, low opening] school was another Army school and the only place we could learn military free-falling.

While at HALO school, our highest jump was something over 21,000 feet, more than high enough to require oxygen to keep from passing out. The Army instructors were a bunch of great guys and our confidence was way up, but there is something about leaving an aircraft flying more than four miles up in the air. Looking down, there isn't much to see, everything is just too small. But you exit the plane and do your maneuvers, falling for over a minute before opening your parachute.

Training of course gives you the ability to leave that aircraft at such a high altitude, but there is a definite feeling unique to doing such a thing. It is definitely an achievement and accomplishment relatively few people can share.

After attending HALO school at Fort Bragg, a number of us took up skydiving as a hobby. A lot of guys in the Team had been sport jumping before even going to HALO school, and the local clubs had a lot of SEALs and frogs in it. Just about everything we had learned in the Army school we could use while skydiving. That way we could both get in some practice and have a lot of fun in the process. We also tested out new rigs and techniques, not necessarily following established Navy procedures.

Some of us were jumping rigs that were more than pushing the envelope, and we were completing the jumps just by the hair of our chinny-chin-chins. Jim Watson and some of the guys from the Team had gone up to someplace in New Jersey and scrounged up a bunch of surplus parachutes that were considered too old for Navy pilots to use but were just fine for our little experiments. We started modifying the chutes as well as dyeing them all sorts of different colors out back of the Team headquarters. Some of those chutes became a little bit too modified and weren't the safest things in the world to jump out of a plane with.

UDTR training ended for me when I graduated in January 1963 and was assigned to UDT 21. The graduation date meant that I didn't spend a lot of time with UDT 21 in Little Creek before we left for winter training back in the Caribbean on St. Thomas. My time with UDT 21 was short, though—I was soon assigned to SEAL Team Two, which had only been commissioned the year before.

While down on St. Thomas, old Sam Bailey, Mr. UDT and the prototype Bullfrog, called over the PA system in his deep gravelly voice, "Rowell, come to administration. Now!"

Such a command was not to be ignored. While jogging over to the administration building, I wondered what was going on. I had made the swim that morning, so I couldn't be in trouble for skipping out on that. As far as the night before went, well, I couldn't remember what I had done then but thought that I couldn't be in too much trouble or they would have nailed me that morning. So it was with a little bit of puzzlement that I arrived at the administration building and Sam Bailey.

"Sam," I said, "what's up?"

Without any fanfare, Sam said, "Pack your shit."

"Oh no," I said, more than a little shocked. "What have I done?"

"You're going back to the Creek," Sam continued.

"Why?" I asked. "I don't understand."

"You're going to SEAL Team something. . . ."

"What the hell is 'SEAL Team'?" I asked. "Have I got to go? I'm having fun down here."

There wasn't any use arguing with orders. "Get your shit together," Sam repeated. "You're going out in the morning. There's already a flight laid on."

Down in St. Thomas then, before we were asked to leave the island, something about accidentally blowing out all of the windows in the Corning mansion from an over-loaded demolition target, it was party time practically from the moment you left the airplane. There was training, of course, and some very hard training. But St. Thomas was a prime vacation spot, especially for lovely ladies needing an escort. And we were in the best shape of our lives at that time.

Partying did seem to wear thin after a while. After training, you would go to evening chow and just want to lay down in the barracks for a couple of hours. You'd tell yourself that you weren't going out that night and mean it. But by the time seven o'clock rolled around, you'd find yourself wandering out of the barracks and out to the Grand Boco Hotel or maybe the Silver Bullet Bar. By nine or ten o'clock, you'd be feeling pretty good and decide on just one last beer. And with that, your responsible plans would be out the window and you would be off making the rounds of the tourist bars seeing what may be available. Then you'd finally get back to the barracks by three or four o'clock in the morning. We partied hard and worked hard. If we hadn't been in great shape, that life would have killed us. You were in top condition, looked good and felt good, but there were times that maybe you didn't feel so good.

So it was very enjoyable down in St. Thomas, and I wasn't looking forward to going back to the Creek. Especially not going back and reporting to some unknown type of special Team. But I went back to Little Creek and, in

May of 1963, found myself just down the road from UDT 21 at SEAL Team Two. The SEALs were a very top secret outfit back then, and very little, if anything, was known about them publicly. I hadn't been in UDT 21 long enough to be up on all of the scuttlebutt, so I hadn't heard anything about them. Sam Bailey was concerned with what happened to UDT 21 and anything outside of that wasn't of enough importance for him to take notice of it.

After arriving back at the Creek from St. Thomas, I reported in to the command. From there, I was given my orders to report in at SEAL Team Two and now was told where they were. When I got to the SEAL Team Two building and reported on board, Rudy Boesch was on the quarterdeck.

"Seaman Rowell reporting, Chief," I said, and my time with SEAL Team Two had begun.

It wasn't for some time that I found out why I had been transferred to SEAL Team Two. Team Two had been going through some trouble getting their radio communications systems developed and manned for the kind of guerrilla warfare they were intended to fight. My records from radio school showed me as a competent high-speed CW operator, and that was what they needed.

"Rowell," I was told, "we're going to start sending you to all these different kinds of communications schools. What you're going to do for the Team is get a handle on the situation and help set up what we need."

Being a seaman there, I didn't have any rate or rank preference and I was sent off to schools right away. The first place I went was Fort Bragg, where I worked with the Army Special Forces and learned about field antennas and the AN/GR-109 radio. The Angry-109 was one of the more common long-range portable radios back then and was supposed to become the center of our communications net. Power in the field for the 109 came from a hand-cranked generator that the powerman would sit behind and turn the two bicycle-pedal handles with his arms.

The Angry-109 was the baby that they put in my hands. My orders were pretty simple and direct. "Jack," they said, "we know you can communicate. Now we want you to do it."

That was my stepping-stone into the Navy SEALs. The powers that be had looked long and hard at the records of a number of UDT men, and mine was the record that stood out. Today, I feel that it was very fortunate that I had the skills that they needed in SEAL Team Two. Those abilities helped me enter a career that I enjoyed.

Everybody in the Team then left a mark in the tree that grew into the legend that became SEAL Team Two. From Gallagher to Jim Finley to Jimmy Watson, everyone contributed their part. There are a lot of little things that were done along the way, but I feel strongly that my greatest contribution to SEAL Team Two was to help them communications-wise.

We used to compete with the Special Forces platoons, who really considered themselves hot stuff in every aspect of unconventional warfare. But the weakest aspect of many of the units was communications, especially CW. It seemed that I was always being put up against the best radioman in an A-Team, and the results were often the same. We always made commo, established communications, often well before the most experienced men the Army Special Forces had. The SEALs were one of the new units on the block, but our communications were at least as good as those of the older units.

But even for us, communications could be an iffy thing, especially over long distances. One experiment we tried at Team Two was to establish communications between a group of SEALs who were training down at Eglin Air Force Base in Florida and our home base at Little Creek. It seemed that Jim Finley, though he didn't really hate me, had a case against me when it came to the radios.

The AN/GR-109 had a generator that weighed in the neighborhood of fifteen pounds. As the radioman, I usually packed the radio, batteries, accessories, and antennas to our system. But someone else had to pack the generator along. Not only did someone have to carry the generator, they had to crank it when we tried to establish communications. And the generator of a 109 had a few idiosyncrasies of its own.

Cranking the handles of an Angry-109 generator took a good amount of strength and endurance at the best of times. If the radio operator was doing a lot of dits and dahs, the current draw from the radio made turning the generator handles that much harder. If the radio operator had a very heavy hand on his Morse key, turning the generator handles could be real work with the sudden resistance.

To this day, I can remember the comments of some of the guys back then, Jim Finley especially. As he was cranking the generator handles, Finley would say, "Jack, get that fucking message out, will ya? I'm dying here. This thing is killing me."

Of course, even with his bitching, Jim would continue to crank the generator handles. After all, that was part of the mission, to establish communications. And the mission comes first. But it was amazing to me how the guys would just keep turning the handles of the generator, for twenty, thirty, or more minutes. Whatever it took to get the message out.

You didn't want to stay on the air for a half hour or so. What you wanted to do was establish communications quickly, get your information transmitted and acknowledged, and get the hell off the air. Enemy forces could have DF [direction-finding] equipment on you at any time, and the longer you stayed on the air, the greater the chance of your being detected and located.

So the key to good military communications is to get your stuff out quickly and cleanly. To do that, you had to be able to set up your antennas properly and run your gear correctly. And to do that, you had to practice, and training was something the SEALs did constantly.

For anyone who was the radio operator's helper, they had to throw that Angry-109 generator into the sack along with their parachute and all their other gear. And those guys with the generator knew that they would be cranking that sucker. Not a fun job. But my job was always to be the radio operator. I never had to crank the generator.

Being the key man was much better than being the crank man, one of the more pleasant memories I have of those early days.

That was one of the comical situations that arose back then. Humor was always important in the Teams, especially given the serious nature of so much of what we did. And we tend to remember more of what struck us as funny, even though the situation may not have been funny to anyone else involved. Many of the older guys remember being the crank man on the generator while I was working the key. Lenny Waugh, Jim Watson, Jimmy Wallace, even Hoss Kucinski had their turn at the handles. And even big Hoss got tired out cranking the generator handles of an Angry-109. But soon enough, we were finally being put in a situation where our training could be really tested.

Vietnam had been a situation that SEAL Team Two had only been involved with slightly by 1966. We had sent a number of men over to Vietnam, both as members of SEAL Team Two MTTs and as men assigned to SEAL Team One MTTs. But as far as active combat went, Vietnam had been a SEAL Team One party for almost a year before SEAL Team Two received the go-ahead to start sending direct-action platoons to the Southeast Asia theater.

When the word finally came down to SEAL Team Two in mid-1966 that we were going to start being involved in combat, things became much more intense at the Team. Where we normally would train hard, now it was balls to the wall in an all-out effort to become as good as we could be. Before, we were training to be better at our mission in general. Now it could literally be a matter of life and death.

Our commanding officer at that time was Lieutenant Commander Bill Earley, only the fourth CO SEAL Team Two had since it was commissioned. Earley was one hell of a strong swimmer, and in the Teams the officers would swim right alongside the enlisted men during training. At that time, I thought I was pretty good in the water, but Earley was really awesome, with a strong kick and powerful stroke. On one night swim I was Bill's swim buddy, and at the start of the swim, I figured it was just another time in the water. By the end of that particular evening's training, I was really tired and more than glad to leave the water.

When the announcement came down about our going to combat in Vietnam, we just started working all that much harder. Just as Earley's example had forced me to put out that much more on my swim with Earley, the thought of going to war forced us all to put that extra percentage into our training.

Just about everybody at the Team was excited about going into combat and proving that we were the best. There were some apprehensions about facing combat and thinking about your own mortality—just because we were SEALs didn't mean we weren't people too. But for the most part, we were all looking forward to testing ourselves in the ultimate classroom, combat.

But there were a lot of other classrooms and schools we had to go through before being shipped out for Vietnam. The operational platoons at SEAL Team Two were numbered from two through ten at that time, and we were going to deploy to Vietnam on a rotational basis. Our platoons were going to be part of Detachment Alfa, operating mostly in the Mekong Delta. At the start, two platoons were going to be deployed on a six-month tour of duty starting in January 1967. Before those first platoons were rotated back to the States, their relief platoons would arrive in-country early enough to get introduced to the operational area before the first platoons left.

Before any of us left for Vietnam, we did a lot of operating in the field together. Night navigation and combat patrols were commonly done, with all of us in a squad working closely together and learning about each other as well as how to operate. Training closely as a squad developed even more unity inside the Team. Even if you were working with a guy you weren't as close to as another buddy of yours, you still learned to respect each other and know one another's strengths and weaknesses.

You had to develop that kind of closeness and unity to survive in Vietnam with the way we were going to operate well inside of enemy territory. We had to depend on each other within a squad or platoon and know how each other would think and act if the situation changed suddenly and we didn't have a chance to communicate with one another. And we had to know each other's jobs, not only to develop the closeness we had to have but also to be able to pick up and carry on if one of us fell. As a key radio operator, I didn't just train with my equipment, I also learned how to handle the Stoner light machine gun and the XM148 grenade launcher. And the other guys learned how to handle the radio and call for support or extraction.

Our plan was to go out on patrol primarily as a squad, half a platoon. On a combat patrol, we would be inserted into enemy territory and search out the Viet Cong in his own backyard. The thought of that kind of combat was a little bit like skydiving for me. Getting on board an aircraft bothered me, as did the ride. Even today, I don't like to fly without a parachute. It wasn't the jump itself, it was the long ride up where you had time to think about everything and wonder if you had anticipated all of the possible problems. Once I unassed the plane and was in free fall, all of the anxieties and nervousness were gone.

All of the training we were doing in the States was a little like getting on board the plane for a parachute jump. We were busy enough but you had time to think and wonder about what was coming up. Finally, in the fall of 1967, my platoon's rotation came up and it was time to leave. Now that we were actually on our way, the anxieties were a bit sharper, but we would soon be in a position to act on them.

Seventh Platoon arrived in Vietnam on 24 October 1967. Lieutenant Pete Peterson was our platoon leader and directing Alfa squad with Warrant Officer Charlie Watson as his assistant leading Bravo squad. One of the big advantages we had in the platoon was in our platoon chief, Bob Gallagher. The Eagle, as he was known, had already been on one deployment to Vietnam. Gallagher had been with Second Platoon when it was one of the first two SEAL Team Two platoons to arrive in Vietnam in January 1967. Less than seventy men from SEAL Team Two had been deployed to Vietnam for combat when Seventh Platoon arrived in-country, and Bob Gallagher was the first chief from a platoon to return for a second tour. His experience was going to be a great help to Seventh Platoon once we entered into combat, but first we had to get to Southeast Asia.

The plane ride across the Pacific Ocean to Vietnam had to be the longest, least comfortable, and most boring flight I have ever been on. That flight is the most vivid pain-in-the-ass memory I have of that first tour. To get off that plane, I would have taken on King Kong bare-handed, and I wasn't the only member of the platoon who felt that way.

We were all stuffed on board a military transport with all of our equipment, weapons, miscellaneous stuff, and our scout dog, a German shepherd named Rinnie. We stopped off at what seemed like every island in the Pacific in order to refuel, and let the dog relieve himself. A lot of reading, sleeping, and laying on a steel Conex box went on during the flight. And the surface of a Conex box becomes pretty hard after the first eighteen hours or so. That trip felt like we went halfway around the world, which we did if you consider we started in Little Creek, Virginia.

When we finally arrived in Vietnam, my first impression was not what you would call a good one. "Holy shit," I said as we flew over the Mekong Delta. "We're going to be out in this garbage?"

It looked like the whole of Southeast Asia was nothing but rice paddies and coconut trees. In other words, big open puddles of water over stinking mud surrounded by tree lines where the enemy can hide. And the way of living over there is so close to the earth, almost biblical in a way. The majority of the people in Vietnam at that time were simple peasants. They didn't have much and made their living from the land, working their gardens, rice paddies, and fishing the waters. It was a shame that a war was going on in a land where the people had to work so hard just to eke out a living to begin with.

At first, I wasn't so concerned with the people and how

they lived. I was more looking at the terrain features and thinking about how to react in such areas. We first landed at Tan Son Nhut airport near Saigon, but we didn't stay around long enough to see anything of the busy city. We hopped aboard some trucks after being briefed on being in Vietnam and traveled south to Vinh Long, where Sixth Platoon was. After spending the night with Sixth, we gathered all of our gear and climbed aboard the Mike boat, an armed and armored landing craft, for the remainder of the trip to our assigned posting.

Our assigned base was at My Tho, where we relieved Fourth Platoon. Accommodations weren't too bad—we stayed in a small hotel near town and kept our gear and Rinnie at the PBR base down on the Song My Tho branch of the Mekong River. My Tho was considered a city by Vietnamese standards but wasn't much more than a town to those of us fresh in from the States. But Bob Gallagher had operated in the My Tho area with Second Platoon when he was over on his first tour, so that did give us something of an edge when we first arrived.

Gallagher himself gave us an edge just by being our platoon chief, I thought, and I figured we were fortunate to have him. Bob and I went back a ways together and we had always seemed to hit it off fairly well. Gallagher is another Mick Irishman like myself and senior to me. From me, just like everyone else in the platoon, the Eagle demanded top-of-the-line performance in everything, and he normally got it. His reputation was such that anyone in the platoon, if not all of SEAL Team Two, would go anywhere Bob led. He was the man you wanted at your back in a combat zone, and you knew he would always get you home. I had that feeling when we first arrived in-country, and it was a good one.

Later on, for my second tour in Vietnam, I would be part of the Sixth Platoon, and there was only one man I felt real comfortable with during that time, Jim Watson, our platoon chief. There were other guys in the platoon I was buddies with, and I was proud to be a part of the Sixth, but it never quite held the same feelings for me as did being with the Seventh Platoon on that first tour. Having Pete Peterson as our platoon leader and Bob Gallagher as our chief just made that first tour different and gave the platoon a real solid feel.

My first impressions of My Tho were soon reinforced as we saw more of the city. The streets were busy with everyday people going on with their lives. But there were barricades across some of the streets and people walking around with weapons. It was a relatively peaceful scene, but you could see that there was a war going on. Our hotel was an old villa-like affair with four of us being assigned to a room and all the amenities of the country available to us. On top of the roof of the hotel was a water tower supplying pressure for our showers, a nice feature until it was blown away by mortar fire some weeks later.

The matters of day-to-day living were attended to with the guys from Fourth Platoon showing us where the chow hall was, the ammunition stored, and where the better beer halls were located. It wasn't long after we had settled in at My Tho that we began operating in the field. Standard operating procedure then was that the new platoon would be led on their first few operations by the platoon that they were relieving. That way, we could learn the lay of the land and avoid the more obvious problems from the unit that was already familiar with them.

The early operations helped break in the rookies, which were most of us then, and pick up the tempo quickly and get us relaxed and calmed down from finally being in an active combat environment. Fourth Platoon stayed over about a week to help us get our feet wet operationally. After that initiation time, we helped Fourth get their gear up to Tan Son Nhut and aboard their flight back to the Land of the Big PX.

Now it was time for Seventh Platoon to start going to work seriously. One of the first things I recall from a mission was the night of our first operation, where we were operating with Fourth Platoon. Today, I wouldn't believe that there was an enemy force within a hundred klicks of us. That op was just to get us used to the terrain, how to work as a unit, and build up our confidence. It was supposed to have been a pretty good operation—we were told that enemy forces were in the area—but we didn't see anything the whole night.

On that operation, I met Chieu Hois for the first time. They were ex-VC Vietnamese who were considered friendly forces and would guide us into the suspected target area. Those Vietnamese guides were dressed in just standard street clothes, which should have told me that this wasn't going to be a night for a great battle. But the level of nervousness about being in the enemy jungle for the first time kept me from noticing things like clothes until I thought about them well afterwards.

After a long night waiting for an enemy who never came, your nerves can get a little bit on edge. When the first crack of daylight appears and you can start seeing clearly what's around you, life can get exciting. All I could see were a couple of the Chieu Hois that had led us in—there wasn't an American within my sight. And I was anything but used to seeing Vietnamese faces the first thing on a jungle morning. Son of a bitch, I thought, Charlie's got me. I didn't know whether to start shooting or what. The thing was that you were so psyched up that the enemy could appear at any time that you were ready to react to anything. Yes, I was nervous on my first operation, and anybody who says that they weren't is full of shit.

Looking around in the daylight hours, all I could see were those Chieu Hois looking at me. But my second wind came in quickly enough and I recognized my neighbors as the guys who had brought us in the night before. But that sudden wake-up call on my first operation is a memory I'm going to carry vividly for a long time to come.

When my first real firefight came up I learned a lesson that lasted to my last firefight in Vietnam some years later. When it isn't your imagination and the bullets start flying, you don't have time to be scared or to worry about your reactions. Things are happening so fast that you don't stop and think—doing that would get you killed and possibly take some of your Teammates along with you. Instead, training takes over and you act accordingly. Without a lot of conscious thought, you do what you were trained for.

Just like back during HALO training, when the jump itself is going on, you pay attention to your altimeter, count down the seconds on your stopwatch, and adjust your attitude to track to the target. When you finally pull the ripcord, it's because that is the next step in the operation, just like opening fire in a firefight.

The actions in combat happen so fast that your body reacts quicker than you have time to think about it. Where is the fire coming from? Is it in your field of fire? What is firing at you? How many are there? These are all questions you can answer moments later, but during the firefight itself, you can't be thinking about such things. That is where the intense training we did in the SEALs back at Little Creek paid off. And the side benefit of such training was that you were too busy reacting to even have any time to be scared.

After your first firefight, then the time to think comes in. At first, we all had a sense of elation—we were still alive and the enemy wasn't. How many kills did we get, what did we do and what did we accomplish, what kind of intel did we pick up were all questions that we asked after the fight. And that was also the time to get a little nervous. Looking at what had happened, especially if the fight was a real hot one and your Teammates had been hurt, that could get to you if you dwelled on it at all. But I didn't think about that a lot in Vietnam. An active firefight wasn't what bothered me the most in Vietnam, it was an enemy that you couldn't fight, only try to anticipate.

Booby traps were the real dangers that I hated during my tours in Southeast Asia. Moving along on a patrol or a search, you never knew when you would get the trap that you didn't find. You had to contend with these ingenious, deadly devices, and that meant staying alert and thinking constantly. In a firefight, when the shooting started, it was time to act as your training had taught you.

Everybody had a part to play during and after a firefight. Immediately afterwards, some members of the patrol would search the bodies for intelligence, others would check the body count, and still others kept up perimeter security. You never let your guard down for a moment out in the field. It was back at the camp or even on the extraction boat on the trip back that the time came to be congratulatory to each other.

Even the next day at chow, the subject would center around the platoon's activities the night before. "Shit, man, the bullets hit right here!" would be heard in regards to an action. But all of this would happen later when we were back in a relatively safe area.

During this still early part of the tour, I had my first close-in, personal kill. That is something that happens to many military men, and you never forget it. We had been going into this village area, coming out of dense jungle and passing through some rice paddies. It was a combat patrol—we knew Charlie was around and we were hunting him in his own territory.

When we had just come out of the rice paddy, I spotted these two VC looking right at me through an opening in the brush. The VC fired first, but I was the better shot. The one VC immediately dropped in the loose-limbed collapse of death, and the other guy just scurried off. Roy Dean Matthews, Mikey Boynton, and Gallagher were also with me, and we all moved out to the hooch where I had seen the VC.

We met a few more VC at the hooch and made short work of taking them out. Inside of the building we picked up some intelligence as well as a number of weapons, so there wasn't any question of these guys being VC. But that had been my first kill, the one where you see your man go down. Rounds had been flying right past me, kicking up dust, but my training held true and I just shot straighter than he did.

How a man fired depended a lot on the situation. Some of the guys liked to fire semiautomatically from their M16s, while other guys preferred full automatic. For myself, I put out a lot of semiautomatic fire, especially when I had a single clean target and could get a straight shot. Of course, going into a hooch where the shit can start flying suddenly, you would flip the selector on your rifle over to full auto before ever entering. For a fast reload in a hot situation, we would butt-tape our magazines together—that is we taped one magazine upside down and against the side of another magazine. This way, to reload your weapon, you would just remove the empty mag, flip it over, and stick the loaded mag into the weapon. The only drawback to this system is that the lower magazine was more exposed to dirt and mud. But if you just took a little care you could keep your ammo clean and keep your weapon running fast.

We had the twenty-round magazines for our M16s for the most part. There were thirty-round magazines available, but they were few and far between in '67 and '68. Scrounging up a thirty-rounder was a premier accomplishment. I found out later that fifty-round magazines had been made for us during the Vietnam War, but I never saw any of them in use. Finally, the thirty-rounders became a lot easier to get and everyone in the platoons had them.

When going out on operations, we had a good deal of freedom in choosing our personal weapons. Because I was primarily the radio operator, I carried the XM148 grenade launcher mounted underneath an M16 rifle. This gave me a lot of firepower with the 40mm grenade launcher, but the M16 rifle mated to the launcher kept me from having an empty weapon once I had fired a grenade. Originally Bob Gallagher wanted me to carry the XM148, and I soon agreed with him on the decision.

Other weapons were carried on other missions. There were times I carried a Stoner light machine gun for the squad, but Mike Boynton and Hook Tuure were usually the machine gun men, each packing either a Stoner or an M60. But most of the time I carried the XM148 with a load of 40mm HE [high explosive] grenades for it. The 40mm grenade was not intended for real close combat—the blast and fragmentation could take out the firer as well as the target—so additional ammunition was developed and issued to us for close-in work.

For up close with the 40mm, we had both flechette rounds and buckshot rounds. I didn't carry the flechette round much. Most of the time, Bob Gallagher had me packing HE rounds as the most all-around useful 40mm ammunition. Later on, and during my second tour, I would sometimes load up a few buckshot rounds for close-in work, but by and large I carried HE rounds, and a hell of a lot of them. The 40mm ammunition came packaged in cloth bandoleers that each held six rounds. Normally, I carried five or six bandoleers, thirty or thirty-six rounds of HE. On some hot missions I packed as many as ten or twelve bandoleers, sixty or more rounds of ammunition, depending on what we expected to run into.

In addition to 40mm grenades, I carried ammunition for the M16 portion of the weapon, usually several hundred rounds packed in twenty-round magazines. On top of all this, I didn't have anything special, just a K-BAR knife and a Mark 13 Day/Night flare, and my radio. The radio was a PRC-25 FM transceiver in a backpack rig that weighed in at around twenty-two pounds. An extra battery was an additional two pounds. This all added up to about a fifty-seven-pound load of equipment on the average.

Back during my Vietnam days, I was in much better shape than I am in now, so packing a large amount of ammunition was just part of the job. All of us would put out one hundred percent and more during a tour, and the cost showed up on our bodies. It wasn't uncommon for a man to lose twenty, twenty-five, or even thirty pounds of weight during a tour, depending on how big he was to start with. The hot, humid environment of Southeast Asia could sweat several pounds off of you on just a single operation.

When I went over on my first tour, I weighed about 175 to 180 pounds. When we came back in 1968, I was down to about 155 pounds. The amount of weapons and ammunition we carried added a lot to the weight losses we had during a tour. When we went out on a heavy combat operation, where we expected to fall in the shit to start with, we carried all the ammunition and weapons we could. Men in the squad would carry an extra couple of belts each for the machine guns, in addition to the hundreds of rounds in belts carried by the gunners themselves.

To carry and operate with all of this gear, we had to be in pretty much top shape. One thing was for sure—the

Vietnam environment didn't encourage putting on a lot of body fat. Eating a lot was also something we didn't do much of, though we ate well enough for the most part. With our operations going on at all hours of the day and night, getting a meal at the chow hall could be hard at times. Often we grabbed a bite on the transport boat prior to insertion, if it was a long trip, or after extracting. For myself, I kind of developed a taste for the standard C rations. When you could get them, the dehydrated [freeze-dried] Long Range Reconnaissance Patrol [LRRP] rations were tasty. But you needed a lot of water handy, and the chlorine tablets used in our canteens would quickly take away any of the good taste to the ration.

Personally, I would eat most any of the C rations, even the ham and chopped eggs, which some guys could barely look at, let alone eat. But my favorite probably was the potatoes and beef chunks in gravy. The fruit cake dessert was great, but the pecan roll was a little dry.

It was kind of funny how the guys would barter with each other for the different components in the ration packs. Trading canned peaches for the pound cake or whatever was common. Personally, I liked the canned peaches quite a bit. You could always get a can of peaches from one of the heavy smokers for one of the four-cigarette C-ration cigarette packs. For myself, I wasn't much of a smoker and could usually spare the cigarettes.

It was very rare to see a guy smoke on an operation except maybe on the extraction boat. But we all carried cigarettes, and not just to smoke. The burning end of a cigarette was just the thing to burn leeches off your body with. And after say a canal ambush, where you could be in water up to your chest for hours, leeches would be all over you. Bug juice [an oily insect repellent] also worked for getting rid of leeches, but you couldn't trade it for C-rat peaches.

Funny stories aside, there were some very tight situations for Seventh Platoon during that first tour. In late January 1968, the Tet offensive began and shit started breaking out everywhere. Earlier, there was a fair idea in the platoon that something was coming. Being a junior man in the platoon didn't make me privy to all of the available intel. But we had prepared for some eventuality.

The flat roof of the hotel was surrounded with a wall, and we had built some sandbag bunkers up there. The bunkers were relatively small ones, just walls really—the roof couldn't take the weight of much more. But we had installed more than a few weapons, including 81mm mortars, .50-caliber machine guns, and boxes, cans, and crates of grenades and ammunition.

When Tet broke out on 31 January, the fighting opened up everywhere. Once things started, Tet just kind of snowballed, getting bigger and bigger as time went on. There were short, fierce firefights breaking out in the streets of My Tho—you could see the tracers criss-crossing all over the city. Chicom tracers were green and U.S. tracers were red, so it was a colorful sight, but the shit was hitting the fan big-time.

And the fighting wasn't like what our fathers faced in World War Two. The bad guys didn't wear gray or tan uniforms—they didn't wear any kind of uniform for the most part, just the black pajamas that all the Vietnamese wore. Sometimes you just didn't know who to shoot at, at least not in the immediate My Tho area.

Operating out of the town was different—the enemy was plainly the guys who were shooting at us. Inside of My Tho, we held the hotel and put up with the incoming fire that we couldn't do anything about anyway. The hotel received a lot of mortar fire, some of the rounds taking out our water tower and shutting off the showers. But using the showers wasn't on anyone's mind at the time—ducking mortar fragments was. Most of the guys in the platoon received their first Purple Heart from mortar fragments during Tet. That was when and how I received my first of three Purple Hearts.

How you were hit wasn't always from someone firing at you in particular. It was more of a to-whom-it-may-concern sort of thing. However, wounds were received from enemy projectiles, the guys bled, and pain resulted from the hits. It didn't really matter that some of the guys were hit in the head while in their racks or taking a piss.

Looking back on the situation today, perhaps I don't feel as proud of receiving that first Purple Heart as maybe I could. Even though the fragment I was hit with could have killed me, most of us who received our PHs during that particular shelling don't feel we earned the medal the hard way. The mortar rounds were a lot harder on the roof and the water tower than they were on us. But some of those rounds did penetrate the roof and floors within before detonating. I took fragments in my chin and head, but nothing serious. Some of the guys were hit with larger fragments than I was, and we were all picking pieces of mortar shell out of ourselves for days to come.

We went out on some ops during Tet to try and take the war back to the enemy and nail him before he got into the city. U.S. forces were being spread pretty thin, so support for an operation came from wherever you could get it. There was an operation we were on where we had friendly backup support in the way of ARVN artillery. The accuracy of the ARVN artillery turned out to leave a lot to be desired. When we finally called them in on a target during the operation, the ARVNs were working real hard, in support of the Viet Cong! That heavy artillery was walking in right on our location. Communications chose that moment to break down, so all we could do was ride out the storm.

Gallagher held us in position. With all of the rounds impacting around us we didn't know which way to go anyway. All we could do was hold tight to our position until the ARVNs finally got back on the phone and we could tell them who they were shooting at. That was kind of a hairy mission. There's something really wrong with being shot up by your own side.

But not all of the artillery and mortar fire we saw was coming in on us during Tet. Seventh Platoon managed to give back better than we received. At one point, the Mike boat from MST-2 [Mobile Support Team 2] was moving up and down the river, along the My Tho waterfront, putting out fire from all of its weapons to support our ground troops moving against the Viet Cong. At one point, the Mike boat was taking fire from a warehouse and some large house in town. The boat had to fire over the heads of a bunch of civilians in the area to get them to move away and open up a clear field of fire. Once the civilians had moved, a barrage of 7.62mm and 40mm grenades silenced whatever VC had been in those two buildings.

Besides directing the defense of the Carter Billet, the official military name of our hotel, Seventh Platoon went out on some operations during Tet and coordinated efforts with other forces. Bravo squad advised and coordinated U.S. air and artillery support for the 32nd Vietnamese Ranger Battalion while they were under heavy attack until a U.S. advisor could get to the unit and take over.

In another action, Seventh Platoon recovered a very large VC weapons and ammunition cache just northwest of My Tho. We ran into about three VC snipers while moving in on the cache, but they were soon dealt with, and we picked up about twenty-eight weapons, mostly old U.S. M3 submachine guns, M1 Garands, and M1 carbines, as well as a couple dozen mortar bombs and RPG rounds.

Beside doing combat and fire control duty, Seventh Platoon disarmed twelve Viet Cong duds that were lying around My Tho threatening both the military and civilians. Gallagher was EOD-qualified [trained in explosive ordnance disposal], so he was in charge of much of the dud handling, a nerve-racking job at best. All in all, Seventh Platoon destroyed eight Chicom 82mm mortar duds, two RPG-7 duds, and two Chicom grenades.

All of this happened in the first week of February 1968. Tet turned into a military disaster for the Viet Cong—we pushed them back everywhere they attacked and damned near wiped them out in some areas. And as exposed to the enemy as we were, Seventh didn't lose a man to enemy fire. A lot of the guys were wounded, but no one really seriously.

We did end up losing one man after Tet, but it didn't have anything to do with the fighting. Charlie Watson had caught one of those bad tropical infections the jungle managed to grow. It finally had gotten so bad that they couldn't treat him in Vietnam, so they sent him back to the States in February. Watson had been the assistant platoon leader, so we needed a replacement. Little Creek sent us Ensign Ron Yeaw, and he took up where Charlie had left off.

Not all of our time in Vietnam was spent in combat operations, though it sure seemed like that during Tet. On our down time between ops we relaxed a bit just like all of the other SEAL platoons did. We had a little club where we would go and drink beer, mostly keeping to ourselves and the Navy units who supported us. In spite of being off-duty, none of us ever really relaxed completely while in Vietnam, at least I never did. You never forgot that you were in a combat zone. Unlike back at the Creek, where you could go to the chiefs' club or whatever and just get shitfaced, in Vietnam that didn't happen very much. We were always on call. If intelligence came on a target, you had to act on it right away. A hangover, or worse still being drunk, could get you and your Team-mates killed.

There really wasn't a whole hell of a lot to do off-duty in My Tho. Around the base you would pull maintenance on the platoon's equipment and keep the weapons clean. But other than the occasional bar call, we just didn't socialize with any but our own, and that made for a very tight group.

There were the intermittent calls on traditional sailors' establishments, the same kind of places that sailors in a strange port have visited for centuries. There was a fairly famous place up near Saigon they called the Green Door, but almost every major Vietnamese city had a Green Door of its own. There were a few times that we went kind of wide open at certain establishments, but you never forgot where you were.

All of us went around armed at all times, off-duty or not. There was a reward offered by the VC for any SEAL being taken out, and you never knew if a local was about to try and earn some extra cash for himself. I carried a 9 millimeter, the Team-issue Smith & Wesson Model 39, when I wasn't carrying an M16. Other guys would carry standard .45s, 9mms, or the other Team-issue handgun, a Smith & Wesson Model 15 Combat Masterpiece .38 Special. Some of the guys even carried personal weapons they had either captured or brought from the States with them. The SEALs were pretty open about such things. The regulation about off-duty U.S. military personnel not being armed in civilian areas was not one of the regulations we paid much attention to.

Though there were some rules that we wouldn't pay much attention to sometimes, there were certain people who we listened to all of the time. Bob Gallagher was probably the single most influential SEAL I ever met. Even today, if Bob called me up and asked me to back him up on something that had to be done, I wouldn't hesitate to do it. Gallagher just developed that kind of loyalty among the SEALs he led. Though he wasn't anything like my idol, he was the man I most looked up to and respected from anyone I met during my military career.

At one time or another, Bob Gallagher asked each man in the squad or the platoon to do something that the individual didn't want to do. And each man did what he was asked gladly, because it was the Eagle doing the asking and he wouldn't have said anything if it wasn't important. In every firefight or shitbag situation we got ourselves into, Gallagher just seemed to know just what to do and when to do it to both complete the mission and get us out alive.

As I mentioned earlier, Bob Gallagher was EOD-qualified. The disarming of bombs and booby traps, EOD work, was interesting and something that I thought I wanted to do. But something that had happened in training years before had turned me off the idea. Henry Speigle also witnessed the event and would verify the story.

Years before in UDTR class, there was a young trainee who decided one day not to use the standard M2 cap crimpers to attach a blasting cap to a fuze. Instead, this young man thought he would save a little time and crimp the cap to the fuze by biting down on the soft metal blasting cap with his teeth. This was not considered a good idea and was something of a safety violation. That young man—yes, it was me—never forgot what followed that event.

My instructor at the time was Henry Speigle, and he just stared at me for a moment and then said, "I can't believe you did that." Things went kind of downhill from there. After Henry pulled his foot out of my ass, I had to go see the boys in charge. This was such a gross safety violation, and demolitions was something you never treated disrespectfully, that it was a near thing for me not to be thrown out of UDTR and bounced back to the fleet. Luckily enough, I was allowed to continue training, but that was one lesson I never forgot.

So after that little training episode, I had my respect for demolitions set in concrete. Bob was just tremendous at EOD and I really did think I wanted to try it. But even men like Gallagher can be caught out. We had already lost one man to a booby trap, and the trap was one of ours.

Eugene "Gene" Fraley had been one hell of an operator from the moment we arrived in-country. Fraley worked a lot of rear security for the squad on patrol, and he was very good at it. We depended on him a lot and he never let us down. Personally, I found Gene to be just as funny as hell, and I liked him up to the moment he was killed. Though he claimed to be a lucky guy—Gene had been the only one to walk away from some helicopter accidents in his days before the Teams—Fraley had to be one of the unluckiest guys I knew. If there was an accident anywhere on the base, you could be sure that Fraley was either involved in it or had caused it somehow.

Fraley was kind of like a character in the Li'l Abner comic strip. There was this one little guy in the strip who would walk around with this dark cloud over him. He would always be all right, but anyone with this guy would have their luck go all to hell. Gene was kind of like that, only his last bit of bad luck happened just to him.

For a guy known to be a walking disaster area, it just stood to reason that Gene would like to play with the most dangerous materials we had, demolitions and booby traps. Fraley was actually pretty good at putting together nasty little surprises for us to leave as calling cards on operations. He was always fiddling with some kind of fiendish device, so it didn't come as a big surprise when one day something went wrong.

One day in January, about a week or so before Tet began, Roy Dean Matthews and I were up in the chow hall when somebody hollered in, "Hey, some guy just got killed down at the hooch!" We immediately ran down to the base where our operational hooch was, and some of the base personnel there had already lifted Gene from where he had been killed and taken the body to the sick bay. By the time we arrived at the hooch, there wasn't anything there but the rest of the platoon. Somebody, it may have been Pete Peterson, told us to go over to the sick bay and officially identify the body.

Inside the hooch, there was shit everywhere, scattered by an explosion, so we didn't particularly want to hang around, but the situation down in sick bay wasn't a whole lot better. Gene was lying facedown—of course, he really didn't have a face left, just kind of a blurred flatness. But we were able to identify him by the back of his head. "Yeah, that's him," I said, and Roy agreed.

There wasn't much question about what had happened, but nobody knew the exact sequence of events that led up to Fraley's death. Gene had built a little sandbag enclosure in the hooch where he could insert his arms and assemble booby traps. We had a lot of different kinds of booby-trap devices and fuzes that were made for us back at China Lake, California. Most of the devices didn't have any explosive in them, so you had to load the booby trap and test it before taking it out in the field.

Gene had apparently been loading one of the China Lake booby traps, had taken it out of the sandbag enclosure, and it detonated while still in his hands. The blast had blown materials all over the inside of the hooch, and Gene probably never even knew the bomb went off. That accident, and the investigation afterwards, caused orders to come down suspending the use of some of our booby-trap materials for an indefinite time. So Gene was the first loss for SEAL Team Two of the war. Though Art "One-Lump" Williams of Sixth Platoon had been hit the week earlier, One-Lump didn't die of his wound until months later back in the States.

Even though Gene was gone, he still managed to make life interesting for the platoon one more time. Each of us had a locker in our hooch on the PBR base where we kept our weapons and operational gear. As our platoon chief and EOD expert, Bob Gallagher took it upon himself to empty out Fraley's locker.

Gallagher had been in a lot of situations where other men would have been scared spitless, and he just kept going. But this was the first time I had seen the Eagle literally in a cold sweat. Gene had already been killed by one of his own devices, so you knew something was wrong going in, and he had been known for always causing disasters. Now Bob had to empty out the locker that Gene had filled with all kinds of booby traps and fuzes.

Moving very carefully and intensely, Bob was very, very professional and more focused than I had ever seen him before. Bob removed every piece of material in Gene's locker, and it was a regular hell's kitchen of booby-trap and explosive devices. Gallagher removed each device and carried it down to the end of the pier, where he dropped it off.

What had actually killed Gene was a special flashlight that had to be filled with C4 explosive before being taken out in the field. This thing looked just like a regular flashlight, only the body was filled with C4 and surrounded with ball bearings. Once the fuze was armed, any movement of the flashlight would detonate the charge inside. To arm the fuze, you moved the flashlight switch to one position. Once moved, you had thirty seconds before the fuze would arm and you couldn't touch the light from then on. When you first loaded the booby trap, you moved the switch to another position and it signaled that the circuit was okay.

From what I understand, Gene had tested the light already, otherwise he wouldn't have removed it from the little sandbag bunker. What he must have done was move the arming/testing switch too far past the safe position and started the arming circuit. As soon as the fuze armed, the flashlight detonated. And I remember that the day before, Gene had mentioned that he was going to set up one of the flashlights for our next op, and none of us had thought anything about it.

It was a shame the way Gene went out, accidentally killing himself the way he did. But it wasn't surprising to anyone about what had happened. Some time later, I ran into Gene's wife and told her in what high regard we had held Gene as an operator and how well he had done in Vietnam. It may have been some slight consolation to her. Life in the Teams was dangerous even when we weren't involved in a war. The Navy paid us to work on the edge, and it was part of the job.

Training was what helped us complete the missions that were given to us, and each SEAL's training began with UDTR and Hell Week. That miserable week would burn something into the mind of each man who completed it, something that could never be erased by time or experience. That something was the knowledge that you could do anything as an individual or a Team. In some way, whether an individual's skill, a coordinated plan, or just a balls-to-the-wall effort, we could handle any assignment given to us. That knowledge led to its own kind of high, probably something like what catches druggies and makes them addicts.

We operated hard and functioned hard and we trained hard to be able to do what we did. Few if any other military units could have continued to work the way we did and accomplish what we did, in Vietnam and elsewhere. When we first went to Southeast Asia, there were only a couple of us who could be combat-experienced. But because of the way we worked, trained, and the quality of our leadership, the SEALs had very few losses, and the great majority of us came home.

But not all of us who came home did so all in one piece. Some of our wounds were minor while others were far more serious. One casualty that could have had a great deal of effect on the platoon was when Bob Gallagher was injured on one of our very early operations.

It was late in the first week of November, we hadn't

been in-country more than a week or so, and this was only
our fourth op. We went down the Mekong in the Mike
boat, traveling almost to its mouth at the South China Sea.
Changing to STABs for our insertion, we landed A squad
and then B squad in the same place about thirty minutes
later. The platoon set up an area ambush, keeping an eye
out for any VC forces that may still have been moving
even though it was starting to be daylight. After we had
made sure the area was secure, both squads moved out for
the main objective of the operation, a search of Giong
Ong Ban village.

During the search, we discovered a bunker complex in
the village that was heavily covered with booby traps. One
squad was watching the village perimeter some distance
away from us, while the balance of the squad I was in
held security around the bunker complex we had found.

All through the bunkers and surrounding area were trip
wires and small foot mines. The mines weren't enough to
kill you outright, just blow off a foot. Charlie had learned
that if you injured one soldier, it took several other troops
out of the action to take care of the wounded man. To
make sure that the booby traps didn't do their planned
job, Bob Gallagher was taking them apart, disarming the
whole area.

About half of the booby traps we found were trip wires
attached to homemade VC grenades. The grenades were
silver and looked as if they had been cast up in some
jungle workshop. The explosives for the grenades had
probably come from some U.S. dud bombs or other ordnance. One thing you had to say about the VC, they didn't
lack for guts. It would be no small thing to cut open,
say, a dud five-hundred-pound bomb and steam out the
explosives, just to fill up hand grenades.

Bob was just a short distance from me as I kept watch,
and I could see him clearly as he went about disarming
the grenades. Only something went wrong and a grenade
went off, blowing Bob backwards.

The grenade went off in Gallagher's hand, and I saw
the explosion knock Bob over. The blast was a small one,
but more than enough considering how close Bob had been

to it. Getting up from the ground, the Eagle just stood there holding what was left of his hand while Riojas, our corpsman, came running up to him. The grenade had only gone off as a low-order explosion—that is, it had burst but without all of the force of its explosives going off. But the blast was more than enough to amputate a few of Bob's fingers and leave his hand a bloody mess.

We called in a medevac helicopter right away, but then we had to move our secure zone down to the beach so the bird could put down. We put out a secure perimeter down by the beach and the medevac came in and took Bob away to the 3rd Field Surgical Hospital in Dong Tam. Now our platoon chief was out of action and a good-sized amount of our combat experience had gone with him. That left an emptiness with a lot of the guys.

It wasn't like "Oh, shit—there goes our number one guy." Most of us had some patrolling under our belts now. Everyone in the platoon had matured in combat, and we realized that our missions would continue. We were confident that we would continue and succeed, due in no small part to the fact that Pete Peterson, our platoon leader, was just a super officer. But as the medevac bird lifted away with Gallagher on board, there was a feeling that the game would continue, but our Team had just lost its best quarterback.

The good news came later for us. Bob was going to be all right and wouldn't lose the use of his hand. In fact, Gallagher came back to the platoon only a few weeks later, a bit the worse for wear but ready to go back out operating with us. And seeing Bob come back was a good sight and it did cheer up the guys quite a bit. It seemed like nothing could put the Eagle down for long.

There was one operation towards the end of our tour that did take the Eagle down for a while, though this time I wasn't with him when he was hit. In the platoon, I really wasn't much more than another bump on the log and wasn't privy to what our upcoming plans were or where our intelligence came from. But the scuttlebutt had it that we were going in on a VC prisoner of war camp, and had a possibility of getting out some American POWs.

At that time, March 1968, there were all sorts of channels you had to go through to set up a POW rescue op. Later in the war, a special setup was made, code-named Bright Light, just for POW ops, so that you could act on intel very quickly while it was still fresh. But in early '68, it practically took orders from the CNO [Chief of Naval Operations] himself to get a clearance for a POW op.

The operation was called an area reconnaissance, and we went in heavily loaded with weapons and ammunition. For myself, I carried many HE 40mm grenades for my XM148. The weight of the ammunition wasn't so bad, at least not on the trip into the insertion point. We traveled downriver in the Mike boat and transferred to our smaller STABs for the actual insertion. For the operation, after patrolling in from the river, we were going to split the platoon into two squads in order to cover a much larger area. We were going to go in about three klicks, almost two miles, from our insertion point before splitting up the platoon. My squad, Alfa squad, were going to conduct our recon to the northeast while Bravo squad moved to the northwest.

We inserted fairly early in the evening, around 2200 hours, and followed our plan, moving north from the insertion point. Now the ammunition load I was carrying grew a bit heavy. We had traveled inland quite a ways in order to reach our objective area, moving slowly and carefully, since we suspected Charlie was all around us. This was an uncomfortable situation for us—as SEALs and frogmen, we always liked to have the water at our backs, it's our escape route and means of hiding. This time the water was at least a mile or more away. But we did have plenty of support for our operation in the form of a pair of Seawolf helicopter gunships waiting for any call from us and fire support from the Mike boat that brought us in.

Our search was going to take place in the jungle, which started about a mile in from the river. It was the jungle canopy that was supposedly hiding the POW camp. We patrolled at a very slow pace, moving only a few meters at a time and keeping alert for signs of the VC we knew were all around us.

Hours later, we had crossed the last of a bunch of rice paddies and were facing the tree line of the jungle, our starting point for the area search. Lieutenant Peterson and our squad split off to the right, and Ron Yeaw moved with the other squad off to the left. Bob Gallagher was with the other squad, so there was no problem there with any lack of experience on the part of the leadership. Yeaw was a tough young officer, but he had only been in-country for a short while as a replacement for Charlie Watson, and he still needed to get some more operations under his belt.

Our squad moved into the jungle and carefully continued our patrol. The strain of slowly moving and constantly being alert for every sound can really take it out of a man. But we had been in-country for almost a full six months, and moving like this was just part of our job. But it was the strain and just physical work of a patrol like this that proved out just why most of our training involved physical workouts. If we hadn't been in shape, we could have never completed an op like this one, or probably even survived given what happened.

The squad had moved less than a klick by 0200 hours and had almost reached our objective area when we were compromised. The squad ran into two VC on guard duty that we couldn't avoid. Pete Peterson took care of both VC silently, one with a shot from a hush puppy [silenced pistol] and the other in fast hand-to-hand. Now the cat was out of the bag and things were going to start heating up fast.

As we approached an opening in the jungle where there was a coconut grove, we could hear Charlie way over on the right of us, maybe half a klick to a klick away. The VC were calling to each other, and it was obvious that they knew we were in the area and were hard at work looking for us. The other platoon was way over to our left and had to be in just about the same situation we were in.

The VC were really trying to locate our position and were firing everywhere, hoping to get a response from us. Pete finally made a decision that we were done and that it was time for us to get the hell out of there. We began moving north to find an opening where Seawolf and our

support slicks [unarmed helicopters] could come in and
get us. Now we were hauling ass with about fifty VC
chasing us. They still didn't know exactly where we were,
but they were getting mighty close. Even though we were
moving a lot faster than we had, we were still keeping as
silent as possible while on the move. We covered about
three hundred meters inside of an hour, looking for a place
to hole up and call for help.

Breaking out of the jungle, we came across an area of
rice paddies with this little grove of trees near the middle
of them. That grove was going to be our haven, and we
headed for it. The rice paddies were open enough that a
helicopter could come in to pick us up. But now the VC
had found us. We reached the grove and hunkered down.

There were little bunkers and hooches all over the
damned place. Some of them had active VC in them, and
now there was fire going out all over the place. I was
putting out rounds from my XM148 as fast as I could
load, aim, and fire. There wasn't any problem with targets—most of the hooches were small barracks, and I
could put a round into the building and see guys falling
out of them as the grenades went off.

While the squad established a fast perimeter to hold off
what looked like about twenty approaching VC, Pete was
on the radio calling in the Seawolves for an air strike.
Until some of the incoming fire was suppressed, any slick
coming in to get us would be one big target. The mission
was over, we were compromised big-time, and the helicopters were going to be our only way out. We were way too
far from the river to make any kind of break for the water.

Peterson made our situation clear to the birds in the air,
something along the lines of ''Get down here and get us
the hell out of here!'' We were right in the middle of a
well-populated VC area and they knew we were there. The
hornets' nest had been kicked and they were swarming
around in numbers.

There had to have been thirty or forty Charlies in that
area of jungle right around us. The longer we stayed, the
more enemy we would have been facing. But well before
the mission had started, we had Seawolf 66 and 69 locked

in to give us support. In addition, there were two Army slicks, Outlaw 66 and 26, ready to come in and move us out.

The biggest thing right then was to suppress the enemy fire, using what rounds we did have to their maximum effect. I had my XM148 pumping out 40mm grenades as quickly as I had a worthwhile target. Another man in the squad had an M79 and he was also putting out 40mm fire. The two M60s we had were running hot with controlled but heavy firing. Now the ammunition we had dragged through the jungle didn't seem very heavy. We were glad of what we had and would have been even happier with more.

While Pete directed a Seawolf strike into the VC around us, the slicks came in to get us out. Ammunition was starting to run mighty low by the time the birds came in to get us out. But the Seawolves kept the Charlies' heads down enough that we were able to get on board the slicks and leave with no losses to the squad. It had been a hairy mission for us and a very close thing. But we soon learned that the situation was even worse for our teammates in the other squad.

The other squad had found a VC barracks area much like we had, only they had walked right up to it in the jungle. While they were checking out the inside of the building, a firefight broke out and a grenade went off, wounding most of the squad. Yeaw was badly wounded in the arm and legs but could still walk. Gallagher was very badly wounded but could still move. The Vietnamese interpreter the squad had with them was badly wounded and he couldn't walk at all. Mikey Boynton and Hook Tuure were hit, but nothing like the others.

With a bunch of VC after them, Bravo squad hauled ass away from the barracks. They were also looking for a place they could hole up and get pulled out by the helicopters. But unlike us, they had a longer way to go, over a klick, before they could find a clearing where the slicks could come in and get them out. Mikey Boynton is a big fellow and he carried the wounded interpreter in his arms that whole way. Not that it was much easier for the rest of the squad.

The squad found a hooch among some rice paddies that they could put a perimeter around and called in the Seawolves. Things were pretty tense, but they finally got out. After everything was done, it was estimated that we took out around twenty-six VC between the two squads and the Seawolves. Apparently, we had been facing a full VC battalion. Even for us, those odds were a little too much. I guess the Navy thought so as well. Mikey Boynton received the Silver Star, a bunch of us got Bronze Stars, and Gallagher was later awarded the Navy Cross for that op.

Yeaw was hurt so bad that they sent him off to Japan and later back to the States. It was touch and go with Gallagher for a while, but he stayed in-country and recovered well enough to come back to the platoon before we returned to Little Creek. We still went out on some good operations, but now the platoon was getting short and we were all looking forward to going home.

Just like anyone else, most of us looked forward to going home and were counting the days to our relief. As the number of days got smaller, you could get nervous if you let yourself dwell on it. There would be the question of "the bullet with your name on it" being out there somewhere. Myself and a few other guys did feel things get a little more intense towards the end of our tour. Maybe it was just that we were a bit more cautious when we went out on an op. One thing was for sure—none of us let the others down, no matter what we thought.

The intensity of being in Vietnam never changed no matter how short or new you were. I hadn't done as many combat tours as some of the other guys in Team Two did, but from the time that you arrived in-country to the day you left, the feelings of being in combat stayed the same. At least that was how it was in the Teams. The actions that we did and the way we operated constantly kept us sharp, and none of us ever let his guard down while in-country. It was almost like you took a deep breath on the plane flying in and you didn't let it out until you were on the plane heading out.

In spite of the feelings of relief, the flight home wasn't much better than the flight to Vietnam. That was the longest single flight I ever took in my life and a real pain in the ass, literally. It would have been nice if Vietnam had been a little more convenient, like maybe down in Roosey Roads, because the Pacific is a wide ocean. But even though it was a long flight, it was enjoyable to know you were going home.

None of us really brought much home with us in the way of souvenirs, except maybe booze. For myself, I had never been much of a souvenir collector, and the tour hadn't changed me. It did seem that there were a hell of a lot of AK-47s that managed to find their way back to Little Creek, so maybe more than a few of the guys brought back a weapon or two.

Actually, the weapon situation did start getting out of hand after a while. Finally, the skipper put out the word during a formation one day. It was told in no uncertain terms to all of us that anyone with any foreign weapons at home, be they AK-47s, grenades, or whatever, if they were brought in to the Team building and turned in, there wouldn't be any trouble. There was an unspoken part of that little speech that if you were caught with something after the turn-in, life in the SEALs would be very short for you.

More than a couple of guys had brought home enemy ordnance. I seem to remember holding a brand-new AK-47 myself. But all of the hardware was turned in. Legal items, such as pistols and bolt-action or semiautomatic rifles, could be kept, but any automatic or explosive weapons had to be turned in. Some days it was pretty funny how suddenly a small mortar or other nasty would appear under the XO's desk in the morning.

In spite of the jokes and the funny memories, Vietnam was anything but like a trip to Disneyland. Some of the guys said that they really liked going over to war, but it was a really ballsy situation. What I had seen in Vietnam was death, a lot of it, and the SEALs contributed their part of it, sending more than a few VC to an early grave.

But that situation is what war is, and you can't put a good
face on it no matter what you do.

There had been one particular time during Tet that I
was with Bob Gallagher near a small Army airstrip. Charlie had a bunch of Army people pinned down with heavy
fire. There were six or eight VC in ditches on either side
of the Army position, keeping the position in a crossfire
and just cutting it to pieces. The Army people were taking
it pretty badly and were losing men without being able to
get out of the situation themselves. Finally this one lieutenant climbed into a jeep and drove out to the position,
under fire all the way, to try and get some of the men out.

The lieutenant loaded as many men as he could into it
and started driving back through a withering hail of fire.
That jeep just took so many rounds it didn't look like it
would hold together, and neither would the people inside
of it.

When that jeep finally got to our position, there wasn't
much left, except for parts. Heads and other body parts
had been chopped apart by the bullets. The lieutenant was
still alive, but his jaw was shot away and he had other
wounds that were taking him out fast. Seeing death like
that affects you no matter who you are.

The Vietnam War had been pretty horrible. We had
seen things that the VC had done to villagers who
wouldn't cooperate with them to make an example of them
to others. That didn't cause us to go out and commit our
own atrocities—the SEALs are better than that—but we
didn't have much trouble taking the war to the enemy. I
never did anything that caused me to lose much sleep, and
most of what the U.S. Army, and even the ARVN forces,
were accused of were just that, stories. But Vietnam had
been a particularly nasty bit of business.

But most of us had gotten home from that first tour.
Some of the guys came home from that first tour to a
different situation than the one they had left. Either they
were changed, whether by experience or wounds, or their
home situation had changed. I was one of those who came
home to the latter.

I didn't go back to Vietnam on another tour until Sixth

Platoon was manning up to deploy in late 1968. Bob Gallagher wasn't around, and Jim Watson was putting his platoon together in the fall of '68, so he looked like my best chance of being deployed. Jim and I had been friends in Team Two for a long time, and now Jim had made chief and was in charge of Sixth Platoon. I wanted to go in-country with Jim, feeling he was another Bob Gallagher, a chief I could depend on and who would give me an opportunity to join his platoon.

Things had changed in my personal life since I had returned from my first tour. I needed to get back to Vietnam and I needed somebody like Jim to say, "Come on, you're the guy I want." My confidence had been shaken a bit with the trouble I was having in my personal life. My marriage had been going badly, not a particularly unusual occurrence in the Teams, but there was a Teammate involved and that really made things bad. Finally, I had to go back in part just to prove to myself that I still could.

What I did feel confident in was that Watson would give me a chance if I talked to him. My love for the Team hadn't changed, no matter what happened. I felt I was still an operator, and I needed to function, to do what I was trained for. Quitting the Teams wasn't what I wanted to do, though I had thought about it. Instead, I had to do what the SEALs were created for, and I had to do it in combat.

Another option would have been for me to go back into UDT, perhaps one of the SDV [Swimmer Delivery Vehicle] platoons or something like that. In the SEALs back then, you had quite a name to carry, and I was questioning whether I was worthy of it or not. That's a bad question to ask yourself, and the only way to answer it is to either back away or return to the jungle. I chose the jungle to prove to myself that I was still an operator and that wearing the SEAL name was something that I still earned.

Jim Watson didn't come back to me right away and say I could join the platoon. The platoon chiefs had a lot of input as to who operated with their platoon, and even with our past friendship, Jim had to consider what was best for Sixth Platoon. But finally, he did come back to me and

tell me I could join in with Sixth Platoon, and he told the
Team skipper that he wanted me to deploy with them.

That was something that I felt good about. I was tickled
and told Jim that I would never forget the opportunity that
he had given me and that I would never let him down,
ever. Now I was going to operate with Sixth Platoon as a
Stonerman, carrying one of the Stoner light machine guns
that added so much to the firepower of the SEALs in
Vietnam.

The Stoner was a belt-fed light machine gun that fired
the same ammunition as the M16, only it carried between
100 and 150 rounds at a time. The Stoner spoke with
authority, spewing out its ammunition at a rate of around
800 rounds per minute. Only the SEALs had the Stoners
in any numbers during the Vietnam War, and I had become very comfortable with the weapon. You had to have
a certain taste for the Stoner—the weapon needed more
care and attention to operate at its best. For me, it just
became another part of my uniform.

To me, the Stoner was easy to break down and maintain.
Other guys preferred other weapons, like the M60 machine
gun, which fired at a slower rate than the Stoner but put
out a heavier round of ammunition. Some guys just liked
the M16, and some, like Jimmy Watson, preferred the
shotgun. In predeployment training, all the members of a
platoon became familiar with all of the weapons we carried or could expect to run into. But that was just so that
anyone could pick up another man's weapon if he went
down and carry on with the mission. Each man developed
his own tastes as to what he preferred, and those tastes
were catered to as much as could be allowed.

As we said in Vietnam, the Stoner had "boo-coo" firepower and "tee-tee" weight. A lot of bullets without a
lot of weight. It wasn't like the XM148 I had carried in
my first tour with all of those heavy 40mm HE rounds.
Of course, if they had offered a 40mm grenade launcher
that mounted under a Stoner, I would have hung that
sucker under there in a hot minute. We were always looking for ways to increase our firepower, preferably without
increasing the weight we carried around with us by too

much. But sometimes you just accept what is available and then keep your eyes open.

Sixth Platoon arrived in Vietnam on 12 December 1968 in time for me to spend another Christmas in Vietnam, my second in a row. We were assigned to Nha Be, where we would be relieving Third Platoon, who had been in the area since June. Lieutenant Rick Woolard from Third stayed back to introduce us to the area and get our feet wet operationally. Watson and Woolard had been friends back at the Creek, and we picked up the ops where Third had left off pretty smoothly. We went out on our first operations within a week or so of arriving in Vietnam. One squad went out on a canal ambush, and I was with the other squad, who did the same thing in another area. Our squad was being led by Woolard, but that didn't seem to help things much—both ops came up a dry hole with no contact being made.

A Christmas cease-fire had been declared, which cut way back on the number of operations we did in December. I went out on another canal ambush under our platoon leader, Lieutenant Bruce Williamson, with Lieutenant Woolard still lending support, just a couple of days before Christmas, but again we didn't make contact with the enemy. A few days after Christmas, we went out on an operation where we were emplacing what were called Duffel Bag devices, kind of a listening device that could tell us if the VC had been operating in the area.

The Duffel Bag devices were just another piece of high-tech equipment that was supposed to help us do our jobs by detecting VC movements without us having to be in the area. I never did learn how well the darn things worked. After that first op, artillery fire was called in on the position, but no results were ever confirmed. Mostly what we did was a lot of combat patrols as well as trail and canal ambushes. On the other hand, our platoon chief, Jim Watson, was having a field day operating as an advisor to the local PRU unit as well as the platoon.

As in my first tour, I was one of the lower-echelon guys who worked on weapons, gear, and hooches and wasn't privy to all of the intel we had coming in or what plans were being made. One thing we all noticed right away was how often our platoon chief was going out on operations with the Nha Be PRU unit. The PRUs were provincial reconnaissance units, put together and paid by the Agency to operate in a province and attack the Viet Cong infrastructure [VCI]. The VCI was made up of the leaders of the local Viet Cong units. Taking out individual VC guerrillas didn't affect the VC's operations very much—they could always replace cannon fodder. But if you took out the leadership, then the body of the unit didn't have any direction and couldn't operate effectively. The same protection given to the VC by their underground/undercover method of operating worked against them when it came to replacing their leadership.

A PRU was made up of local Vietnamese and could even include ex–Viet Cong and North Vietnamese Army regulars. Among the Vietnamese were Humong [montagnards] from the mountains, and even ethnic Chinese. These guys were effectively mercenaries, and pretty good ones.

The leadership for a PRU was normally a U.S. advisor who passed out the money and directed operations. A lot of SEALs liked working as a PRU advisor, some because it could put you out in the field operating damn near as much as you wanted to. It wasn't long after Sixth Platoon had arrived in Nha Be that Watson was working part-time as the PRU advisor while still holding up his end as the platoon chief.

That was Jimmy—he never liked to stand still for very long. It wasn't long before PRUs were operating with our platoon, acting as local guides and supplying us with intelligence. One type of operation worked very well with the PRUs as support, and Jim picked up on it right away as a preferred method of operating. That technique was known as a parakeet op.

A parakeet op only worked if you were operating with hard intel, and usually had a guide along who personally knew the target. The guide, a SEAL leader, often Watson, and another SEAL for fire support would go into the target in an unarmed slick helicopter along with a couple of PRU men for additional manpower. The slick would just fly along, not standing out at all in the sky of Vietnam, until the guide pointed out the target. The slick would get in as close as it could to the target and the men would jump out to snatch up the prisoner. When the slick went in, the two or more helicopter gunships that had been trailing along, flying just above the treetops, would zoom up and act as fire support and security.

Jim started using parakeets in the first week of January 1968, originally taking McQuillis along as his SEAL backup. Pretty soon, Jim started taking me along as his Stonerman on parakeets while McQuillis operated with the platoon. There wasn't anything I wouldn't do for Jim, who had given me a chance to prove myself again to me and the others in the Team. But there was one operation, though it turned out well enough, that was more than a little tight.

Jim and I had gone out on a parakeet operation on 14 January to snatch up a suspected VC leader and his bodyguards. The operation was lightly manned, only Jim, myself, and three PRUs from the Nha Be unit. A parakeet op is a real fast-mover. We slid in practically on the target's doorstep. That was when the two helicopter gunships that were dogging our trail rose up and started circling the target area. Even with the gunships for support, your ass feels mighty vulnerable down there on the ground. But one thing can be said about a parakeet, it's faster than hell, but you can get in trouble on one just as quickly.

I had just come off an op with the squad where we had been up all night and most of the next morning running a patrol and searching hooches for suspected VC. We hadn't run into any opposition, but it had been a long night. When the PBR pulled into Nha Be, Watson was hustling around putting together a parakeet based on some hot intel he had just received.

"Jack," Jim said running up to me, "get your shit and your Stoner. Come on, you're going with me. We've got a hot op and we have to move now!"

"Oh, shit," I said, "here we go again." And I grabbed up my trustworthy Stoner. That was always Jim—he al-

ways had to move right now. That didn't matter, of course.
Parakeets had been going on for some time with Jim and
the platoon and they were something you had to react
to quickly.

There was some real good intel on a supposed VC com-
mandant, the hooch he was in and everything. But that
kind of information is time-sensitive. You have to act on
it quickly or the target will move. That kind of quick
reaction was what the SEALs were for, and we moved on
such things like they were made for us.

On such an operation, my job would be to give direct
fire support to the team commander, who was Jim in this
case. The circling helicopter gunships could keep back any
incoming VC, but the ones who were already in the target
hooches we had to control with overwhelming firepower.
That was the kind of thing we preferred the Stoner for,
and that was why I carried one. The VC feared the Men
with Green Faces, and they knew the sound of a Stoner
meant we were around.

A strap around my shoulders supported my Stoner
within easy reach. For ammunition, I would feed the
weapon from either a 150-round drum or with 100-round
plastic belt boxes. When I carried a drum, I would drape
several hundred rounds in belts around my shoulders like
Mexican bandoleers. During an ambush or whatever, I
would save the ammunition in the drum and feed from a
loose belt. The drum would be saved in case we had to
move quickly and break contact. Probably I used the plastic ammunition boxes the most, as they were the easiest
to reload from.

Jimmy was square on for this op. The situation was a
hot one and it warmed up quickly. Once we set down, we
started taking fire from the tree line around the target
hooch. Jim was busy taking down and securing the prisoner. The fire from the tree line was my problem, and I
dealt with it, returning fire with my Stoner. Now we
started receiving fire from another tree line, and one of
the PRUs took a hit in his leg.

Now we had fire coming in from two areas, and I could
see VC running around among the trees. I just started

taking charge of both areas, standing in the middle of a real hot crossfire and putting out fire to both sides. Everybody else was busy—the PRUs were dealing with the target's bodyguards in another hooch, and Jim was on the radio while he was also dealing with our wounded man. While Jim was yelling into the radio that we were under fire and that the helicopter was to come in and get us now, I did my job, standing up next to him and laying down a field of fire.

We captured our VC target, snatching up his weapons and documents as well as taking out his two bodyguards. Things got pretty tense until the slick set down to pick us up. But we managed to get out of there with no more wounded than our one PRU. As soon as we had landed on that op, we had come under fire, which hadn't let up until we pulled out. But that was the nice thing about a parakeet op. What had seemed like an eternity on the ground under fire had actually been only something like fourteen minutes. But that can seem like an awfully long time when the bullets are passing by.

Personally, I had been too busy on the op to notice how long it had been. Things were fast, but I had been covering Jimmy and the wounded man. The other two PRUs were dealing with the prisoner, who Jim had practically knocked unconscious with one punch when he captured him. As all of the other guys piled on the extraction bird, I remained on the ground putting out fire from my Stoner. Finally I climbed on board, standing on the strut and hanging out the door, returning fire even as we pulled up and away. It was great working with Jim on operations that were that successful, but personally I would have liked to have had the entire platoon with us on that one, or even SEAL Team Two if they had been available.

The prisoner turned out to be some VC commander, so the op was considered a successful one. For my part in the operation, Jim put me in for the Silver Star medal, but that was later downgraded to the Bronze Star. But the medal wasn't what mattered to me. Jim had given me my chance to re-prove myself with Sixth Platoon, and there was no way in hell I was going to let him down on any op.

There was never a dull moment with Watson around. Jimmy liked to move fast and hated standing still. From that one prisoner, we got some good intel that led to other ops, which was why we preferred taking prisoners in the first place.

About the third week of January, Jim's constant operating and leading from the front finally caught up with him. We had done some good ops, one of which resulted in our capturing a wounded NVA soldier and blasting four suspected VC tunnels. But Jim was really hot for the PRU program and he supported those men big-time, considering them a prime source of intelligence for the platoon.

On January 17, Jim was taking a rare break that night when word came in that his PRUs had run into a lot of trouble and needed support fast. While he was headed for the Tactical Operations Center [TOC], Jim grabbed me and told me to get George, our interpreter, and some of the PRUs and send them up to the TOC. All I knew was what Jim wanted, and I moved out to get it for him. When I got back to the TOC, all hell was breaking loose. A group of Jim's men were under fire and he was going to move out and support them. This wasn't something I was going to be able to help with, and Jim had the situation under control. The last I knew, Jim was moving out with a couple of PBRs to support his PRU men.

What came next was pretty bad. Apparently, the PRUs had gotten the situation under control and had captured some kind of mine. Some explosive ordnance disposal men had gone along with Jim, and they had all towed this big mine back behind one of the PBRs. While the EOD men were examining the mine on the beach at the base, the hundred pounds of explosives in the mine detonated.

The EOD men were obliterated in an instant. Jim had been walking away from the mine when the explosion picked him up and slammed him down. Jim was very seriously wounded, and the EOD men were well beyond anyone's help. A helicopter took Jim to Ben Thuy to the Army field hospital there while the rest of the platoon just tried to figure out what had happened.

We knew that Jim was in critical condition, and the

leftovers of the mine explosion were more than hard to deal with. Body parts and fragments of the three killed EOD men were spread out all over the area. Bits of meat were hanging in trees, on the ground, and everywhere. The expression "blown into dog meat" holds a whole new meaning for me now, because we shot the dogs who came into the area, drawn by the scent.

For me, the wind kind of went out of the sails of the platoon after Jim was hurt. I had lost a friend and my leader. Operating with Jimmy had always been balls to the wall, but it felt right doing that with him. I had a confidence with Jim that I just didn't feel for any of our officers. Not that Lieutenant Williamson or Thames didn't rise to the occasion and were not good leaders in their own right. It was just that Jim and I had a working relationship and a bond with each other. If Jim asked something, I didn't hesitate to step up and be there.

Having the kind of confidence in your leader that I had in Jim Watson allows a man to concentrate on his job and not have any worry about what was happening with the higher-ups. All of the training we received in the Teams showed up in the results we attained in Vietnam and in other places since. But the key to those results is the leadership you follow and the bonds you develop with your Teammates. Somebody always has to be the leader and someone the follower. For myself, I was mostly the follower.

Now with our chief gone, we had to depend on our officers even more. Lieutenants Williamson and Thames pretty much met the challenge. They still had the support and experience of a good leading petty officer, Larry "Doc" Johnson, our first class corpsman. Doc Johnson acted as the assistant squad leader for a number of ops after Jim was hurt and finally sent back to the States for treatment. For that matter, I acted as an assistant squad leader myself on a number of ops.

But even though we had some good operations after Jim was hurt, we never seemed to pick up that same snap that we had before. On one operation just a few weeks after Jim was injured, one squad uncovered a large supply cache that included another big water mine like the one that had blown up at Nha Be. This time no chances were taken whatsoever with the mine and it was destroyed in place.

Some of the ops went well enough and others were just short of disasters. Twice in three weeks, friendly forces initiated firefights with one of the squads from Sixth Platoon while they were out on ops. No one was hurt in the fights, but even Charlie hadn't been that lucky against us in two months of operating. On another operation two RPG [rocket-propelled grenade] rockets passed within inches of one of our Light SEAL Support Craft [LSSC] while it was traveling down a river at about thirty knots. No one was hurt and fire was quickly called in on the site the RPGs were fired from. But it was obvious that things had taken a downturn for us operationally.

All in all, after Jim was gone, I never got into another firefight like the ones that I had gotten into with him. And I didn't go on operations that were as successful as the ones he led. Of course, not all of the operations we had gone on with Jim had turned out so well either.

During the early part of our tour there was one hooch search that we were on where one of us must have missed something. After we had searched the area and were burning the VC hooches, there was a sudden explosion from one of the fires. Apparently we had missed something in the search and it detonated from the heat of the fire. I caught some grenade fragments in the back, but that was nothing compared to the chewing out I got from Watson. That incident did earn me another Purple Heart and a trip to a field hospital near Saigon. That incident also increased my level of detail in a hooch search.

But after Jim was sent back to the States, it seemed that we had a lot more casualties. Durwood White was injured so badly that he lost his foot and finally had to leave the Teams entirely. On another operation, somebody tripped a booby trap that killed an LDNN who was with us and wounded three SEALs. On that operation, one of the men injured was carrying the radio, which also took damage from the booby trap, putting it out of commission and making commo a dicey thing.

I hadn't been on a number of the ops where Teammates from the platoon were hurt, but injuries are something that can affect the entire platoon, not just the men concerned. Of course, losing our platoon chief made morale drop like an anchor for a while. Maybe it was worse for me because I had known Jim for so long. But we got back up fast enough and continued operating. In my first tour, we had lost Gallagher twice operationally, but both times he was wounded, he was never sent back to the States. It always seemed that there were certain SEALs that stood out more than others. And when these guys were hurt, you suddenly didn't feel quite so invulnerable anymore.

We had some great guys in the platoon. Some were real operators and others were just a whole lot different from anybody else. We had a reinforced platoon—that is, we had an extra man so that we could supply a PRU advisor or whatever—and that meant we had the room for some extra characters. Clayton "Gary" Sweezy was one of these, a very good operator but just as crazy as a hoot owl, a lot of fun to have around.

But it would be hard to pick out the SEAL who I found stood out the most during either of my tours in Vietnam. That is, people who really stand out in my memory as individuals. What did stand out was the men who were operators and those guys who were hunters.

In a way, any of us in the Teams were operators. That's what we called ourselves for the most part—we went on operations, so we were operators. But some of the guys were more aggressive than others and they tried that much harder. Jim Watson was one of the more hard-core ones, and that was part of what made it so important to me when Jimmy called on me to go out on operations with him. Ops with Jimmy were very often all-out, balls-to-the-wall kinds of things where any mistakes were likely to be costly ones.

At those times, we weren't acting as operators, we were hunters, actively going out and hunting the enemy in his own territory. This was different from going out with the

squad on a straightforward mission. Going out with the
squad on an operation was part of what made us operators.
But platoons differed a lot, whether it was from the people
who made it up or just the luck of the draw on the area
you were assigned to.

On my first tour, I was lucky to be with Bob Gallagher,
Pete Peterson, and the other guys in the squad. That gave
us a hell of a platoon with great leaders. There was also
more action on my first tour than on my second. That's
not to take anything away from operating with the Sixth
Platoon. Just because I cannot remember the details of
many of the ops we went on in Sixth doesn't mean we
didn't have our share of the hairy ones. But operating with
Seventh Platoon back in the days of the '68 Tet offensive
just can't compare with my second tour.

If you were looking for the walking definition of what
a hunter was to those of us in the Teams back then, you
wouldn't have to go any farther than Bob Gallagher. A
hunter was a SEAL who went out against the enemy,
prepared for any situation. Your ass would be covered by
the men with you, whether they be a whole platoon, a
squad, or just one or two Teammates. When you went out,
you would be loaded for bear and your training would be
enough to help you make something happen. You would
literally hunt the enemy.

A lot of times we would go out like that, patrolling and
setting up to look for whoever may be there. On many of
the operations we went on in Seventh, we didn't have a
lot of intelligence as to just who or what may be out there.
Intelligence didn't just tell us who might be out there in
a given area. It would also warn us about booby traps or
whether it was a suspected VC platoon or even battalion
area. It was a lot like deer hunting—you knew where the
herds were and where they were likely to pass by. The
difference in this hunting, though, was that the quarry
could shoot back.

Being a hunter meant you might score and score big on
a target. It also meant that you just might walk into a
hornets' nest and be seriously outnumbered. That was what
happened to us in Seventh when we went out on our POW

op. But in those times, you let your training take over and just carried on.

A lot of the operations I went on with the Sixth Platoon consisted of canal ambushes and night listening posts or installing electronic listening devices for the folks in one of the other services. Operating with Watson out of the Sixth Platoon made you a hunter just by being along with him. But it takes some experience to get away with operating like that and still get home in mostly one piece. The other leaders we had in Sixth after Jimmy was hit were good, solid SEAL officers. They just didn't have the experience at that time to pull the more outrageous kinds of hunter ops against Charlie.

And Charlie was no enemy to fool with or take lightly. Charlie was very professional and acted like an animal all at the same time. We could be sly in the Teams, but Charlie was outright sneaky. He would operate on hardly anything, little support and almost no fire support he couldn't carry with him in the Delta. But the VC were as tough and deadly an enemy as you could face.

The VC were a lot like we were back in the days of the Revolutionary War. Our army back then wasn't made up of professional soldiers. It was mostly farmers and civilians who picked up what weapons were at hand to fight with. Charlie was like that—what little training they got was mostly in the face of the enemy. It was a live-or-die situation for them.

The VC were a lot like the Japanese during World War Two. Death was part of their culture and they didn't seem to fear it like we did. Death in Vietnam was an everyday occurrence. The VC just didn't seem to mind dying.

Charlie certainly wasn't a "stupid slope" no matter who says it. The VC weren't dumb or didn't have intelligence—they were very intelligent. At the same time, Charlie was very barbaric. Many of the atrocities that were talked about back home had been committed by the VC when they were terrorizing a village or other Vietnamese area. That was how he had an effect much larger than his numbers could account for. For the training and weapons he had available, Charlie could be a very efficient fighter. And he could hide among the population. The fear the VC created among the civilian population of Vietnam could help Charlie hide in a crowd. It was easy to hide among the people when the people weren't sure whether you had friends nearby who would gut anyone who talked, just to make an example of them.

Charlie was very hard to get ahold of sometimes. He fought well and he could hide very well. But when the SEALs took the war to the VC's backyard, and played Charlie's game against himself, that was when we really started to shine.

We tried to play the guerrilla game every time we went out. Whenever possible, we wouldn't go into an area by the easy way. We would find the hardest way possible to enter an operational area, and that was how we would go in and surprise Charlie. The VC wouldn't expect us to suddenly show up after having traveled through mud, swamp, and jungles, bypassing booby traps and whatever we would encounter, and that was how we turned the tables on him.

That was something Bob Gallagher always swore by. That we would never go in the easy way, we would always go in by the most difficult route. And that method of operation worked for us and is what helped build the reputation the SEALs earned in Vietnam.

For myself, the two combat tours I did in Vietnam had another price besides the three times I was wounded. I came back home from my second tour with my home-life problems anything but corrected. Though I had been able to operate with Sixth Platoon, and held up to the faith Jim Watson had shown for me when he said I could join the platoon, operating with the Team at Little Creek just went downhill after Sixth returned in June 1969.

My situation at home was just the same as when I had left. My marriage was bad and I had to deal with some things that none of my training was ever intended to help with. Vietnam was easy for me compared to my home life. Finally, things got to the point where I just wasn't able to function as a SEAL. I left the Team and went over to Research, Development, Testing, and Experimental, the diving unit that examined and checked out all of the new diving techniques and equipment that would be used by the SEALs, the UDT, and Navy divers as a whole.

Falling back on my old diving skills gave me some time to get my head and my life back together. At the experimental diving center up in Washington, D.C., at the Washington Naval Center, I spent a lot of time in the water checking out new equipment and techniques. The time away from the Team helped me get my life back on track. Once I had my problems behind me, I had a very hard question that I had to ask no matter what the answer: Could I go back into SEAL Team Two?

Before I put my papers in to go back to the Team, I went down to Little Creek and talked to one of the men whose respect meant a lot to me, Bob Gallagher. When the Eagle said that he couldn't see any problem with my coming back to the SEALs, it was time for me to officially ask if I could return. There were channels to go through, but one of the most important answers was going to be the one I received from the chief of the boat at SEAL Team Two, Master Chief Rudy Boesch.

What Rudy said was what went at SEAL Team Two. He had been there since the very first day and knew everything that could, or should, be done to get me back into the Team. Bob had wanted to know if I had gotten my home life, and my head, together, and that was the same question Rudy asked. "Rudy," I asked, "I want to come back to the Team. I have my things straight, my divorce is complete, and I have full custody of my son."

"Jack," Rudy said back to me, "the door is open."

So I managed to come back to SEAL Team Two, the place I felt I really belonged. And that was no small thing. When we had first received our orders committing SEAL Team Two to combat in Vietnam, a number of SEALs packed up and left, either back to the UDT or even out of the Navy. Later, in the seventies, when the Vietnam

War was over, some of these guys tried to come back into the SEALs and were not exactly welcomed with open arms. But I had proved myself in the jungles and swamps of Vietnam more than once, and that made me welcome back at the Team.

There was another sign that I would be all right back at SEAL Team Two. About when I was able to return, my old radio buddy from Italy, Rick Marcinko, was preparing to come back to SEAL Team Two to take over as the commanding officer. It had been a long time since Rick had helped me get into UDTR training, and our careers hadn't exactly followed the same path. But now I was able to stay with the Team until I retired from the Navy just a few years later.

My final years at SEAL Team Two were again taken up with training, but things had taken on another flavor now that there wasn't any visible fight for us to get ready for. Prior to and during our deployments to Vietnam, we were too busy getting ready and training for combat to pay much attention to the normal competitive nature of things in the SEALs. We were getting ready to go to war, and the situation was a whole different ball game. Before, we acted like some of our field training was an adult version of cops and robbers. But when it came time to go where the bullets flew, everything was taken very seriously.

After Vietnam was over, we still trained hard, but things were back to being competitive in nature. We did a lot of operating after the Vietnam War—things like Solid Shield [a joint training exercise] took place every year.

Straight-out competitions were also held between the SEALs and our sister units such as the Army Special Forces or the Marine Force Recon teams. We did a lot of work hand in hand with those people and respected them greatly, though that respect never got in the way of a good-natured rivalry between the services. But I take my hat off to those other units even now. They all did a hell of a job in Vietnam, and the competitions afterwards helped keep us all sharp.

THE MISSIONS OTHER THAN DIRECT COMBAT

The Teams conducted a great many more missions than just those involving combat. In the years prior to the Vietnam War, the UDTs continued to operate primarily in the water, as they had been doing since the very beginning. After their commissioning, the SEAL Teams of both coasts spent much of their time training and developing the variety of skills they thought they would need for future operations.

It was long known that the best way of knowing a subject is to teach it. The SEALs demonstrated this axiom by conducting Mobile Training Teams and instructing allies all over the world in the skills the SEALs had been developing. The UDTs continued working in support of the fleet and Marine amphibious operations. UDT operations centered around reconnaissance and demolitions. On many occasions, the UDTs supplied detachments of men to conduct demolitions of expired munitions, beach and coral clearances, and the destruction of ruined piers and other structures.

With the advent of the space program, the UDTs were called on for additional duties besides those missions that they were already conducting. Known for being among the most physically fit units in the U.S. military, the UDTs supplied men for a number of experiments in the 1950s to see if man could withstand the rigors of space flight. Once manned space capsules were an actuality, the UDTs trained special detachments to assist in the recovery of returned space vehicles.

Though known for being the first people to greet the astronauts when they splashed down on every space flight, the UDTs had done a lot more to assist the U.S. space program. In some of the tests in the 1950s, NASA had used operators from the Teams to test G-forces in centrifuges to see if a human being could even stand up to the rigors of a rocket launch. To simulate a man in zero gravity, UDT volunteers were kept submerged in pools for hours. The tests did little more than bore the UDT operators and wrinkle their skin from the water exposure.

There were other even lesser known assignments given the UDTs in support of the space program. Due to their location, the East Coast Teams located at Little Creek, Virginia, supplied the bulk of the men who worked with the earliest astronauts.

CHIEF ELECTRICIAN'S MATE

FRANK MONCRIEF

U.S.N. (Ret.)

Frank Moncrief is one of the more experienced men in the Teams on the East Coast. He started with the UDT in the early 1950s and was one of the first UDT skydivers. In addition to being a highly qualified skydiver, Moncrief continued to work in his first love, the water. As an instructor for underwater swimming, he taught many of the first SEALs about diving and helped test the equipment they would use in the future. He also taught others how to dive, men who would soon make their own marks in history.

Part of the time I was in the UDTs at Little Creek I was assigned to work in sub ops [submersible operations] at UDT 21. In the fifties and early sixties, it was a bit of a feather in your cap to be one of the guys assigned to sub ops. We were the department that did the testing and evaluation of all of the diving and underwater equipment used in the Teams then.

Because of the importance of sub ops, you had to be very good in the water in order to be considered for the department. Diving with scuba gear was still in its relative infancy, and a lot of equipment we take for granted today was brand-new and unproven then. I had built my own Aqua-Lung from instructions in *Popular Mechanics* magazine well before I ever joined the navy. Even as a young man in the Teams, I had shown myself to be very competent in the water, so I managed to get into sub ops early in my career.

We tested a lot of new equipment while I was in the department, some of which was so developmental that we practically made the stuff ourselves. In the fifties, we used dry suits to protect swimmers from the cold of the water. A dry suit is little more than a man-shaped rubber bag that keeps the water away from your skin. For insulation, you usually wore long underwear or something like it to give you a layer of air between yourself and the rubber suit. Any slight hole in a dry suit and water can leak in, ruining the insulating properties of whatever you're wearing and changing your buoyancy a lot. If a dry suit flooded, you quickly found yourself cold and overweighted and had to fight your way to the surface.

To eliminate the drawbacks of the dry suit, the wet suit was invented. A wet suit is made from foam neoprene rubber that is much stronger than the thin rubber of a dry suit. The foam neoprene insulates you from the cold water, and the little water that gets in under the foam is quickly warmed by your body heat. You can tear a wet suit and only get a little cold right around the tear. And a hole doesn't cause you to sink like a dry suit would.

The first wet suits we had in sub ops didn't show up as a suit at all but a set of instructions and patterns, a roll of foam neoprene, and a container of neoprene cement. This was more of a do-it-yourself kit than anything else. With the skipper's say-so, I was going to make the first wet suits we had. The skipper, Mr. Gaither, didn't have any trouble with the suit, but he did say I had to make the first suit in his size.

Going up to the skipper's office, I showed him what we had. "Here's the three patterns," I said. "There's small, medium, and large. Which do you want me to make?"

"Medium," the skipper said.

"But sir, I think the large . . ."

"Medium," he said emphatically.

"Okay, sir," I answered, "I'll make you a medium." Mr. Gaither was a heavyset guy, considerably larger than

I was. I didn't think that a medium was his size, but who am I to argue with the Boss. Cutting out the patterns, I glued the material together according to the instructions and thought my first tailoring job came out fairly well. When I took the finished suit up to the skipper, he had a slightly different opinion of my work.

"Here you go, Skipper," I said, handing him the suit. Trying it on in his office, the skipper ran into a little trouble—he couldn't get the legs of the suit to even fit over his calves. "Goddam it, Moncrief," he said, "why did you make this so small? I'll bet it fits you perfectly."

"I haven't tried it yet, sir," I answered.

"I'll bet you it fits. Here," he said, handing me the suit. "Put the damned thing on."

Boy, was the skipper pissed. That suit fit me perfectly. Of course, I was about forty pounds lighter than the skipper. So I had to make another suit, a large size this time, to satisfy the skipper.

The suits worked fine, but Bennie Solinski in sub ops shot them down. Bennie said the dry suit was preferable and that was that. He had a higher standing in sub ops than I did, so it turned out to be another year before the Teams received wet suits. Today, the form-fitted wet suit is the standard cold-water protection for both the Team and the civilian sport divers.

Personally, I think Bennie's opinion may have been colored by professional jealousy a bit. Bennie always thought that I had come into sub ops too early in my career. It had taken him several years to get into the department, where I had jumped the gun a bit and came right into sub ops after leaving St. Thomas.

Bennie and I were friends and Teammates, but I think I rubbed him the wrong way. A lot of that just came from my being so good in the water. I had been a scuba diver since before I joined the Teams. And in the early 1950s, scuba diving was a very rare sport. By my second year in the Teams, my skills were recognized and I was made an underwater swimming instructor down at our training site in St. Thomas.

So I had established myself as an experienced man underwater. This helped get me one of the more unusual instructing jobs that came up in the Teams. One day at Quarters, volunteers were asked for some additional instruction duty. Sub ops was used as the source of the men, which, along with Bennie and a couple of chiefs, included Salerno, Hugh Petty, McAllister, Marlow Proctor, Jim McGee, and myself. There may have been some others, but time has taken their names from me.

We were told they picked us to instruct the astronauts. "Instruct the astronauts?" I said. "You have got to be kidding. We don't know anything about being an astronaut."

As it turned out, they didn't want us to teach these guys anything about flying a space capsule, we were supposed to instruct them in scuba diving. NASA had the idea that being underwater would simulate weightlessness, that there was a similarity between the buoyancy of being underwater and the weightlessness of space. The idea turned out to be one of the more efficient ones and working underwater has been used to help train astronauts since those first guys on the Freedom 7 crew.

We had to teach the astronauts how to scuba-dive to help NASA prove its theory. Teaching guys to dive had been something we had all done for years. I was something of a fish, which is what made me want to join the Teams in the first place. But even though I was good in the water, teaching those first astronauts was a real job.

It wasn't that the guys weren't good students—far the opposite. But they asked more questions than anyone else ever had. You take a regular sailor in the Teams and all you had to do was show him the Aqua-Lung. You put this thing in your mouth and breathe normally. You can work at this depth and you have to be concerned with an embolism, recompression, and all of the other details of being underwater. That would be it, and you could take the sailor into the water and get him some experience. That was not what you did with the astronauts.

When I first showed a demand valve to John Glenn, he was not satisfied with just the instructions on how to use it. "That's very interesting," he said, "but how does it work?"

I had to take that demand valve completely apart. Every part, spring, and tube had to be explained as to what its function was and how it accomplished it. Glenn was thorough—all the astronauts were.

These guys were sharp and in good shape. The only trouble we had with them was the bunch of photographers who were constantly about. These photographers weren't Navy men, they were civilian newspeople and something we weren't used to at all. They circled all of the time, like buzzing flies, and they were just about as popular as flies with us. The only thing is that with all of those photographers around, I never did get even one picture of myself with the astronauts.

In spite of the photographers, we continued with the training. In the pool, we started off getting our students used to working with swim fins and face masks. These guys were sharp enough to pick up on the techniques quickly. The physical end of training was never a problem with the astronauts. All of them were in excellent physical shape and they were all athletes in their own right.

After the mask and fins training was completed, we went on to put the guys in the water with their Aqua-Lungs. Lessons in clearing the mask of water, clearing the breathing hoses, and how to control your equipment and deal with emergencies were all covered. The guys picked up on everything, and training went pretty smoothly.

Finally, it was time for the testing stage of pool diving. We rigged up our "trainees" with full loads of air. We may have been still using the triple-bottle rigs then, so the guys had a good deal of bottom time, especially in a relatively shallow pool. Then we gave them their instructions for the test. "Once you go under," we said, "don't come up for anything. You can deal with every kind of emergency or accident you might run into. So just do it, and no matter what happens, don't break the surface."

Our students understood, and down they went. Now we started harassing them. As the guys swam in circles in the pool, we would go in and take their face masks off, dropping them on the bottom. Not only did the astronauts have to put on and clear their face masks, they had to grope around on the bottom of the pool and find them first.

Hoses would be squeezed so that they couldn't breathe. Panic had better not set in or they would shoot straight to the surface. Tanks would be turned off, mouthpieces pulled out, or fins stripped off. And all of this was done while they continued swimming in circles in the pool.

Of course, we would give them time to correct whatever we had done to them. They could reach back and turn their tanks on again or put a swim fin back over a foot. We weren't just harassing them without purpose. Everything we did could happen to you underwater. It was much better to learn how to deal with things while still in the pool rather than in the dark, open waters of the ocean. This was the kind of training we did with everyone in the Teams. Only with the astronauts, it ended up backfiring on us.

After their training with us was over, the astronauts invited us to Langley, Virginia, to take an airplane ride. McAllister, Marlowe Proctor, Petty, and myself took the guys up on their invitation and drove up to Langley. The planes we were going to fly in were T-33 training jets. I thought the planes were fine, but the astronauts were bitching about not being able to get a more high-performance aircraft. That should have been something of a warning to us.

After borrowing Wally Schirra's flight suit and Deke Slayton's helmet, I joined Gus Grissom, one hell of a guy, who was to be my pilot. "Okay, Frank," said Gus, "I'm going to explain the whole system to you. When we're done with this, you'll be able to fly this baby all by yourself."

"I've never had any interest in learning how to fly an airplane," I said, "I'm just coming along for the ride." Skydiving was a big thing for me then, so it wasn't a fear of heights that bothered me. I just hadn't been interested in learning how to fly then.

"Okay," Gus continued, "we're going to taxi out to the end of the runway now." The canopies were open and we were moving along while Gus continued. I was sitting in the backseat of the craft carefully behaving myself.

"By the way," Gus said, "sit there with your hands on your knees and your feet off the pedals. Just like you were sitting on a toilet. And don't touch anything!"

There was kind of a bucket spot on the floor for your feet, and my shoes were in there, nowhere near the pedals. "Yes sir," I answered. "I'm not going to touch a thing. I'll just sit here and watch you fly the airplane."

The cloud cover that day was at maybe three thousand feet, a gray overcast. When we reached the end of the runway, Gus was talking to the tower and going over the checklist with me. Again, he repeated for me to keep my hands on my knees and away from the controls. This wasn't going to be a problem. Even though he was telling me everything that was going on and I could hear all of the conversation through my helmet, I had no idea about flying a jet.

"Okay, I'm going to drop the canopy now," Gus said. "Watch your fingers."

My hands were still on my knees and not moving. As we continued, Gus spoke to me about every step of the takeoff. "We're on the runway now," he said. "We'll start off slow and build up to about 180 miles per hour. When we hit that speed, I'll pull back on the stick and we'll lift off."

Just as he had said, Gus talked me through every step of the procedure. Pointing out to me which gauges to watch. I knew when we were flying when the wheels extended and locked. Feeling the wheels bump as the pressure came off them and they closed into their wells, I could see the ground starting to fall away.

Moving out over the Chesapeake, Gus said that we were going to look for a hole in the clouds in order to climb. As we flew over the Chesapeake, the fun started. "Well," Gus said, "I can't find any holes for us to climb through. The flight plan I filed says we're going to Richmond, so I guess we better be on our way." With that, Grissom threw that plane into a turn and tried to drive me through the seat.

We were pulling maybe three or four G's during that turn. My hands were still on my knees as I felt my helmet drive down to my shoulders and my bottom push into the seat. He had told me to sit there like I was on the toilet— he didn't say he was going to try and flush it.

Gus heard my grunt over the headset. "Don't worry about it," he said to my concern. "We're fine." And we continued under the clouds towards Richmond.

"This helmet felt like it was made out of lead," I told him.

"Oh, don't worry about that. We just pulled a couple of G's."

I wouldn't have wanted to feel a whole bunch of G's right then. While Gus continued to talk to someone over the radio, we continued on our way. "We'll pull up as soon as we reach a break in the clouds," he said back to me.

That break must have been coming up. It didn't seem like more than a moment went by when suddenly Gus sat the jet on its tail and launched us straight up. We were hauling along about as fast as that T-33 would go. Leveling off at about ten thousand feet, Gus settled back into a fast cruise. That had been a beautiful fast climb, and now the scenery had taken quite a change. The clouds extended from three thousand feet to around ten thousand feet. We scooted along just above them as they billowed all around us. It looked like big white coral heads and mushrooms were growing around us.

It was beautiful up there, and I really was enjoying the flight. Then Gus started in on me. Suddenly the plane was sliding up on the left side till just the wingtip was pointed down. Then we were slipping down and up onto the right wingtip. We sideslipped back and forth, all across the sky. He kicked that jet all over the place, without warning me once.

Gus heard me gasp and called back to ask what was wrong.

"Oh, nothing," was my slightly strained answer.

"Frank," Gus said to me, "I want to tell you something. This is my swimming pool. Just sit back and relax."

Relaxing wasn't the easiest thing to do right then. That man wrung me out with every kind of aerobatics he could do. Gus turned me every way but loose. Then, all of a sudden, Gus said, "There's Richmond."

"It looks like a city," I asked innocently. "How can you tell it's Richmond?"

"Let's go get a close look," he said, and he flipped the plane over and drove us straight down, pulling up at about two thousand feet.

I just said, "Oh my God!" And Gus didn't just come out of the dive straight, he sideslipped us in big arcs through the sky. We just swayed back and forth across the sky. And the swaying was ended when he turned the plane over.

After all of this was done, Gus called back to me and asked how I was doing.

Gulping, I answered, "I'm okay."

"Don't throw up!"

"I won't throw up. The last thing I'm going to do is throw up in this plane." That was, it was the last thing I was going to do just before I died, but he didn't need to know that.

"Okay," Gus continued, "I'm going to give you a break. Put your hand on the stick in front of you."

My feet were still in the bucket, but I grabbed the stick just like he told me to. "Okay, now put your feet on the pedals."

"Gus," I said, "if it's all the same to you, just what are you trying to get me to do?"

"Do you see the dummy horizon on the instruments in front of you?"

"Yeah."

"Just keep the wings level with the horizon."

Hey, I could do this. Now I was flying the jet along, just keeping the wings level.

"Well, do something," Gus said.

"I am doing something," I answered. "I'm keeping the wings level."

"No, I mean do something."

"Well, what do you want me to do?"

"Push the stick over to the left and pull it back."

I didn't even really push the stick over. It was more like I thought about pushing it over. Suddenly, we were slipping over to the side. Now he had me doing that stuff to myself!

Pulling the stick back to where it was, I leveled off. "You didn't do anything," Gus complained.

"I did plenty," was my retort.

"Just push the stick over and pull it back. Go on, do it!"

To show him I wasn't a complete rookie, I whipped that dude over and pulled it back hard. I didn't know a plane could do that without falling apart. "Gus," I called up, just a bit stressed.

"What?"

"I'm going to bring it back. You've got it."

During my little maneuver, I had come very close to blacking out. Now, as I let go of the controls, the plane was suddenly falling out of the sky. "Gus!" I shouted.

"It's all right," he called back, laughing. "I've got it."

What a flight that was. We went back to the field at Langley without any further incident. McAllister had been in one of the other planes and he'd lost his lunch in his helmet. It was just the astronauts' little way of getting back at us for their pool training.

When we finally landed, I was as white as a shirt. Looking at me, Gus asked how I was feeling. "I feel, wow, like my head is this big," and I held out my hands shoulder-width.

"Frank," Gus continued, laughing, "I've got to tell you. We don't do that stuff to trainee pilots until they've been in the air for at least a month. I really wrung you out."

But he just hadn't been able to resist the opportunity to nail an instructor. I was seasick for something like two days after that. But Gus had been one hell of a guy. It was a shame how he died in the capsule fire on Apollo 1. But in all of the books and the movies done since, the training we gave to the first astronauts, the Freedom 7, has never been shown. Since then, the public has seen

UDT men jump into the water to recover every U.S. space capsule to come home. We were always the first to greet the returning travelers.

THE END OF THE VIETNAM WAR, DIFFERENCES BETWEEN THE COASTS, AND THE POSTWAR LIMITING OF THE TEAMS

There has long been a friendly rivalry between the Special Warfare Teams of the East and West Coasts. To any outsiders, all operators, no matter where they are from, are Teammates and must be shown the proper respect from "nonquals." One slight bone of contention retained by SEAL Team Two is that it is older than SEAL Team One. Commissioning orders were backdated to be effective 1 January 1962, but the original mustering formations were not held until 1300 hours on 8 January. Because of the difference in time zones, SEAL Team Two claims to be the senior team by a matter of three hours.

In reality, there was a noticeable difference between the Teams of the East Coast and those of the West Coast, especially in the SEAL Teams. The East Coast Teams were made up of older men with an average age being around twenty-six to twenty-eight years. The older men also were more established in their careers and in their home lives; because of their greater age and time in service, the average rank in SEAL Team Two was E-5, while in SEAL Team One it was E-4.

One large difference between SEAL Teams One and Two stood out during the Vietnam War. As Southeast Asia was considered primarily a SEAL Team One operational assignment, the brunt of supplying direct-action platoons fell on this Team. Platoons began deploying from SEAL Team One in February 1966 for combat duties in Vietnam. SEAL Team Two soon followed, with their deployments beginning in February 1967.

As a part of their overall commitment to support of operations in Southeast Asia, SEAL Team One had as many as five platoons operating in-country simultaneously.

SEAL Team Two primarily worked with fewer platoons in-country at any one time. Because of the higher level of commitment, it was not unusual for veteran operators from SEAL Team One to have five tours of duty in Vietnam by the war's end. In comparison, SEAL Team Two had very few operators with five tours in Vietnam, three being the more common maximum.

The younger average age of the SEAL Team One operators, combined with the higher number of deployed platoons, caused SEAL Team One to have a much lower retention rate than was found in SEAL Team Two. Older operators tended to already have a longer commitment to a career in the Navy, so reenlistment was not as great a concern in SEAL Team Two.

By the Vietnam War's end, the SEAL Teams, and Special Warfare as a whole, were larger, with much greater numbers of operators in the Teams than had been there six years earlier. These numbers had to be brought down to reflect the lower mission profiles given to SpecWar during the 1970s. With the guerrilla war of Vietnam over, the regular fleet Navy saw even less use for the unconventional warfare conducted by the Teams. This was very much a repeat of the situation following World War Two when the 3,500 men of the UDTs were cut back to a few hundred within only a year.

A much larger percentage of the men in SEAL Team Two were close to having sufficient time in the service to retire. Normal attrition through retirement and voluntary returns to the fleet Navy were enough to reduce the numbers of men in the East Coast Teams. That situation wasn't found to be a solution for the West Coast Teams, and more drastic cuts were made in personnel.

JAMES JANOS

U.S.N. (Left 1974)

Well remembered by his Teammates, Jim Janos is better known to the public under his professional name, Jesse "the Body" Ventura. Jesse Ventura was a professional wrestler who fought in the ring for a number of years until finally retiring in the 1980s. As an actor, Jesse is recognized as the man who carried and fired the minigun in the film Predator. *But it was his career prior to his public life that paved the way for his future success. As a member of UDT 12, Jim Janos served in the waning years of the Vietnam War and through the Team cutbacks of the early 1970s.*

The thing I liked the most about being in the Teams was the fun stuff, the characters that I met and the good things we did together. Sure, there were bad times, hard training, and even harder missions. But we were a conglomeration of pirates at heart, and sometimes action as well.

It seemed to me that it was the attitude of the men in the Teams that really made the difference. Once you completed training and entered a Team, you were a Teammate for life. You knew what you were and were proud of it. And some were a little more proud of it than others. Today, my wife Teresa has even commented on the fact that she has never met a Team guy who was not an eccentric.

"Every one of them, in their own way," Terry said, "is so off the wall." And I met Terry after I had left the Teams, so she has only met just a few of the guys really. My brother had told me about life in the Teams and what the guys were like, and I think that was a big part of what made me follow his lead.

My brother and I grew up in South Minneapolis, Minnesota. It wasn't much of a surprise that my brother and I ended up in the service at some point in our lives, as both my mother and father were World War Two veterans. My dad, George W. Janos, Sergeant E-5, served in the infantry under General Patton as part of the crew of a tank destroyer, fighting in North Africa, Italy, and Europe.

Dad would talk a lot about being in the Army, but he never said much about being in action. It was a long time before I learned about why my dad never spoke much about the part of war that is exciting to a young boy. Simple fact is that when you get older and face combat yourself, not talking about it afterwards isn't something that takes a lot of explanation.

Mom, Bernice M. "Lenz" Janos, First Lieutenant, was a nurse in North Africa and held a commission as an officer. My dad was a sergeant, so whenever they had a fight when I was a kid, that fact came out. Dad would always call my mom "the lieutenant," which would irritate my mother no end. Something about the standard story that enlisted men would always blame the officers just because they were officers.

Going through my dad's papers after he was gone, I found a small laminated card that was a shrunk-down version of his DD-214. It was so small that I had to use a magnifying glass to read the card, and I learned some things that I never knew before. He had been through seven major battles, including the Battle of the Bulge.

As it turned out, I was not the first member of my family to appear on television—Dad made it well before I did. There was a documentary of World War Two showing on a Sunday night, and my entire family was gathered around the TV watching it. The big story that night was the battle at the Remagen Bridge. As the show was play-

ing, suddenly there was my dad up on the screen crossing
the bridge with the other GIs. We knew it was him because
almost immediately afterwards, the phone rang and it was
my mom's parents out in Iowa.

"Were you watching?" they asked. "We saw George
crossing the Remagen Bridge."

That was pretty neat, and it impressed the hell out of
me. But even though both my parents were veterans, and
Mom and Dad both served in North Africa, they didn't
meet until after the war. And Dad had gone through the
war the long way. First, he enlisted at the oldest age they
would accept, thirty-six, and then he served through four
years of the war until it was over.

Years later, my aunt was going through some archives
and found out that my dad was one year older than he
thought he was. That was quite a surprise, finding out at
age sixty-five or seventy that you're one year older and
never would have had to serve in the Army in the first
place.

When my folks were married, Dad was forty and Mom
was thirty. Mom was still a nurse and was working at the
University of Minnesota, so they bought a house in South
Minneapolis. My brother came along in January 1948 and
I was born in 1951.

My brother and I were different in a lot of ways. Jan
was always immaculate, kept his room and things clean
and neat. On the other hand, I was more of a relaxed sort
of housekeeper. Later, in UDT 12, Lieutenant Commander
Bruce Dyer, then our XO, nicknamed us Janos the Dirty
(me) and Janos the Clean (my brother). The nicknames
came from how our personal gear lockers were kept in
Subic Bay in the Philippines. Apparently, during one
locker inspection, Dyer was looking at Jan's locker and
noted that everything was clean and properly stowed away.
When my locker was opened up, stuff fell out on Dyer,
and that apparently made some kind of impression on
him.

From that day forward, on any UDT duty rosters would
be found the names Janos the Clean and Janos the Dirty.
Actually, the nicknames were needed, since both my

brother Jan and I have a first name starting with J, and most of the duty rosters only put down a man's first initial.

Before any of this happened, both my brother and I had to be in the service. Our joining the Navy was directly from my father's advice. It wasn't that Dad wanted either one of us in the service—actually he didn't want us to join at all. But if we were going to insist on joining the military, there was no way any son of his was going to enlist in the Army and slog along in the mud like he did.

Vietnam was going on big-time, and what I was being taught in school wasn't quite what my dad thought back home. At that time, my teachers were saying that the Vietnam War was a good fight and that we belonged there and were stopping Communism. As far as my father, the combat vet, was concerned, that whole idea was bullshit and the only reason we were fighting in Southeast Asia was because somebody was making money. That was his perception, and time later proved him a lot more right than some of my teachers were.

My dad thought we had no good business being in Vietnam, and I think he also feared for his kids. Today, I would feel the same way about my son going off to war. But my dad figured our choice was ours to make, so if we wanted to go, he wouldn't stop us. He would guide our choice, though.

Today, I wouldn't want my own son to go to war, but if he wanted to join the military, I would allow him his wishes. I wouldn't agree to making a young man go to war like the draft did. As a firm believer in the professional, volunteer military, I think there would be more than enough young men and women who would serve their country in a time of need. Both my brother and I were dumb enough to go into the service, so there must be other suckers out there.

But well before either Jan or I went into the service, we fought about it over the kitchen table. Dad was unmovable about one thing—we would not be going into the Army. My dad's observation was that the Army always built their bases on the worst available piece of shit real estate that could be found. In any state in the Union, if the Army put up a base, it was on a chunk of dirt that nobody else wanted or could stand.

If Jan and I wanted to join the service, it should be either the Navy or the Air Force. According to my father, those two services would teach us something, while the Army or the Marine Corps would only teach us how to pound gravel with our feet—that and charge, in the case of the Marine Corps.

If we were going to go into the service, we might as well let the government pay to teach us a skill or two. So Jan joined the Navy a couple of years out of high school and I followed soon after.

So my brother led the way into the Navy and the Teams. Jan had decided to join the Navy and volunteered for UDT. Both of us had been swimmers and scuba divers while in school, and, like so many of our generation, we had learned about the UDT from the Richard Widmark movie *The Frogmen*. It seemed like a natural thing for us to gravitate to the Teams in the service.

I did ask my brother just what had made him think of volunteering for the UDT, and it wasn't just that Widmark movie. When we were little kids, my mom had bought the two of us these little plastic frogmen that swam in the water. Swimming might be too big a word for what they did. You filled up part of this little plastic man with baking soda and he would rise and fall in the water as the soda fizzed into bubbles. That was Jan's favorite toy when he was a kid, and it stuck with him for years. When Jan told me that was what he remembered, I still laugh to myself, amazing what motivates someone.

Neither one of us really knew anything about the SEALs at the time. If you studied the available literature enough, you could learn little things about the SEALs. We knew that the frogmen of the UDTs were leaving the water to conduct missions on land, but that was about the extent of our information. While I was in high school, Jan attended training out in Coronado with BUD/S Class 49. He graduated in March 1969, and when he came home on leave, I learned a lot more about the UDTs and the SEALs.

By the time he came home on leave, Jan had not only

graduated training, he had been assigned to UDT 12 and already done a tour of duty at Da Nang. A friend of mine, Steve Nelson [BM1, Seal Team One], was also interested in the Navy and the UDTs, so when Jan came home, he had a solid audience for his stories. Of course, what Jan had to say was not necessarily what we wanted to hear. "Don't go in," Jan said. "Go to college. Just go to college and have fun."

Both Steve and I were already enrolled in the local college and were intending to go. About a month later, my brother returned to Coronado. After Jan was gone, Steve called me up.

"Jim," Steve said, "I've made a decision, and I want you to come with me."

"What are you talking about?"

"I've decided that I want to be a SEAL. I want to do what your brother is doing, and I'm joining the Navy. I want you to join with me on the buddy program."

There was only one way I could answer this. "Are you crazy?" I blurted out. "Didn't you listen to Jan? He told us to go to college."

There was no way I was going to argue Steve out of what he had decided. At that time, there was no difference in our minds about being a SEAL or in the UDT. And out in Coronado, there was little difference as well. Men were trained and part of the Teams, they could serve in either the UDTs or in SEAL Team One after they had their qualifications behind them.

Jan told me what I needed to know about training and the Teams. Probably he actually told me less than I needed to know, looking back on things. His words were pretty much all it took for me to decide I was going to follow in my big brother's footsteps.

After Steve had called me, I agreed to go with him to the recruiter's office. "But I'm not going to sign anything," was what I told him before I agreed to go. "We'll just hear what they have to say." I came home that night with a military ID with my name on it.

So much for my careful decision-making. Back home, I just looked into the mirror and said, "What the fuck did

I do?'' Welcome to the Navy—I was enlisted. We didn't have to report for a while yet—we had joined under the new 120-day delayed-entry program—but we were considered members of the reserves, and there was a good thing that came out of that.

Near the Minneapolis airport used to be a little Army post, the 13th Artillery. With our military IDs we could go onto the post and drink legally, and cheaply. Drinks were only about a quarter each then, so Steve and I would go over to the post and get shnockered up before hitting the town.

Since I had already decided what I was doing with my life for at least the next four years, I was going to make the best of what time I had on the outside before reporting in. Quitting my job with the highway department, I decided to go into the service without a dime to my name. Everything I had was going to be blown on a good time before I reported in.

Finally, Steve and I flew out of Minneapolis and arrived in San Diego for boot camp. Our first night on post was spent standing underneath this goofy shed they had while some little guy ran up and down the ranks yelling at us.

Physically, I was in great shape well before I arrived in boot camp. Swimming and playing football had made the 190 pounds I had on my six-foot-three-inch frame muscular enough to make the boot camp physical training not much of a challenge. Jan had told me what to expect in BUD/S, and I had spent some of my last months as a civilian getting ready for the ordeal.

But all of that was in the future. Right then I was standing with a bunch of other fresh recruits being chewed out by this little shit. Turning to Steve standing next to me, I voiced my thoughts on the situation to him.

''Steve,'' I said, ''you're lucky I don't kill you right now. We could be back home chasing women and having a good time. Instead here we are standing under this fucking hut being yelled at and we haven't done anything.''

My opinion of boot camp didn't change much during the training. Every day, after the instructors were through harassing us and showing us how to fold our socks and whatever, we were being taught every facet of being in the Navy. One day you would learn about electronics technicians and what they did. All these different instructors would come in and tell us about all of the jobs, or ratings, that were available to us.

Soon after Steve and I completed our battery of screening tests, and passed it with high marks, we were gathered in a big auditorium with all of the other recruits to listen to some lecture. In front of something like three companies of recruits, three hundred men seated in their dungarees and black shoes, out onstage came these two guys wearing spit-shined Corcoran jump boots, starched and pressed fatigues, and pressed Marine Corps hats. These were the recruiters for BUD/S, and just looking at them you knew they were hard cases.

"We're here to tell you about the Underwater Demolition and SEAL Teams," was what they said, and they proceeded to tell us all of what they were about. After the talk, we were all shown the Navy SEAL recruiting film, *The Men with Green Faces*. Now Steve and I were more than a little interested. I was pumped—this was what we had both joined the Navy for. This was my day.

All before this one lecture, I had constantly been asking our boot camp company commander about when would we be seeing the UDT/SEAL presentation. And each time I asked, the commander looked at me with the same "What the hell is wrong with you?" look in his face. And now my chance was here.

"All right," the recruiters said when their presentation was done, "anybody who wants to volunteer for BUD/S, stay in the room. The rest of you, get the fuck out of here."

There were guys in the recruit companies who couldn't get to the door fast enough. It was like they were thinking, get me away from these nutcases, this is not what I joined the Navy for. Others just moved out smartly. After the two hundred fifty or so recruits had left, there were maybe forty or fifty guys left in the auditorium along with Steve and myself to take the screening test.

Out of that number of guys, I think there were maybe

ten to fifteen of us who were really serious about what the upcoming opportunity meant. The other guys were just staying there partially to break the monotony of daily training at boot camp. Now we took the physical screening test to see if we could qualify for BUD/S.

Before coming into the Navy, I had been a competitive swimmer in high school. For my swimming test, I swam like I was in the Olympic trials, and burnt myself out like a dumb shit. I didn't need to go that fast. Knowing what I do today, I would have been much better off just falling into a nice easy breaststroke and done my three hundred meters inside of the needed time. That would have been a lot smarter than coming in almost a pool length in front of the next swimmer.

What I was going to do was show the SEAL instructor just how good a swimmer I was. Which is part of what they want to see anyway. But I should have saved some of that energy for the run.

Steve was an okay swimmer, but he had quit the swim team back in high school in order to take a job, which he considered more important. In spite of that, Steve did okay on the testing.

On the rest of the screening tests, I shined. The push-ups were as many as you could do in two minutes, resting only in the up position. Sit-ups were the same, as many as you could do in two minutes. There were other exercises, and then we did a mile run. The test exercises were done one after the other with no space in between to rest. We had paired off, and the only rest we got was when we switched places and you had to count the repetitions while your partner tested out.

All through boot camp, I had been working out in order to be prepared for this day. When we were done with the day's training, I would go off in a corner somewhere and do sit-ups, push-ups, and other exercises with Steve right alongside me. This made sure I was in good shape for the tests. In spite of that, I didn't come in first on the run, I came in third. Running is not my forte, and I couldn't believe how badly I hurt after that lousy little mile. My lungs were burning badly, and that was something I would never forget. It was all I could do to cross the finish line.

Maybe I shouldn't have pushed so hard during the swimming. But the swimming alone washed out thirty guys from the group. There were only about twelve of us who continued the testing. Most guys just weren't able to swim three hundred meters, especially not in a fifty-meter pool where you have less turns.

By the time we completed the screening test, there were only four of us left who passed. Bueler, Brettlinger, Nelson, and myself. When the instructor walked along the line, he got to me and just said "Passed" right away. Coming to Steve was another matter.

When that instructor got to where Steve was standing in line, he looked up at Steve and then back down to his clipboard. He must have looked up and down several times before he finally said "Passed" and went on to the next man. Steve damned near collapsed with relief. Now we went back to our boot camp company knowing we were going to where we wanted to be.

When we arrived at the company, our company commander came up to us. "I heard you two passed the SEAL screening test," he said to us.

"Yes sir, Mr. Bondi," was all we could answer, wondering what was going to happen next.

"Are you really going into that shit?" he said. "You really want to become a pole-carrying assassin?"

That's what he said, and I'll never forget it. He must not have known that I had a brother in the Teams. "Mr. Bondi," I said, "that's the only reason I joined the Navy."

He just looked at me, rolling his eyes with this "You're gone from me" expression on his face. "Look, you two," he said. "I'm not going to bother either of you for the rest of boot camp. Just do your stuff and don't get in my way. Let me do the stuff I have to do with the rest of these people. For yourselves, just fold your clothes and stand at attention when you're supposed to. With what you two are going into, there isn't anything I can legally do to you that will even come close to what you're facing.

You have no idea about what you're letting yourselves in for."

To this we just agreed, thinking it sounded like a good deal. And Bondi was a man of his word. For the rest of boot camp, he mostly left Steve and me alone. We did what we were supposed to do and mostly marked time.

Something like three years later, I ran into Mr. Bondi while standing in line for a San Diego Chargers game. Walking up to him, I said, "Mr. Bondi, do you remember me? You pushed me through boot camp three years ago. I just wanted to tell you that I made it. I'm a SEAL and I'm in the Teams."

He just looked at me like he was petrified of me. There was this look of fear in his eyes. And all I wanted to do was say hello to the man who had pushed me through boot camp. I didn't hold any grudge or anything. Of course, he didn't know that, and I must have had another twenty or thirty pounds of muscle on me as I stood in front of him. It was just the reputation the Teams had among the regular, black-shoe Navy. They didn't know who we were, and most of them didn't want to know.

Passing the screening tests wasn't a free ticket into the Teams, or even training. Disaster almost hit even before I could report in. The results of the whole thing made me even a stronger member of the Teams and helped resolve in me the Team spirit of no matter what the job is, if you want it bad enough, you will get it done.

The particulars of the incident were simple enough. I was given a physical before being officially allowed into BUD/S. It wasn't just me, of course—all of us were given the same physical. But I'm color-blind, and the physical just about washed me out. Suddenly, I was unqualified to be in the Teams no matter what I did.

Suddenly I was getting washed out of BUD/S before I had even made it to the compound. This was devastating. When I received phone privileges later, I called home and talked to just the right person, my mom.

Mom was a very strong-willed woman—she had to have been to survive her own military career with her personality intact. The conversation soon turned to what the recruiter had told me before I had enlisted, and that was that there would be no problem in getting into the Teams if I had the heart for it. "No problem," the recruiter had said, even after I had told him about my color-blindness. "You have an A physical profile. That's all you need."

At the BUD/S physical, they had given me the book test, where you look at fourteen circles made up of colored dots. Certain colored dots make up numbers if you can recognize the colors. This test has nothing to do with resolve, heart, or "fire in the gut"—you can either do it or you can't, and I couldn't.

The conversation I had with my mom was pretty abrupt about my future plans. "I'm going over the hill if I don't even get a chance to get into the Teams," I said to her. "If I quit on my own, that's my business. But if they take this from me, I'm going over the hill, Ma. The first chance I get, I'll leave school and become a criminal."

That's not exactly the way to have a conversation with your mother, but it did show just how resolved I was. What I didn't contend with was my mother's resolve. There was no way she was going to let me screw up the balance of my life if she had anything to do about it. Senator Hubert Humphrey's office soon received a phone call from my mother, and she talked to the senior senator from Minnesota himself.

What my mother did was tell Senator Humphrey that the local recruiters had told me that I was qualified to take BUD/S training. That got me into the military, and now that I was in, they were taking that away from me and telling me that I couldn't go.

And while my mother was working her way down from the top, my brother was coming up from the bottom. Jan had been on deployment while I was taking the tests for BUD/S. Even before I could report to BUD/S, I had to attend my Class A school and have a navy rating. For me, A school was storekeepers school on 32nd Street in San Diego. Even though my mom had talked me out of going over the hill while at storekeepers school, I kept trying to argue my case at BUD/S.

While I was at school, I kept trying to volunteer for

BUD/S. When my brother came back in-country, he heard about what was going on and looked me up at school. "Put in another chit for BUD/S," Jan said, "because you still have to take the pressure test."

The pressure test was one where they checked your tolerance to high-pressure oxygen and being deep underwater. When they had first washed me out of the selection process, I had never taken the pressure test. To take the test, I had to go over to the BUD/S training area itself, across the street from the Naval Amphibious Base at Coronado. What my brother wanted me to do was take another physical screening test in the Team area.

Anything that was a chance sounded good to me, so I put it to Master Chief Mooney that I had already passed the screening test for BUD/S but still needed further testing over at UDT 12. Mooney okayed my request, so I jumped on the bus, went over to UDT 12, and reported into the quarterdeck. Chief Kinnard took me from the quarterdeck over to the diving tank and proceeded to give me the pressure test. "So," the chief said to me, "you're Janos's kid brother, huh?"

"Yeah," was about all I could say before the test began.

Chief Kinnard put me into the diving tank and ran up the pressure. There was no problem with the test, and I passed it. Taking me into another room, the chief ran me through another physical and then took out that damned color-blindness test book.

Opening up the book, Chief Kinnard handed it to me and told me to read off the numbers, and he flipped the pages. After I was done, the chief closed the book and said, "Well, you're certainly color-blind. You missed thirteen out of fourteen." This was not what I needed to hear.

As a man was passing by the area, the chief yelled out to him, "Hey, isn't so-and-so in Team such-and-such color-blind?"

"Yeah," the man answered, "I think he is."

"Is he a good operator?"

"One of the best."

Standing there, I had sweat just pouring down off me. This was my life these guys were tossing around. Finally trusting myself to speak, I told Chief Kinnard that all I wanted was a chance to try, and all that was holding me up was this one damned test. And the chief just started typing out my physical report. When he came to the color-dot test, he typed in "14 out of 14, passed." Then he signed the form, handed it to me, and said, "Good luck in training, kid."

Right then I was ready to kiss that chief's ass and let him draw a crowd for the chance to get into training. And here he just handed it to me. What I found out later was that the chief was a corpsman my brother had served with overseas. My brother had mentioned to the chief that I had a problem and wondered if there was anything that could be done about it. The chief had taken it from there.

To me, Chief Kinnard's actions were the essence of what being in the Teams was about. In the Teams, it wasn't what you said that mattered, it was what you did and who you were as an individual. If I quit, I would be nothing but a puke and be gone. But I deserved at least a chance, and they gave it to me.

Going back to storekeepers school, I gave my paperwork to Chief Mooney. Mooney was a master chief from the old school, which basically meant he knew every other chief in the Navy. Calling up BuPers [Bureau of Personnel] himself while I was in his office, Mooney bellowed into the phone, "Bob, this is Mooney. Look, I got a young kid in here who's breaking my walls down and tearing up my pictures. He wants to be one of those damned SEALs. I don't know why he wants to do that but he's tearing me down to get there."

Earlier, I had explained to Mooney what I wanted to do and he'd suggested that maybe the Teams just didn't need me. "But they're crying for qualified men, Chief!" was all I could say to him.

Master Chief Mooney had been in the Navy since before World War Two. He was an E-9 with more time in the service than the battleship *New Jersey,* and they were finally just throwing him out. After thirty-one years in, guys like Mooney don't retire—it takes a direct act of the Navy to finally get them to leave. There were worse guys I could have on my side.

"Can you get this guy into the next BUD/S class?" Mooney said into the phone.

"Yeah," was the answer that came back, and my heart started beating again.

The next week I spent cooling my heels in the X division. That was where they kept all of the guys who weren't assigned to a unit yet. On Thursday, my orders came through and they read that I started BUD/S on the next Monday. No pretraining or anything else, but I had my chance. Going from 32nd Street, I jumped on a bus and headed over to BUD/S on Friday. Arriving at noon, I had checked in and been issued my gear by four o'clock that afternoon. My training class started Monday morning.

Now that I had a chance to breathe and think about what was going on, I realized just how fast things had moved. Jeez, I said to myself, couldn't they have let me start with the next class? But I had my shot and there was nothing else for it but to continue on.

Halfway through training, I got a letter from Senator Humphrey's office stating they had started a senatorial investigation. I had to quickly call my mom and have it stopped. She told the Senator that everything had worked out [thanks to a couple of salty chiefs], and thanked him very much for his concern.

This was back when the Teams still had buildings in the Amphibious Base, on the bay side of Coronado facing San Diego itself. Those old shacks aren't standing anymore, and all of the BUD/S training now takes place in a separate facility across the street facing the (cold!) Pacific Ocean. You had to go pound on the door to Building 207 and wait until you were called. These voices inside would bellow out, "Who the fuck is it?"

You had to shout out your name and then you were told, in the same gentle tones, "Get the fuck in here!"

In that building were all the first-phase instructors. And these men had to be the scariest people on the planet. They were certainly the most frightening individuals I ever met in my life. After I handed my orders to Gunner's

Mate, Guns [GMG] Olsen, he took them in this big paw and growled at me, "Did you have some damn uncle or brother or dad or something come through training here?"

Prouder, and dumber, than anything, I answered, "My brother did. Janos, UDT 12."

Terry "Mother" Moy, one of the instructors, was sitting in the corner of the room. "What did he say his name was?" Moy asked.

"It's another one of those stupid damn Janoses," Olsen answered.

"You mean that puke brother of his made it?" Moy asked in an incredulous voice. "That piece of shit made it through training? How the hell did that happen?"

These two instructors had just started playing the head games of BUD/S on me. And all I could do was stand there and take it. Leering over at me, Moy growled, "Well, boy, you better be twice as tough as that screwed-up brother of yours, because we're going to find out Monday morning. Dismissed!"

Oh, did I screw up, I said to myself later. Why did I ever admit to having a brother in the Teams? That weekend, I was talking to my brother and told him what Moy had said. Jan was immediately pissed off.

"That jerk Moy said that?" Jan exclaimed, and then he went on being soundly derogatory about Moy. There wasn't much question that things changed once you completed training and entered the Teams. Jan had already completed a deployment to Vietnam, so he was in a position to say just what came to mind about the men who were going to be my instructors. The thing was that I hadn't gotten into the Teams yet and still had to face my first day of training, and those same instructors.

The very first day of training we faced the obstacle course. I hadn't seen the damned thing ever before, let alone attended pretraining so that I at least knew how to go through everything and not kill myself. The instructors did show us how everything was done, in a quick and efficient manner. Then it was our turn to run the course individually.

Later in training, there is a set maximum time limit you

have to beat in order to pass the obstacle course. Roughly around the ten- or eleven-minute mark. That time seemed an eternity away when I ran the O-course my first time. In the startling time of forty-three minutes. And that was forty-three minutes of unadulterated hell. Never before had I faced such a mess of painful, grueling obstacles that you had to pass over, under, around, and through. After my run was through, I stood there looking at that fiendish assembly of logs, nets, ropes, and pipes and just felt the four flapping, torn-open blisters on each of my hands.

This was only the first day of training! When did time-out come up? Surprise—time-out never came up in training. Things just got faster, harder, and worse. I was injured, and no one cared.

By the end of that first day, someone did care about the torn blisters on my injured hands. Mother Moy set down a table in front of all of us. On the table, Moy opened up a big box with the red cross of first aid on the cover. Turning to us, Moy grumbled, "Okay, which one of you pukes has got flappers?"

What he meant was the torn sections of skin that used to cover my blisters. Like the dumb shit that I could be, I called out, "I do, Instructor Moy."

"Come up here, boy."

At least during that run to the table, I should have thought about what I was doing. Moy looked at me and asked, "Are you right-handed or left-handed?"

Puzzled, I answered, "I'm right-handed, Instructor Moy."

"Then hold your right hand out."

Moy was going to do something painful to me, that I was sure about. But I figured all he was going to do was pour mercurochrome on my blisters. Bracing for that, I put out my hand. Seems I didn't brace quite hard enough.

Reaching out, Moy ripped the loose flaps of skin off my palm. Tears were running down my face. "Painful" wasn't the word for how my hand felt. It was like I had dipped it in fire. And then the worst part came. "Okay, boy," Moy growled. "Now you rip the other ones off."

Standing in front of the class, I had to tear my own

skin flaps off my left hand. "Now get back in line, you big dummy," Moy snarled.

Running back into line, I learned my lesson that day. You stay small in training. The rule is to get inconspicuous and blend in as much as you possibly can. Bring no attention to yourself if you can possibly help it. Any attention that you will bring down on yourself will come with a payment that you don't want to make.

With my hands bleeding, I went to see my brother that night after training was done for the day. Sitting there, I was crying as my hands bled. With a silly kind of grin on his face, Jan just sat there looking at me. His roommates in the barracks, Big George Merrill among them, just looked on with what you might call sympathy. Big George spoke up and told me, "Don't worry, kid. It'll get better. You can make it."

That was a lot better than what Jan said. All my own brother did was look at me, laugh, and say, "And you still have twenty-one weeks and three days to go yet."

Training is the big equalizer in the Teams. It seems funny just who the guys are who are standing in the formation when graduation comes about. You sure can't pick them during those first days. There are muscle-bound athletes who look like Arnold Schwarzenegger in that first formation who are gone by the end. And there would be this little guy, who on the first day you said didn't have a chance. Hell, some of these guys you wondered how they got through the screening tests. But come graduation, that little guy would be standing tall and the muscle men would be long gone.

In my class, Class 58, we started about 125 men. And we graduated a big group, around forty guys. My class was a summer class, which some of the guys say is a lot better. My brother's class, Class 49, was a winter class and had a much lower graduation rate. Class 49 graduated about nineteen guys, though they started with about ninety. In the winter in San Diego, the waters offshore are colder than in the summer. This is true even though there's a current that brings down water from off Alaska all year round.

In San Diego during the winter, there's a penetrating kind of dank, wet cold that just seeps into your bones. This is a kind of cold that just saps your strength and makes you want to do almost anything to get warm. And during training, the instructors would have you dipping into the Pacific during the night and then rolling in the sand onshore to complete your misery. That would chill you to your core.

My first day of training was bad enough. When Hell Week came around, I just went numb. Inside, you just kind of die. What you can say for Hell Week is that, in a way, you get stronger as those miserable days crawl by. More and more, as you just keep going, the resolve to complete the course just continues to grow in you. Finally, you numb out completely and there's nothing more that they can do to you. You just go on automatic and complete each evolution as it comes along. No looking forward to the next exercise, problem, or evolution. Just making that next step and the one after that is enough to occupy your mind.

Far back in my own mind was the resolution not to quit. How would I have been able to face my brother, or my mom and dad, if I quit? How could I go home? That was a question that I just couldn't answer, so it helped keep me going. Later, I told Moy at a reunion about something else I remembered from Hell Week.

During those miserable days, you had to do rock portages and other evolutions in front of the Hotel Del Coronado, just north of the base. The Hotel Del Coronado is this big, expensive place in Coronado, right on the beach overlooking the Pacific. They filmed part of the movie *Some Like It Hot* at the Del Coronado in the fifties.

While we struggled with our rubber boats past the Del Coronado, up on the balcony would be these rich people drinking their martinis and watching us. We were the entertainment for the evening. I promised myself that someday I was going to sit on that balcony, drinking the martinis, and be entertained by the trainees. And now, every time I go back to Coronado, I book an oceanside

suite at the Del Coronado. That way I can look out and
see the rock jetty.

One day on that rock jetty, my boat crew took a monster
wave. The instructors tell you not to look behind you when
approaching the jetty, just paddle. Maybe you're just not
supposed to see what may be gaining on you. You might
just freeze and watch as a mountain of water crashes down
on you. But you had to continue paddling in order to keep
the boat straight into shore.

That monster wave that caught us was not something
we were prepared for. It rose up underneath our rubber
boat and carried us clean across the jetty, past the cement
pylons, and set us down on the beach. That was the easiest
portage we ever did. For sure, if I had looked back at that
wave, I would have at least wet my pants, though I may
not have noticed it.

Funny thing was that when I told Moy about my memory, he said that the Hotel Del Coronado was what stuck
out in his mind as well. Moy had lost his swim partner—
the guy just quit. So Moy had to swim by himself on one
of those long ocean swims. An instructor in a rubber boat
stayed by Moy during the swim, but that wasn't what kept
Moy going. What he said he did was count every window
in the Hotel Del Coronado while going by. There are just
rows and rows of windows in the hotel and counting them
was what kept Moy from going crazy.

It's Hell Week and training in general that remains a
SEAL's standard for comparison for the rest of his life.
Once you have completed that, you know that your limitations are not what you thought they were. You aren't superman, but you do know what you can face and just
keep going.

And this realization doesn't come with the end of Hell
Week. BUD/S stays at a high level of physical demand
throughout the three phases. After First Phase, which has
Hell Week in it, you think you might get a break from
the pressure. But that doesn't happen. The demands made
on you go up, not down. The more you get in shape, the
harder they push you. Things have to be done better and
faster, all the way to graduation.

Chief Signorella was one of my Second Phase instructors, along with one of the really great instructors, Chief Warrant Officer Casey. This guy was one of the really unbelievable characters in the Teams. We nicknamed him Biggie Rat, from the 1960s cartoon pair Biggie Rat and Itchy Brother. Casey looked just like a little rat. He was a skinny warrant officer, an older guy with sunken eyes.

Casey was a great teacher and would lecture you at length on many of the subjects we had to be taught. A haranguing little shit on the strand at Coronado, he went with us to San Clemente Island for the three weeks of demolitions training in Second Phase. After Hell Week, we thought the worst of the physical training was over. It got worse on San Clemente. The instructors would hit you with heavy punishment for the slightest infraction of the rules or anything else.

San Clemente Island was home of the iron butterfly, a huge pallet and helmet with a butterfly painted on the pallet, always carried at arm's length over the shoulders and back. The butterfly was carried five hundred meters up this hill, as steep as a mountain and you had to request a landing coming down. This trip was done for any fuck-up on the demolition range.

But when it came to the demolition instruction itself, there wasn't a finer instructor on the planet than Warrant Officer Casey. That man did a 180-degree turn from being a harassing little shithead that you wanted to strangle to being the calmest, most instructive teacher I had. Casey had two things he used to say: "Gentlemen, you will in fact" and "Without further ado."

It became kind of a game. As we took notes, one of us kept a count of how many times Casey said "You will in fact." When other people talk about the teacher's signal "You will see this again," for us it was "You will in fact." Whenever Casey said "in fact," you should take a note, because he considered it important. The only trouble was that Casey would say that phrase as many as a hundred times during a lecture. His only other tag phrase was that everyone else was a "swinging dick." A hell of an

instructor and one of the coolest men on the block, but a
limited imagination for catchphrases.

But finally, we graduated BUD/S in November 1970.
Half of my class went to SEAL Team One and the rest
to UDT 12. We were given a choice when we graduated
as to which Team we wanted to be assigned to, UDT or
SEAL. Earlier in Third Phase, we had been given a sign-
up sheet to list our Team preference on. If it was at all
possible, after graduation, you would be placed in your
preferred Team. Sometimes that wasn't possible and they
put you where they needed you. For my class, our choices
mostly held.

My brother had already briefed me on what was going
on in the Teams, and I shared the information with my
friends in the class. What I told the guys I was closest
with was that if they wanted to deploy overseas, to put in
for UDT 12. A number of us had already heard the scuttlebutt about what was going on over at SEAL Team One.
At Team One there was a long waiting list of guys who
wanted to deploy, especially to Vietnam. This was late in
1970 and the word had it that the war was winding down.
Fewer and fewer SEALs would be sent to Southeast Asia.

But in the UDT, the situation was very different. All
the West Coast UDT Team were still rotating deployments
on their six-month schedule. The schedule had UDT 12
rotating up for deployment in February of '71. The bunch
of us would just have enough time to complete all of our
advanced, post-BUD/S training and go over to UDT 12
before they went out on deployment.

Our post-BUD/S training was first going to be Army
jump school at Fort Benning, Georgia, SERE [Survival,
Escape, Resistance, and Evasion] school, and SBI [SEAL
Basic Indoctrination] in Coronado and out at Camp Kerrey, the SEAL training camp near Niland.

My first real introduction to the general opinion of the
Teams toward the rest of the services came right after
BUD/S when we were sent off to Army jump school. All
of us who were going were called into this one large
briefing room where a number of the old-timers were waiting for us. What those veteran frogs had to say was a

little astonishing to a young guy who had just barely graduated BUD/S.

"Look," we were told, "we had better get reports back on you guys, because if we don't, you'll answer to us."

All of us were so new we weren't even FNGs—fucking new guys—yet. And here we were being told, in no uncertain terms, that we had a certain reputation to maintain when we reported into the Army. This was more than a little different than the last twenty-six weeks had been. But if that was the situation, we could handle it with no trouble.

We arrived at Fort Benning and reported into the school. There was this little shake-and-bake sergeant running about and generally making a pest of himself. A shake-and-bake sergeant was one of the lesser-known evils to come out of the Vietnam War and infect the Army. These twerps would attend some NCO school for six or eight weeks and come out of it an E-5, buck sergeant. No experience, little skills, but a great big attitude. Here we were just a bunch of E-2s and E-3s, but there was no way we were going to take any crap from this Army puke.

"Okay," the sergeant said, "two of you will go in the top floor of this barracks. Two of you will go here, and two of you will go there." As he went on, he indicated where he wanted us to stay. It was obvious what was happening—the Army was trying to break us up. That just wasn't going to happen.

We all just stood there for a moment. All of our officers were gone over to the bachelor officers' quarters, so we had to handle the situation ourselves. We just looked at this little buck sergeant and told him, "No, we'll just take the top floor of this building here." With the sergeant standing there, we walked into a barracks.

Going to the floor we had indicated, we just told the few Army guys who were there, "Goodbye, you're outta here, this is ours," and they just packed up their stuff and left. But that little sergeant still wasn't satisfied and continued to try and assert his authority over us.

We had arrived at the school a day or two ahead of our assigned class's start date. So we just decided to relax in the barracks for that night. The lights were on and we were playing poker and listening to the radio when our dear little sergeant showed up again.

It seems, because it's a school, there's a strict lights-out policy at Benning for the jump students. We weren't abiding by that, so it seems we steamed up our favorite sergeant. About midnight, that same little shake-and-bake sergeant, with less sense than stripes, came up and started hollering at us. Seems he wanted to know just what we thought we were doing with the lights on and the radio playing. Apparently he thought we were supposed to run in the corners, cower, and hide from his frightful wrath. Things didn't go his way that night.

One thing that we had been aware of was that we were under Navy regulations, even while at the school. The Navy doesn't have what the Army calls an Article 15. That's a unit-level punishment for more minor infractions. The most the school could do to us for the way we were acting was refer us back to our command. In other words, they could call up UDT 12 or SEAL Team One and tell them that we were misbehaving, and that's what the command was expecting to begin with.

We weren't even going out of our way yet, and we were continuing the mission those old frogs had given us. This little sergeant was yelling and screaming at us, wanting us to put the lights out and climb into our racks. One of the guys who was with SEAL Team One, Jim Haskell, turned and looked at the guy and just growled, "Who the fuck are you?"

"I'm Sergeant so-and-so," was the answer, "and I'm in charge of this barracks—"

He was suddenly cut off when Haskell continued, "You've got ten seconds to get your ass down the stairs and stop bothering us."

"What?"

"Time's up," and Haskell got up, grabbed that sergeant by the seat of his pants and collar, rushed him out the door, and tossed him into the dirt. "And don't you ever come back into our barracks unless you have permission."

The sergeant got up and ran off into the night. The rest

of us went back to what we were doing. About a half hour later, another sergeant showed up, this one of a considerably different caliber than our little shake-and-bake had been. This big black sergeant was a black hat, one of the real instructors at Benning, and he had considerably more stripes on his arm than that E-5 had. His attitude was also a hell of a lot different.

That sergeant came into the room with a small entourage and just surveyed the scene for a moment. Dismissing the rest of his men, the sergeant waited until all of the others had left the room before speaking to us. "Look here," he said. "I know you guys are the best. No one is denying that. But I have a school to run here. We would appreciate a little cooperation from you guys."

This was a far different situation than the little E-5 had tried to run on us. "Look, Sarge," we said, "no one told us anything. We didn't know about any lights out. That little guy just came in here and started yelling and screaming. You don't do that to us—you don't yell and scream. Explain the situation to us and we'll act accordingly. But none of this screaming shit."

The black hat just said, "Okay." From that point on, we got along great with the people at Benning. That instructor had established his ground, and we respected it. He actually got to like us in the end because of the example we set. Our standard action was, when one of us was called on to drop for push-ups, we all dropped. For whatever reason, if one frog was told to hit the ground, suddenly they had twenty or so guys pumping out push-ups. When the one man recovered, we all stood up. That kind of Teamwork helped to instill our type of camaraderie in the Army members of the class. Besides, airborne push-ups are nothing after you've done weeks of BUD/S.

We did our own PT in the mornings, before reporting to the Army PT. The bunch of us would get up an hour earlier than we had to and do our own PT in the dark. At 5:00 a.m., the rest of the barracks would hear us working out. Besides messing with the Army's heads, we just felt that the airborne PT wasn't sufficient for us.

Other stuff at the school had a bit of a different reaction

from us. Anyone who tells you that they weren't scared
on their first parachute jump is probably either lying or
crazy. But it wasn't very hard to do the jump.

You always have to pay attention. But we stood up in
the plane and prepared to shuffle out the door for our long
drop. There were a number of set procedures we had to
follow, one of which really struck me as funny. The order
was called out to "check equipment." When that order
goes down the line, you're supposed to look at the man
in front of you and make sure he has all his gear rigged
correctly.

How the hell was I to know if the gear was correct?
Nothing was hanging loose. Looking at the gear, I thought,
Well, shit, I didn't pack it. I hope it's all there—every-
thing's hooked on.

The first jump is something that you always remember.
The order to stand in the door was given, and I was in
about the middle of the stick as the action started. Suddenly, people in front of you start disappearing and you
move forward as the line gets shorter. Then it's your turn
to stand in the door as the wind blows past you. You
throw your static line out and slap your hands on the
outside of the doorframe.

When the jumpmaster yells "Go!" you just pull yourself out of the plane and jump into the air. The automatic
part helps a lot as you step out of an airplane with a
hundred or so pounds of shit on you and nothing between
your feet and the ground except a lot of air. Of course, I
had always been afraid of heights, so running on automatic
and doing what they told me without conscious thought
was the only way I would be going out that door for the
first time.

It was partially because of my fear of heights that I
joined the Teams in the first place. I wanted to conquer
my fear, and I knew that the training would help do that.
What I am proud to say is that my first jump was not
what they call a "night jump." I had my eyes open from
the first moment to the last. There's a vivid memory I have
of watching my fatigues flutter in the breeze as I dropped.

All of us from the Teams had our fatigues tailored before we reported to Fort Benning. Not only does the tailoring make the uniform fit better, we look better in it as well. Instead of having the baggy uniforms the Army wore, our fatigue pants fit more like a pair of Levi's.

So as I hit the correct body position after exiting the door, I could see the edges of my greens just buzzing in the wind. The sight just amazed me. Within just a few seconds, I felt myself being pulled up as the parachute canopy opened up. Looking up, I agreed with the old line that an open parachute is the best skirt you'll ever look up under.

The guy on the ground was bellowing up at us through a loudspeaker to check static lines, and whatever. I was paying him some attention but mostly I was enjoying the ride. As I looked up, I could see that the canopy was nice and open, the risers weren't crossed, and the suspension lines were straight. After making sure of my rig—seems it was packed okay—I tried to do what the instructor was barking up at us and steer the chute. The parachutes sucked in those days, just old T-10s with round canopies. You could steer them, but only slightly and with great effort.

Even in the Teams in those days, we didn't have the sophisticated parachutes of today. We jumped the same T-10 rigs that we had first used at Benning, only with a couple of panels cut out of them to give some better directional control. I was a quick learner in the Teams and ended up doing thirty-four jumps total.

And when we returned to Coronado after jump school, there were no major complaints from any of the old frogs that we hadn't kept up with tradition. There must have been enough reports coming back on us from the Army to satisfy everyone.

Right away after our return from jump school, we had to report for SERE school. We had our first part of SERE training right there at the base in Coronado. We were shown how to build shelters and all of the survival tricks we would need in the field. After our classroom training, we were transported out into the field for some hands-on training.

We were sent northeast of San Diego, up near the mountains at a place called Warner Springs. This area was near the Los Coyotes Indian Reservation and the Anza Borrego Desert State Park, but the training was anything but a picnic in the park.

We got out there and were told to survive for the next week. Survive on what? The area had been run over by guys doing the exact same thing as we were for the last ten years. Anything edible had long ago been picked clean. Finally, we ended up eating acorns. They were the only edible thing we could find. Ever cook acorns? I can't recommend them as a steady diet, or even a snack.

Basically, the training was to go the week without eating anything. We didn't have anything to shoot with, so we couldn't have gotten any game, even if we had found any game. That land had been combed, so we never did get to try any of our snares or other survival tricks.

After our enforced diet was over at Warner Springs, not one I can recommend for weight control, we reported back to Coronado for SEAL Basic Indoctrination. This was the training where we really learned what it took to be a SEAL. The name of my instructor, Chief David Bodkin, is something I'll never forget. Big Dave, six foot three inches and maybe 220 pounds with a big, full beard and maybe five tours to Vietnam behind him. The most knowledgeable man around, with the most boring, monotone way of speaking I ever heard.

The bad guys were always "japs" to Big Dave, a leftover term from the World War Two UDTs. And Dave was so nonchalant about what it was we were supposed to do. "You go in, and then you kill the japs and go on about your business," he would say. It was like the enemy was just there to disrupt the business at hand, whatever the real business of a particular mission might be.

SBI was rugged, we operated nearly every day and night, but one of the most rugged things was just listening to Big Dave drone on in that flat monotone of his. Trying to stay awake might remind you of Hell Week, if you didn't think about the very serious nature of what Dave was talking about.

From sunup to sundown during SBI, we operated in platoons and went on patrols. Even though I'm a pretty big guy, I still walked point for my squad and platoon during SBI. For those seven weeks, you learned everything those veteran SEALs could teach you. And everything you did was constantly critiqued on during your performance so you could improve on your weak spots.

The first four weeks of SBI training was conducted at Coronado and the area around the base. First aid was taught to us by Greg McPartlin. He taught one of the favored classes where you learn how to give each other hypo shots. That's a real eye-opener, especially for the people who aren't comfortable with needles. We had some great instructors and they taught us well. Finally, we had to put everything into practice.

The last three weeks of training were conducted at Camp Kerrey. That's the SEAL training base near Niland, east of the Salton Sea and at the foot of the Chocolate Mountains. Parts of the training area are desert and others swamps and tall grassland. The wet part bore a striking resemblance to Vietnam, which is why the area was chosen in the first place.

Our arrival at Camp Kerrey was a bit unusual. We parachuted in from a helo that had picked us up at the Amphibious Base. Once at Camp Kerrey, we would be living in the bush and conducting live-fire drills and long-distance patrols. The camp was named after Lieutenant Robert Kerrey, now a U.S. senator from Nebraska. Kerrey was a member of SEAL Team One and the first SEAL to win the Medal of Honor. When we got there, Camp Kerrey was still being built and had not been officially named yet. Today, the training area is a vast modern facility with a building named after Billy Machen, the first SEAL killed in combat in Vietnam.

There was no question that the camp was new. A bunch of the firing ranges hadn't even been completed yet. Some of the ranges and such were being built as we arrived. I'm sure of this because they had us do some of the work.

This led to a bad incident when we were approaching the end of our cadre training. We had been working on a range during a very hot day in the desert, not that there are many other kinds of day at Camp Kerrey. One of the instructors, Warrant Officer Jess Tolison, one of the real old-time SEALs and a plankowner from SEAL Team Two, was killed that night in a traffic accident. Jess's truck flipped over on the very rough road that led to the camp. The accident was just one of those things, a bad flip on a gravel road at night, but it made a sobering impression on all of us.

The class was back in the Quonset-hut barracks, cleaning weapons, which is what we did whenever we weren't doing anything else. The instructors had gone into town earlier and we didn't think anything of it, except maybe that we would have liked to go along. Word came to the barracks that the truck had crashed and Mr. Tolison was dead. That was it, he wasn't one of my major instructors, but he had taught me some classes.

The accident left the class numb for a while. There was an investigation and some stupid accusations were made that Mr. Tolison had been drinking. But that wasn't what had caused the accident. He had just flipped his six-by truck on some loose gravel and it killed him. Some six months later, one of my instructors from Second Phase BUD/S, Lieutenant Jim Thames, was killed in an ambush in Vietnam. That incident caused the same kind of numbness to just settle over me.

It was when I was reading *Hunters and Shooters* years later and came to Greg McPartlin's story that I realized I had been there for the accident that killed Mr. Tolison and I finally learned the other side of the story. And some of the SEAL books that have been written now have told me about other things.

Today, when I read the stories written by Jim Watson in *Point Man* and Demo Dick Marcinko in his books, it makes me glad that there were others who had made the same mistakes as my platoon did during SBI. On our first live-fire ambush, we had set up according to our training and practice. When the signal was given, we all opened fire. When the cease-fire was signaled, we all went up and examined the targets in our killing zone. This was a bit of a wake-up call.

Out of all of the rounds we had fired, there were maybe four holes in all of the targets. That's kind of a sobering result. For all of our vaunted abilities and training, we didn't do too well at even a bunch of cardboard targets that weren't shooting back. So training continued and got even harder.

There was an art to conducting an ambush, as there was an art to so many of the actions SEALs did. And we got better as time went on. I never did figure out what it was that made that first ambush such a display of bad marksmanship. Maybe it was you become a little infatuated with the tracers. Every fifth round traced a red streak of light, supposedly to the target. The only trouble was, we missed the target.

Our performance improved considerably since that first live-fire ambush. We didn't hit shit on that first bunch of targets, and that was maybe a good thing. It sure made us notice our lack of experience and skills. So we practiced everything that a SEAL would be expected to do in the field. We practiced, and practiced, and then practiced some more. That was why the training was seven weeks long, to give us enough time to get the basics down pat before reporting to a Team.

There was a lot more to the training at Camp Kerrey than just marksmanship. Everyone in the platoon, from the lowest E-nothing to our officers, took his turn leading a patrol and running his own operation. When it was your op, you had to be the patrol leader, do the patrol leader order, set up everything you were going to do from the order of the patrol, the equipment you would take, the action on the target, and the extraction from the target area. It didn't do any good to complete a mission flawlessly if you couldn't get everyone home safely.

And just because the missions were practice and the enemy wasn't firing at us didn't mean the situation was safe. We often had live ammunition and munitions for attacking the target. And on top of that was just the inherent danger in the way we operated and the environment we worked in. The Teams didn't receive hazardous duty pay for nothing. I was almost killed during SBI training.

A huge investigation followed the incident that almost took my life. There were fuck-ups in training for the Teams just like happened in the other services. It was just that we worked so close to the edge to begin with that our mistakes could get very costly very quickly.

The op we were assigned was the demolition of some bridges crossing a river. The area was supposed to be enemy-held and we were going to insert down the river in a pair of IBSs [Inflatable Boats, Small] at night. Bypassing the first bridge, we would put out security at the target bridges, place our charges, set the timers, and withdraw. Supposedly all without being detected. The instructors picked the site as being just like Vietnam. In fact, the area we were operating in is the same one that they show in the film *The Men with Green Faces* as being Vietnam. The "Rung Sat" swamp the SEALs patrol in during parts of the movie isn't Vietnam, it's Niland.

So we were all set to blow the second bridge on this river. Two platoons in two IBS groups moved out into the river to begin the op. When we put in that night, the water in the river was higher than hell. It was winter in Southern California and there had been enough rain higher in the mountains to seriously swell the river. We had a minimum amount of moon, so the light was low and the waters rushing quickly would easily carry us to our target. This was going to be a piece of cake as far as a practice op went—just watch the security, steer the boat, and stay in the shadows along the shore. As long as we stayed out of sight of any instructors, we wouldn't have to paddle at all.

The IBS groups were just floating down the river, and everything looked fine until Mr. Murphy decided to visit. All of a sudden, we started hearing this dull roaring sound. Nobody was talking—all communications were done with hand signals, so none of us were making the sound. But the roaring just got louder and louder. Just what the hell was this loud shit we were hearing? It was darker than hell and none of us could see anything in front of us more than maybe a foot or so.

In front of me was five-foot, eight-inch Ricky Dees, a phenomenal athlete. If Ricky had my height, he would have been playing in the NBA, he was that good at basketball. Ricky was in front of me and I was hunkered down, keeping security along the tree line on my side of the boat. All of a sudden, Ricky sits up in the front of the IBS and shouts, "Holy fuck! It's a dam!"

The river was pouring over the top of this concrete dam, pulling us in a current that was just racing along. Ricky jumps from the IBS and made it to shore. By the time I had scrambled around and gathered all of my shit together, I got up and jumped for the riverbank, which was a concrete wall by this time.

Ever see in a cartoon how a cat jumps from danger and sticks to a wall only to slowly slide down, claws scraping? Well, in this particular cartoon, I was that cat as I slid down the wall and back into the river. There wasn't a lot of time for me to think about what was going on. I had about two seconds in which to say to myself, "Shit, I'm going over the dam!"

Taking the deepest breath I could, I went over the top of the dam and into the roiling waters below. Dees, I, and five others had been in the lead IBS, so we were the first ones to come up to the dam. I had no idea what the other boats or my Teammates were doing, I was too busy just trying to stay alive.

Fortunately, Ricky made it to shore and signaled the next IBS into shore. The other six of us just went over the dam with our IBS. Along with the boat, we had our weapons, equipment, and a full load of ammunition. Loaded to the gills with gear, I sank like a stone.

The week before, we had been diving and wore life jackets as a standard part of our equipment. On our river patrol, we were also wearing inflatable life jackets, but these were a smaller one used by SEALs on patrol. For some reason that I never found out, the CO_2 cartridges on the diving and the patrol jackets are on different sides. Since we had been diving most recently, I was grabbing for the inflation lanyard, only it wasn't there.

Besides being on the opposite side from where I was

looking, the inflation trigger was underneath my web gear and all of the other equipment I was wearing. Sinking deeper, it was like I had climbed into a washing machine. The turbulence of the water tossed me around until I was completely disoriented. There was no way I knew which direction up was. And my breath was running out.

Just as suddenly as I had entered it, the water tossed me to the surface. I had no idea that I was going to break the surface and the water immediately sucked me back down as quickly as it had spit me up. There hadn't been a chance for me to blow and get a fresh lungful of air. Now I was back underwater on the same stale breath of air I had taken when I went over the dam.

Back into the washing machine I went, tumbling around again. And again, I was tossed to the surface and sucked back down before I could get a breath. Bouncing around ass over teakettle, all of my gear was being torn away, my weapon was long gone, and my hope was fading fast. I resigned myself to the fact that things were over now. I was going to die at SBI and there wasn't much I could do about it. A fuckup had taken place and it was going to cost me everything I had.

Calmly, I asked myself which way I wanted to die. Did I want to inhale water or simply hold my breath until I passed out? That thought was very clear to me. I was helpless and the river was doing with me whatever it wanted to. The decision I made was to hold my breath until I passed out. My lungs were burning and I had no idea how long I had been underwater. This thing had hit us out of the blue and I had no idea what exactly had happened or where any of my Teammates were. I did see my mom and dad looking down at me, I spoke but they couldn't hear me and could only cry.

This was a pretty good example of how the SEALs defy death every day, even in training. Just as I was going to become another statistic, my head popped above water and I was able to exhale and get two quick breaths of air. As I started to hold my breath again, my boots dragged bottom and I was able to stand up slightly. Looking back at the white water, I had to be about seventy-five meters downstream from the dam. Training held for everyone, and we didn't lose a man.

From that day forward, I became a firm believer in fate. To this day, I believe that there is a certain day that you are fated to die, and there isn't anything you can do about it. And that day on the river wasn't my time. Someone should have died that day and we all made it.

We went back later and looked at the dam and none of us could see how we had lived through the fall and that whirling maelstrom of water below. All of us raised hell asking why weren't we told about the dam. And there was a cover-up about the lack of information. Simple training wasn't the answer. If that op had been real, we would have had aerial photographs of the target and every inch of the river leading to it. We would have been told, "Oh, by the way, fellows, there's a dam on the river that you'll have to portage around." There was no way a platoon would be sent out on an op in the middle of the night without being briefed on a great big dam being across their river!

The investigation that followed was based on more than just our complaints. We also lost three or four weapons in that river. A Stoner and several M16s scattered themselves along the river bottom. The water was so turbulent that divers weren't able to be sent in. Even with tanks on, divers would have just been tossed along the bottom like I was. But they would at least have been able to breathe.

The higher-ups wanted to charge me with the loss of a weapon in training. This really set me off. "What about who was supposed to tell us about the dam?" I said. "Someone is responsible for almost killing half a platoon of us. Seven people almost died."

Nothing ever came of the charges that were leveled at me for the loss of the weapon. The whole incident was swept under the rug and the story hushed up.

After we had completed SBI, we finally reported to our assigned duty Teams. Mike Gotchey, Don Erskine, Edward "Dirtfarmer" Robinson, and myself all requested UDT 12 prior to our graduation from BUD/S and we got the assignment. About half the class went for SEAL Team One and a handful of the guys did manage to get in a Vietnam deployment before the war wound down.

We all made it in our own way through the years after. RMSN Mike Harold Gotchey of Denver, Colorado, is today a top doctor of veterinary medicine, specializing in horses. SN Donald Kim "the Big E" Erskine went on with his career to become Commander Donald Erskine USN (Ret.), one of the legends of the Teams with duty in Vietnam with Det. Golf, Granada, SEAL Team Six, and many more places. And Edward Wayne "Dirtfarmer" Robertson today is a computer expert with the Tennessee Power Company.

Even though I was assigned to UDT 12, I had to complete all of the training courses before I was considered qualified to operate. That was why the bunch of us were sent to SERE school and SBI. On the West Coast then there was no distinction made between SEAL Team One and UDTs 11, 12, or 13. A man had to be fully qualified as a SEAL to operate in any of the Teams, and that was what we called them all, the Teams.

During the Vietnam War, SEAL Team One had to supply a much greater number of operating platoons to Southeast Asia than SEAL Team Two did on the East Coast. Those big numbers meant that there had to be a bigger pool of qualified men to draw on. That, and the fact that the West Coast UDT also had detachments serving in combat in Vietnam, meant everyone in the West Coast Teams had to complete SEAL training.

Within only a few months of arriving at UDT 12, I was on an overseas deployment to the Philippines and Southeast Asia. In my short time in the Teams, I spent almost seventeen months on deployment to Southeast Asia. Some of my friends who graduated at the same time I did had gone immediately to SEAL Team One, hoping for a Vietnam tour. After I had completed seventeen months overseas, some of my friends still had yet to deploy once.

Being overseas was the best part of being in the Teams, and I loved every minute of it. You had a direct mission to do and no one barked on your ass about stupid stuff. Things like your boots being polished weren't as important on deployment as the operating you had to do. Normal working uniform was cammies [camouflage] fatigues when you weren't wearing swim trunks and blue-and-golds [T-shirts]. On deployment was the time you did what you were intended to do, not practicing for it, which is what you did back in Coronado.

In Coronado, half the time you could find yourself being pulled out and assembled for some kind of parade in front of a bunch of brass. Overseas, looking good didn't matter nearly as much as doing good work. And that was a big reason why I loved it on deployments.

The deployed UDT would be supporting a number of smaller ARGs [Amphibious Readiness Groups] from out of the big naval base at Subic Bay in the Philippines. An ARG was an amphibious invasion group made up of Marines and their support equipment and ships. The Marines were not doing much more than floating around in the South China Sea off the coast of Vietnam. The higher-ups seemed to be using them as some kind of threat to the North Vietnamese to try and control the war and get concessions from the Communists. The Marines would also have been able to suddenly land a very large force in South Vietnam, cutting off any major North Vietnamese Army incursion. The Marines were all set to land from the sea at any time or place along the coast of South, or North, Vietnam.

To support the Marines for an amphibious invasion, a UDT platoon was assigned to each ARG. The UDT men would map out an invasion beach, conducting reconnaissance and destroying obstacles just like our forefathers did back in World War Two in the Pacific. The ARGs were never used against the North Vietnamese during the war, and for the most part the ARGs just floated around in their ships, the UDT platoon along with them.

So there was always a platoon of us stuck out there with the Marines. In addition, the UDTs ran Det Golf, a detachment of frogs operating out of Solid Anchor in support of riverine operations in South Vietnam. Det Golf had been operating under UDT control in-country since January 12, 1968. Solid Anchor was a UDT and SEAL base in the Mekong Delta at Nam Can, way down on the southernmost part of South Vietnam.

West Coast UDTs still had a WESTPAC [Western Pacific] obligation, even though Vietnam was winding down, that the East Coast UDTs just didn't have. Where the East Coast frog Teams tended to deploy to the Mediterranean, we went to the Western Pacific.

Southeast Asia was considered part of the WESTPAC operational area, so the Vietnam War started mostly as a West Coast action. SEAL Team One sent action platoons into Vietnam starting in 1966, while the East Coast and SEAL Team Two didn't start sending platoons into combat until a year later. That isn't to say that SEAL Team Two didn't run up one hell of a record in Vietnam. But SEAL Team One had the greater commitment to the war and had as many as five or six platoons operating in-country besides the UDT deployments.

An entire UDT of six platoons would deploy to WESTPAC at a time. The West Coast UDTs not only had Detachment Golf operating in the Mekong Delta, there had also been UDT detachments Hotel and India operating with the riverine forces during the war. We also had Detachments Echo and Foxtrot. Those were the UDT dets assigned to the Marine ARGs in the South China Sea. All of these dets were supported by the UDT that was assigned to Subic Bay.

The Subic Bay UDT would send detachments out on two-, five-, or six-month rotations, moving the guys around as needed. The Navy had studied the situation and done their homework, determining that a six-month tour of duty was about the maximum for the kind of work we were doing in the Teams. What the Navy told us was that after six months of operating, our ability to operate and stay at a high level of efficiency dropped significantly.

UDT 12 had four operational platoons, numbered one through four, and an SDV platoon. The SDV, Swimmer Delivery Vehicle, platoon maintained and trained with the small wet minisubs that were used to move swimmers and equipment over long distances, and they mostly kept to themselves. In Subic, the SDV platoon had its own Quonset hut in the area where most of our work took place.

The submarine *Greyback* had been operating out of the Subic base for about a year before I arrived in the area. The LPSS-574 *Greyback* was a converted Regulus-missile-carrying submarine that had been converted into an amphibious transport submarine, the only one of her kind in the world. One of the things that was special about the *Greyback* was that she had these two big hangars in her bow.

The bow hangars on the *Greyback* had been originally made for the Regulus missile, kind of an early cruise missile looking like a small jet complete with wings. When she was converted for her new job, the forward hangars were made into lock-in, lock-out chambers that you could enter from inside the boat. The big hangars were closed with a round clamshell door hinged at the top and operated hydraulically. Most of a UDT or SEAL platoon could fit in one of the hangars or it could be used to transport SDVs and act like an underwater garage.

We all worked off the *Greyback* at one time or another while deployed in Subic. One time we had a particularly memorable experience with her. We were locking into one of the forward hangars after a dive. There were enough hooka [hose supplied breathing] units in the hangar to let a full platoon and several extra men breathe off boat air, so there was no crowding or danger for our platoon from the hangar itself. After we had settled into the hangar, just as we were getting ready to put the hatch down, a shark came swimming right along the deck of the *Greyback,* moving directly at us.

This damned shark was going to come right through the open hatchway into the hangar with us. And it wasn't a small shark either—he was big enough to where he would get your attention quickly enough. As the hatch was closing, the shark headed right for us. That son of a bitch was going to be locked into the hangar with us.

Our concern for the situation would make more sense to you if you knew that the hatch couldn't be stopped once it had begun its cycle. As the steel door was coming down, all of us had the same concern. What were we going to do if that big bastard was locked in with us? That big door had to shut first and then slowly open. What would our situation be like with a big, pissed-off, panicking shark locked in with us in a closed, water-filled hangar?

The pucker factor got pretty high as Lieutenant Jack "the Hawk" Young was trying to call in over the underwater intercom, "Don't shut the door, there's a shark coming in here with us!"

Just as the shark was getting close to the hangar opening, he veered away at the last moment. I saw his white belly as he broke off to the side. The bunch of us just sat there for a minute letting out a big sigh into the water.

That wasn't the only time I had an encounter with a shark. But my other meeting was with a big great white off of Point Loma, outside San Diego Bay. We were out on a 212-foot bounce dive, where you go down to the bottom and remain the minimum amount of time so that you don't have to decompress on the way up. There must have been seven or eight swim pairs in the water as we conducted the dive.

The dive was operating off a PL, Landing Craft, Personnel, Launch [LCPL] Mark 11, a thirty-six-foot boat that we had secured an IBS to the side of. Nothing out of the ordinary happened during the dive, but we must have gotten the attention of something nearby. Just as we were pulling the IBS in over the side, a huge great white shark swam by.

Our last swim pair couldn't have been out of the water for a full minute when the shark came by. Its dorsal fin stuck up a good foot and a half to two feet above the water. The big gray body had to be eighteen to twenty feet long, damn near as long as the boat. And this killer was just cruising quietly by on its hunt.

Dave Bouke had been sitting on the end of the PL, lighting up a cigarette after the dive, and was the first one to see the shark. "Check that out!" Dave called out as he spotted the shark. Everything stopped as we just watched that big mother go by.

I was always happy that the movie *Jaws* had come out after I left the Navy. Diving would have been a bit rougher after seeing that, and seeing that great white go by. But what really would have gotten tighter were those long swims they had us do in the Pacific during training. Those night swims in diving phase consisted mostly of being sent out to sea in pairs wearing rebreathers. The instructors would drop us off in the middle of the night way offshore. On the beach would be a little light and you would take aim at the light, go down to about twenty feet, and swim in to shore.

On those night dives, you couldn't see anything except the glowing phosphorescence in the water. All a big shark would have to do is line up in front of a swim pair and open its mouth. We would have swum right in, not seeing what was in front of us.

While I was with UDT 12 in Southeast Asia, my brother Jan was deployed to the Indian Ocean to help make a whole new Navy base there. It was while he was there that Jan managed to meet some of the really interesting sea creatures.

South of India, just about in the middle of the Indian Ocean, is the Chagos Islands, and just south of them is Diego Garcia. The U.S. Navy built a big base at Diego Garcia, and my brother left with a detachment from UDT 12 late in January 1971 to do the initial work on the base.

My brother's platoon did all the demolition work, blowing up the reefs and such, to open up the approach to what would be the Navy base. Diego Garcia would give the U.S. Navy a forward base in the Indian Ocean where it could support operations all throughout the area, including the Middle East. Even at that time, the higher-ups in military planning knew that we would need a base in the Indian Ocean because that would become a hot spot for future conflicts. The base did a lot of action in support of our ships in the Persian Gulf during the 1980s, and Diego Garcia was probably one of the busiest U.S. Navy bases during Desert Shield and Desert Storm in the early 1990s.

The demo job at Diego Garcia was great work, according to Jan. He showed me pictures of the clear blue water—fantastic visibility and a lot of interesting critters. The operators were out swimming with the stingrays and just having an outstanding deployment.

While Jan was blowing up coral and swimming with the rays, we continued to work at Subic Bay. Keeping up our skills was one thing, and to support those, we worked out every day to keep up our strength and stamina. Frank Perry was over at UDT 12 when I arrived there. As soon as Frank was on board, he was naturally put in charge of our PT program. It is my opinion that UDT 12 soon became one of the most in-shape Teams in all of the Navy. I can say that easily because we had regular Team competitions along the Strand, the length of land south of Coronado.

The Team competitions were mostly physical ones, where you worked against the other Teams, including SEAL Team One. For one contest, we lined up on a tug-of-war with a limited number of men on the rope. Moy had also left training and was then in UDT 11, our opposing team in the contest, as the anchor man. I had been into weight lifting for a while before this particular contest and had built up pretty well, so I was anchoring for our team.

We had been doing PT under Frank Perry for two years by then. It was nothing for us to just pull that other team across the line. Now it was my turn to yell at Moy. Laughing, I said, "You better get in shape now, Moy." There wasn't anything he could do—it was obvious who was the winners hands-down. Boy, was he pissed.

Our physical capabilities we could lay right at the feet of Frank Perry. On a Perry PT, you did push-ups, fifty at a pop, and multiple sets. Flutter kicks were three to four hundred during a workout. And if we didn't do that many, it was because we did five hundred.

That kind of exercise level was continued every morning during the week. I was always grateful for Frank teaching me the value of good, hard physical exercise. And our PT was hard no matter where we were. One time when we had deployed to the Philippines, Frank was running us through PT in the tropical heat and humidity. A SEAL Team One platoon had come down to Subic from Okinawa. They were going to operate with us for a while and thought they would be taking things easy. You don't take things easy under Frank Perry's direction.

That SEAL platoon was being directed by Lieutenant Everett Green, the same officer who recently came close to being the first black SEAL admiral and my best friend, Steve Nelson. Green told his platoon to just join with us for PT every day. We just sat back and smiled at what was going to come. It was ninety-eight degrees and humid normally. We had been in this environment for several months, all the time building up with Frank's PT. This SEAL platoon was in for a surprise.

Frank had that little glint in his eye for that first PT. He suggested that we were going to do things just a bit stiffer than we normally did, in honor of our SEAL Teammates. By the end of PT, that entire SEAL platoon was sprawled out on the grinder [exercise area], each man just laying there in a spreading pool of his own sweat. "Gee," Steve Nelson said later, "I guess we've been sluffing off on our PT, haven't we."

"Yeah, I think so," I answered. "Now that you're with us, we'll get you SEALs back into shape again. You guys brag about how rough and tough you are, but us frogs wore you into the ground."

That PT had been a bit rough, so Perry had something more for us. "Okay, you guys," Frank called out after PT was over, "line up and we'll run down to the post exchange and back." That was a distance of five miles. We all lined up and went out on the run. I don't think there was one of those SEALs who even started the run with us.

But to give good Team credit where it is due, those SEALs kept working out with us. Within a month or two, those SEALs were doing a proper Frank Perry PT right alongside of us. They even went out on the run. They just had to get put back in focus was all.

The SEAL Team One platoons then were just a small number of guys, just twelve or fourteen. And PT wasn't run by Team One as a whole. Each individual platoon ran their own PT. It seemed that SEAL Team One never started the day with PT. For UDT 12, PT under Frank Perry was how we started the day. And that was as a whole Team. After PT was when we broke down into platoons and went about our individual business.

Frank Perry had been an instructor for my brother's BUD/S class. The men all called him Superman. In my day Third Phase was where we all learned underwater work and diving. First Phase was all physical and Second Phase was land warfare and demolitions, where you learned weapons, patrolling, and explosives. Frank Perry was one of the Third Phase instructors.

Frank never harassed anybody—he was a very quiet man. What he did do was just go out and complete his normal PT. And Frank would just dare you to complete his PT with him. Chief Frank ''Superman'' Perry was all of forty years old then and had a washboard stomach with four rows of abdominal muscles and a wiry build. There was this tall set of poles with a climbing rope hanging down between them in the training area. Frank was one of the very few men I ever heard of who could climb up this rope, using only his arms, while wearing a pair of twin ninety-cubic-foot air tanks on his back. Those tanks are the big, ugly bastards that are part of the most uncomfortable diving rigs known to man. And Perry could just climb up the rope and touch the cross pole wearing a set of these tanks.

And on runs Perry was just as big a superman. As the sand got softer, your feet would dig in more and running would get very much harder. Perry would just dig in that much more and run a bit faster as the sand got softer. His normal PTs would burn out students who were in the best shape of their lives.

For the majority of my Navy career, Frank Perry was my physical mentor. And Frank was a sea daddy to all of us in UDT 12 as far as our keeping in shape went. There was one time when Frank had to go into the hospital for some kind of operation. A bunch of us went up to the hospital to see Frank before his surgery. When we went into his room, there wasn't anyone in the bed. Frank was down on the floor in his hospital gown doing push-ups next to the bed. After all, Frank knew he might not be able to do any push-ups for a day or two after the surgery. He didn't have the nickname Superman for nothing.

But even Frank Perry's PT couldn't prepare us for everything during my first time overseas with UDT 12. My platoon even managed to see some action in Korea. Infiltrators had been working their way down from North Korea. Command figured we might be able to lend a hand to the South Koreans in dealing with the problem, so UDT 12 sent Third Platoon up to Korea to work on shoring up the situation at the DMZ.

Instead of working in the water, they sent us inland, still close to the shore but dealing completely on land. Korea was a bit of an eye-opener. We had left the tropical climate of the Philippines and Vietnam to find ourselves on the 38th Parallel. Arriving in Korea in March is a bit startling, that country is on the same parallel as Minnesota. I soon developed a whole new respect for the Korean War veteran.

As far as I was concerned, Vietnam was great compared to Korea. Send me to operate in the Mekong Delta swamps, no problem. Just keep me out of Korea. The whole country is one big rockpile, frozen rocks. Little specks of snow were always flying around. The water temperature was maybe a balmy thirty-four degrees, two degrees above freezing. Give me Southeast Asia over that godforsaken place. It was only a ten- or twelve-day mission but that was plenty long enough for me.

The women also had a great resemblance to the countryside, and that didn't do anything to endear the place to me. All those Korean women, at least the ones we saw, looked like they could be middle linebackers for the Bears. They all had legs like Dick Butkus.

Once our little side trip to sunny Korea was over, the platoon returned to Subic. UDT 12 was getting ready to rotate back to the States soon, but something came up that let a few of us stay on in the Philippines. All in all, I ended up staying overseas for nine months during that first trip.

The war in Vietnam was cut back almost completely by the middle of 1971. The UDT dets had been pulled out of Vietnam about halfway through my deployment. Our obligation in Southeast Asia had ended, and cutbacks in the Teams were already starting. UDT 13 was scheduled to be decommissioned, and something had to be done to absorb a number of the guys from UDT 13 into UDTs 11 and 12.

Command didn't exactly know what they wanted to do with us or how they wanted to set things up for the future. What was decided was that half the Team would be sent home and half would remain, and in the future, only half a UDT would be deployed at a time.

Volunteers were called for who would be willing to stay at Subic and complete our assigned tour plus an additional three months. Effectively, the volunteers would be starting a whole new six-month deployment, beginning in the middle of an active deployment.

Whatever they wanted to do was fine with me, as long as I could continue on my deployment. My name was either the first or second one on the list of volunteers who were willing to extend their deployments and stay overseas.

That was how a bunch of us remained at Subic Bay an additional three months while command figured out the new schedule. Looking back on things, those three months of additional deployment were the most wild, happiest, and carefree of my life. The commanding officers had gone back to the States with the other half of UDT 12. We were left at Subic with my old platoon commander, Lieutenant Jack Young, an Annapolis graduate, and BM1 "Honest" John Ervin as our leading petty officer.

Honest John was probably one of the most "give a damn" senior enlisted men. He just didn't care what we did as long as the work schedule was met and we didn't cause any trouble for him. John fell under one of the big problems that existed in the Navy as a whole and in the Teams. A lot of sailors ended up being consumed by alcohol, and John fell into the trap along with so many others. There probably were a large number of alcoholics in the

Teams now that I look back on things. The cost of working so hard for many of us was paid by playing real hard and sometimes drinking hard as well. John served multiple deployments to Vietnam and survived them all. He later died in a car crash while at EOD school in Maryland.

The officer who was actually in overall charge of the extended deployment was Lieutenant Commander Larry Bailey. Larry was the executive officer of UDT 12 at that time just before a change of command took place. I had begun with Commander Pete Peterson as my commanding officer and Bailey was the XO. Later Commander De-Florio took over as CO and Bruce Dyer was the XO.

Since Bailey was our XO at the time, he was left in charge of the bunch of us. But since Larry was getting ready to change commands anyway, he took advantage of a bunch of back leave he had built up and toured the Orient. He did some wheeling and dealing and caught military hops all over the place. While we were in Subic, Bailey was in Bangkok or wherever having a great old time.

That situation didn't bother us much. It left Lieutenant Young in charge, who was basically a hell-raiser just like the rest of us. Boy, did we have fun in Subic for those three months. All the pressure was off, the war was over, and we really didn't have anything to do.

Subic Bay had been a U.S. military base continuously since the end of World War Two. Just outside the main gate was a mile of road that held something like 350 bars and ten thousand girls, and that was every night. Imagine being nineteen, maybe closing in on twenty, and in the best physical shape of your life. We went out bar-hopping every night. Finally, there was one night when I swore to myself that I wasn't going to a bar that night. You had to draw the line somewhere, and I just wasn't going out that time. Yeah, right.

We had the top floor of Barracks 1, a three-story building. By ten o'clock that night, the barracks was empty except for me. There was no one there but me—I was alone. There were echoes through the empty room. I had to go into town—it was lonely in the barracks.

Finally, we did rotate back to the States. Now, each UDT was going to have a year-long commitment to WEST-PAC and only send half the Team out on deployment at a time. When we got back to the States, there was a new problem for those of us in the Teams, and the military as a whole. The massacre at My Lai had taken place back in September 1969. In March 1971, Lieutenant William Calley was convicted of murdering at least twenty-two civilians and sentenced to prison.

When we were back in the States, our entire Team was pulled into the briefing room. With us all crowding the room, the CO came in and addressed us.

"Gentlemen," he said, "you're all well aware of the Lieutenant Calley situation and the whole situation with Vietnam and the press back here at home." He went on like this for a bit, telling us how the news reporters were sniffing around, each hoping to break another Calley story, whether it was true or not. Then he finished with, "I'm issuing all of you a directive right now that you should consider a direct order. You are to talk about nothing that you saw, nothing that you did, or anything that you heard about."

To this day, I still live by that order. I just don't tell war stories. Because of the way the SEAL Teams operated, it was always very easy for rumors to get started about everything from gathering ears to assassinations. When no facts are available, scuttlebutt tends to fill in the vacuum with whatever. And more than one of those latrine rumors are still making the rounds as facts about the SEALs' operations in Vietnam.

For UDT 12, most of our operations consisted of demolition work. Some of the frogs who were at Solid Anchor would occasionally go out with the SEAL Team platoons and operate as need be. Robert "Andy Gump" Willingham of South Carolina was a real old-timer and a diehard Team 12 guy who was also one hell of an operator. Today he's still probably the toughest man I have ever known. The SEAL Team guys would grab Andy whenever they could and take him along with them on combat ops.

But for the most part, combat was winding down for all of us in the Teams.

My brother graduated with Class 49 in March 1969. Jan managed to do more than a few actions in Vietnam. He was in Da Nang in 1969 where I wrote to him while I was a senior in high school. Besides what Jan had written in his return letters, I remember the mail being neat because you didn't have to use a stamp on them. With an APO address, all you had to do was write ''free'' in the upper right corner instead of a stamp. Jan's letters came to me with the same mark on them. Probably one of the most interesting missions Jan was on was Operation Deep Channel, known to us as the Big Blow Job.

In January 1970, twenty-two frogs from UDT 12 started blowing a channel across the Plain of Reeds in South Vietnam. The plan was to make a five-and-a-half-mile-long channel between Vam Co Day and Vam Co Dong rivers. This was the biggest demolition job in UDT history, and the largest combat demolition job in U.S. Navy history.

The entire demolition job used 230 tons of high explosive in the form of Mark 8 hose. A Mark 8 hose is a 2.5-inch-diameter rubber hose filled with a mixture of Composition A and aluminum with TNT booster charges. The charge is twenty-five feet long and weighs 150 pounds, looking for all the world like a big chunk of firehose. The frogs, my brother included, officially made up Detachment Delta for the operation. Manhandling five hoses pyramided together for each charge, the det blew a channel five feet deep and thirty feet wide, with a turnaround area every thousand feet, connecting together twenty-five-foot charges every bit of the way. The whole operation used something like sixty percent of the free world's supply of Mark 8 hose. That was one of the ultimate UDT blasting jobs, and the Team got the job done in only two-thirds of the estimated time and at two-thirds the expected cost.

The relationship we had between the other services wasn't the best in the world. The fact was that we effectively ruled along the post city, the bars outside the main gate. Fights between the frogs and SEALs against all comers just weren't that rare a thing. There was one brawl we had gotten in where the bunch of us were arrested by the U.S. Armed Forces Police.

When they hauled us into jail, the officer in charge looked like he was just tired of the whole thing. "Nobody denies that you guys are the best," he said to us. "Nobody argues that you aren't all the baddest asses that walk the street around here. Why do you feel the need that you have to take it out on us? Just what is with you guys?"

We had this little Mexican guy named Riojas who hailed from East L.A. He jumped up and gave the officer his answer. While bouncing around and shadow-boxing, Riojas looked at the guy and said, "Man, we just have to keep in fighting shape."

All Riojas was doing was pulling the guy's leg a bit. But it didn't look like he thought so. That officer just shook his head and walked out of the room, realizing that we were a lost cause. There was nothing he could do for us, so he just processed the paperwork and we ended up back in the barracks and eventually back in the bars.

Probably the most traumatic thing for me when I came back off my first tour wasn't the antiwar protesters, it wasn't the lack of acceptance for the uniform in some places or even the Lieutenant Calley situation. When the Team left on my first deployment, I was nineteen. When I returned to the States, I was twenty. As far as the law was concerned, I was still underage, a minor in California and couldn't go in a bar.

The rules were that I couldn't even walk into a bar. Going overseas and putting my life on the line for my country, that was all right. But when I returned home, I wasn't even granted the privileges of adulthood. Fortunately, we had a Team bar called the Hub that didn't bother to check IDs.

But we did have our share of veterans on the West Coast, and some of them had been in the Teams just short of forever.

Most of the guys in the Team had a nickname of one kind or another. A lot of them weren't something you would use in mixed company. Others, like my being Janos the Dirty, just appeared one day and stuck. There were guys like Frank "the Pig" Wagner, who got his name from the late-sixties habit of referring to police as pigs. Frank earned his name by playing cop for the Navy.

Occasionally, the Navy in the States would make the stupid mistake of asking guys from the Teams to stand shore patrol. The assignment wasn't any big deal. A billet would be sent over for so many men to stand as shore patrol officers in the San Diego area and volunteers would be asked for. That was like sending the fox in to watch the chicken house. Frank would always be the first guy to volunteer for shore patrol. The rest of us hated the job. Frank was always sent down to the Tijuana border, where he would have a great time beating up drunk jarheads coming back from liberty in Mexico.

And it was because Frank always was one of the first to volunteer for shore patrol duty that we nicknamed him "the Pig."

But even with some of the good times we had in the area, I couldn't wait to get out of Coronado again. I was supposed to be in the States for a year after my first deployment, but I didn't want to wait that long. Within seven months of my return, my chance to deploy had come up again.

For my second deployment overseas, the situation was a lot different. The war was over and there were cutbacks all over the place. Going on my first deployment wasn't any problem at all, but I had to do some hustling to get out of Coronado again.

The Subic Bay Naval Base had a football team, and a pretty good one. During my first tour, we had a commitment in Vietnam, so we were never sure when we might get called up to go on an operation. That situation kept me from playing on the football team. But when the war ended, we had no more active commitment other than goodwill stuff. The goodwill stuff consisted mostly of working with the Filipino frogmen and other kinds of stuff. I could spend time away from the Team and not short the guys at all.

One thing that always stayed true in the Teams as well

as the rest of the services, if you managed to put one over on an officer, they would always get you back. All I wanted to do was get back overseas. A sure way for me to get back was to play football for Subic Bay. Though I hadn't been able to play during that first deployment, I had met the athletic director for the base. Giving the director a call, I tried to hustle myself a way back to Subic.

For the upcoming deployment, I could arrange the time to play for the football team. Subic Bay took its football seriously. The head coach for the team had been an assistant coach at Stanford, one of the Pac Ten universities. That guy had been paid good money to come and work on the team at Subic. The Navy had a whole football league in Southeast Asia—the teams toured around and played each other. Two teams in Japan, the Marine team in Okinawa, Clark Air Force Base had two teams themselves. Navy football was a big deal in the Pacific, and it was my ticket overseas.

All I had to do was get myself assigned TAD [temporary additional duty] to UDT 11, who already had their people deployed. Once in Subic, I could play football until UDT 12 arrived in the fall. By the time my Team arrived, the local football season would be over and I could return to UDT 12 and continue my regular deployment.

To put my plan into action, I first contacted the people at Subic. They were enthusiastic about the idea of me being on the team and wanted me there as soon as I could arrange things. I went in to Bruce Dyer to talk about what I wanted to do.

"Mr. Dyer," I said, "we're scheduled to deploy in September/October. Football starts in July at Subic because of the rainy season. I would like to go over and play for the Subic Bay team. I wrote Bill Ross and he said that they would pay for a civilian airline ticket to get me over there in time for the season. All I need to do is go TAD to Team 11. I'll play football and when you guys come over this fall, I'll be right there already. I can help get things set up and do predeployment before you get there. It'll be the smoothest transition between the Teams you've ever seen."

Bruce Dyer looked at me and said, "I'll tell you what. If you can go over to Spec War Group and convince the commander that you ought to go over early, I'll let you go."

This sounded pretty good, so I thanked Mr. Dyer and went over to Spec War Group. What I didn't know was that this commander Dyer wanted me to see had a reputation for being a hard-ass. Dyer was setting me up, but me being an experienced SK3 [third class storekeeper], I didn't know any better. All I decided to do was act like a big, dumb enlisted guy. The worst the officer could do to me was yell a bit and toss me out of his office. I'd been yelled at by the best, so what did I have to lose?

Calling over to Spec War Group, I made an appointment to speak to the captain. Going over to the office, I took along my letter from Bill Ross that explained how he would pay for me out of his own budget, supply the transportation, the whole thing. Walking over, I got in past the secretaries and was ushered into the captain's office. Since I was indoors I didn't have my hat on, and so I didn't even have to salute the man. Standing there, I explained my situation to him.

Telling the officer that my Team was deploying later in the year anyway, and that all I wanted to do was go over early, I handed him the letter and waited. He looked at me and said, "You must be a hell of a football player, son."

I was over two hundred pounds at the time and in good shape, so I told him that I was okay and a pretty good football player.

"Let me understand this," he said. "Your Team is deploying in October anyway. Team 12, right?"

"Yes sir," I said. "It will be the second deployment for me."

"And you're requesting to go over early?"

"Yes sir," I answered. "I'll be done with football and go back to my Team. Most of the season will be over by the time my Team gets there, so I'll only spend a month away from them in Subic. After the season, I'll go over to the Team and be ready to do the whole tour."

"And this guy is willing to pay for this out of his own budget?"

"Yes sir."

"Hell, I don't see anything wrong with this. You seem pretty enthusiastic about the whole thing."

"You're damned right I am, sir."

He signed off on it without any problem. Even when I told him to write on it that it was okay with him, since Lieutenant Commander Dyer had specifically said I had to have his permission. The officer signed it and everything was go. Mr. Dyer couldn't change his mind easily, since I had the permission of the higher commander, just like he had told me to get.

Tom Lawson was the commander of Team 11 at that time, and he didn't quite agree with my plan of action when I first arrived at Subic. "You aren't playing football," he said. "If you're TAD to us, you're going to operate right alongside the rest of the Team. If there's any spare time afterwards, then you might be able to play some football."

"But sir," I said, "this guy paid for my flight over here. I have the permission of the commander of Spec War Group. You're going to stand in my way on this?"

"You're not playing football," was all he said.

"But why do you think I'm here?" I continued. "This guy paid for me to fly on a civilian flight just to be here."

My pleading was falling on deaf ears. I had to go to Ross and tell him that my officer was being a prick and wouldn't let me play on the team. "Let me handle that," was all Ross said about it. The next day, Lawson received a personal message from the admiral of the fleet. The message was that the admiral would consider it a personal favor if Mr. Lawson would find it in his heart to let me play football. Football was good for troop morale, the admiral continued. The troops like to go to the games, cheer their teams on, and have a good time.

Lawson was jawed the rest of the time he was there. But this was the admiral—what was he going to do? Besides, he was being a prick about the whole thing. My playing football wasn't going to cost him anything. And

Ross mentioned to the admiral that he had paid for me to come over for the specific purpose of playing on the team.

The football went great—we were all-service champions and never were beat. The Army, Navy, Marine, and Air Force teams were all meat for our grinder. My position was as defensive tackle, and I managed my share of sacks.

That was some of the best duty I ever pulled. All I had to do for two and a half months was go to football practice and play the games on Saturday. There was even enough time for me to go into town a time or two. Ross had his frogman on the football team and I was holding up my end of the bargain. For that period, I was the Lord of Subic, and none of the great old-timers, Marcinko, Gallagher, any of them, could hold a candle to me that time. I practically ruled Olongapo City, the area outside the main gate, for that time.

That was how I spent an additional eight months on deployment. Out of my four-year enlistment, I spent something like seventeen months deployed, which is a real good average. But I had managed to put one over on Mr. Dyer a bit, and paybacks can be a bitch.

The deployment went well enough. I played football and then went back to UDT 12 after they had arrived and the season was over. Now I had two tours under my belt. I wasn't an FNG but a seasoned veteran frog. An old-timer in my own way, considering I was on a four-year enlistment. And what did Mr. Dyer do to pay me back? He put me on the slow surface boat that was carrying our equipment in Conex boxes back to Coronado. I was sent back on the ship, assigned to watch a bunch of steel boxes. Twenty-three days at sea with no sight of land.

Dyer put me on that big, pointy gray lump in the water because I had put one over on him by getting permission to go early. I pulled a fast one, flying a commercial airline and having a good time. Now I was assigned the duty that either goes to the newest man or the worst fuckup in the Team.

Years later, the story developed a different end. By that time I had been wrestling and working hard. My weight was up to 275 pounds and I had sold out Madison Square

Garden three times and was something of a household name in some circles. My old Det Golf Teammate Bill Ranger, who lives in D.C., knew I was coming to the capital and wanted to throw a party for me. Ensign Bill "Bring Home the Bacon" Ranger is, at the time of this writing, fifty years old and the oldest commissioned ensign in Naval history. Most of the old officers we had served with were in the Pentagon by that time, and he was going to invite them. Best of all was when he said that Bruce Dyer was going to be at the party.

I had been a civilian for some years by that time. I was at the height of my wrestling career, twenty-inch biceps,* six foot four inches, and no body fat to speak of. Plainly speaking, I was a monster compared to my Team days. "Mr. Dyer is going to be there?" I asked.

"Yeah."

"You tell him that I'm going to kick his ass for sticking me with those fucking Conex boxes at the end of my second tour when that's an FNG's job." I was all piss and vinegar and convinced everyone that I was going to rip that officer apart. This was the same part that I played as a wrestler, and I was pretty good at it by now. At least I had everyone I could see convinced that Dyer's days might be numbered.

Arriving at the party, I saw Dyer and got right in his face. "Mr. Dyer," I growled, "I want to know why you sent me back with those damned Conex boxes."

With perfect Annapolis aplomb, he looked at me and said, "Well, Janos, the only thing I can say to you is, did the Conex boxes arrive safely?"

"Yes, they did," I answered suspiciously.

"Well, then I sent the right man for the job."

"Great answer, you prick," I said with a grin. "Is that what they taught you at Annapolis? How to come up with the perfect answer for the enlisted men?"

Like Dyer said, when the boat finally docked after that last tour, the Conex boxes arrived safely. That was also about the end of the really good times in the Teams for me. The chickenshit had started big-time since the war had ended. The "dirty thirty" [the thirty or so UDT and

SEAL operators dropped from the Teams in the post-war cutbacks] had already been sent back to the fleet or to the civilian world. Ricky Dees had been caught up in the cutbacks and he was gone. So were a number of the guys I had gone through training with.

The war in Vietnam had ended, and the Teams just had too many guys in them. UDT 13 had already been decommissioned, and the other UDTs had absorbed as many of those men as they could.

To this day I have no idea what the criteria was that determined who was going to leave the Team after Vietnam. Thirty guys ended up being cut from the Team and returned to the fleet. Who it was that made the final decision is unknown to me as well. It could have been just a paperwork examination, a random pick of individuals, or a concerned, thoughtful decision. That was never made public to those of us in the ranks of the Teams in Coronado.

However it was done, thirty of our Teammates left us and returned to the fleet and the Navy at large. A decision had been made that there were too many men in the Teams, and cutbacks had to be made.

Some of the men cut were among the best operators I had ever been with. And at the same time, some of the guys were brand-new and fresh out of training. Among those thirty men were operators who had already deployed with a Team, done a full tour, and come back to the base. There just didn't seem to be any logic to the decision from where I stood.

What did stand out was the war in Vietnam was ending and there were no more platoons, or even individuals, being sent over for combat. In addition, the oil embargo was just hitting hard about then. With people concerned about standing in line to feed their cars, odd plates one day and even plates the other, it was easy to overlook the loss of a couple of platoons' worth of men from SEAL Team One and the UDTs.

From where I stood, the gasoline problem wasn't all that small of a thing. The Harley-Davidson motorcycle I was driving only held so much gas in its tank. That was my sole mode of transportation—if I couldn't get any gas, I was stuck. There were more than a few days where one of those people standing in line was me. And with all of that going on, it's easy to see how the loss of some of the most highly trained men in the Navy could be overlooked.

And, as fate tends to make it, a short time later, the Teams were desperately short of trained operators. Even while I was still in, we had an alert. The Teams went to DefCon [Defense Condition] Three because of the action in the Middle East. The Yom Kippur War in October 1973 fired up, and the Pentagon was concerned that the whole Middle East would explode. We were put on a war footing and expected to be deployed at any moment. "Are you kidding?" I said. "I'm getting out!"

My protests didn't mean a thing to anyone. They could have extended my enlistment if things had gotten bad enough. My enlistment still had two years of inactive reserves to run, so it would have just been a matter of paperwork for the Navy to tell me I was staying. I was one of the last of my class to still be in the service. Most of the guys I had served two tours with were gone. But Israel ended the war in a big hurry, though I understand things got pretty tense for a while there.

During that DefCon Three alert, it had gotten to the point where I had to check into the area at four-hour intervals. Our bags were packed and we had to be prepared to go anywhere in the world in twenty-four hours. We were bitching this time. The last war, Vietnam, had been our responsibility. This one should have been the East Coast's party. They had always been bitching about Vietnam. Now it should have been their turn to go over and chase sand crabs in the desert.

Most of us were wondering just what the hell we were going to do in the sand in the first place. We just weren't that prepared for desert operations at that time. Things have sure changed now—the Teams are prepared to drop in the Arctic, the mountains, jungles, or deserts. It was partly due to that running around we did during that alert that opened the planners' eyes as to just what the Teams might be doing in the future. Now, individual Teams are trained to operate in specific areas of the world. But back then it was they'll send us where they want us, we'll figure out what to do when we get there.

We had been extending our abilities well before all the shit hit the fan in the Middle East. Lieutenant Mark ''Hard Guy'' Cadden, a Det Golf teammate, had gotten it into his head that there was one area we didn't know how to operate in at all. Cadden asked what had we ever done in the snow? The Teams were qualified to operate in the water, we had operated in the jungle for the last several years, and we were even experienced in the desert somewhat because of the area around Niland. But snow and extreme cold was a new area for us.

Going up to Lake Tahoe, we spent a month learning how to operate in the snow. Tents were what we lived in, and we slept on the ground. God, it was awful. I'm very glad I was still just barely out of my teens—otherwise I may not have made it through that one without losing some parts to frostbite. Learning to walk on snowshoes is quite the experience, even harder than soft sand. Cross-country skiing is fun, after you learn how to not fall on your ass every foot or so.

Diving and working underwater, our main reason for being, wasn't forgotten either. Snowshoeing a bunch of tanks and gear up to a frozen lake, we chopped a hole in the ice and did an ice dive. Flopping around in the snow in black rubber wetsuits, we probably looked more like seals than the guys in SEAL Team One. But I bet a bunch of those guys never did some of the things we did for that month.

RM3 Frank ''Lola'' Smarcola of Miami, Florida and I were the first pair to go under the ice on that dive. My God, that water is cold. I don't care that I'm from Minnesota, when the water freezes over, we try to stay out of it back home. Once we got down under that ice, every time you would move you got a rush of that cold water through your wet suit. Frank and I sat there at about thirty feet down, looking at each other, and I could see we both had the same opinion about the water.

The two of us swam about for a bit. We made sure we

were both tied together and to the descending rope from the ice hole. Somehow, the thought of chopping back up through the ice with our diving knives increased our concern about the rope that led back to the only open water in the lake. Once we had enough, we went back up and another swim pair went down. Finally, everybody had completed their little dip in the ice and it was time to head back.

All of us had to put on dry clothes, gather up the gear, and snowshoe back to our camp site. This was not the fun way to do a dive. John Berngasser decided to really demonstrate what a lunatic he could be, so he stripped naked and jumped into the water. That was really just to say he did it, but Berngasser did swim around that hole, naked as a jaybird and blowing like a walrus. And we still had to go down to the base camp. I don't know how long it took for him to warm up, but he was an interesting color when he got out of the water.

My fondest memory of C rations came out of that snow trip. We ate the darn things overseas, but the rations up in Tahoe may have been exceptionally old. Two guys threw up big-time on the morning we were all going to do a big cross-country ski trip. They had both eaten the ham and chopped eggs in water C ration, and it may have turned just a little bit. That particular ration had about half an inch of unadulterated grease on it before you got to the food itself. And the appearance of that ration pretty much looks like it sounds, somewhere between cat food and what my two Teammates were leaving in the snow. The Dr. Seuss book *Green Eggs and Ham* may have been inspired by that C ration.

One bad habit I developed in the Teams, which some people would equate with the C-ration story on the disgusting level, was chewing tobacco. Though I never smoked, I did chew quite a bit while in the Teams and later while I was wrestling. The habit was a fairly easy one to get into. Chewing doesn't make any noise, you can't smell anything, and it helps keep you awake during those long periods at night on patrol or waiting on an ambush.

Nicotine is a stimulant, and it kept me awake on those long drives between wrestling bouts just as it had during my days in the Teams. The habit seemed to be a lot more common on the West Coast than the East, but a lot of my Teammates chewed back then.

We did a lot of things back then that appear pretty bad today, but not all of them were by our choice. There was one time that the higher-ups wanted to use a new technique for cast and recovery rather than the old roll off the rubber boat and pick up with a rubber snare that had been used by the Teams since World War Two. After Vietnam wound down, all kinds of new ideas for replacing old techniques and equipment cropped up all over the place. There was this attitude that if it had been developed during the rush of the war, you had to be able to improve on it during peacetime.

So the old "slow" boat cast and recover was to be dumped and we had to use a new high-speed technique. My platoon was picked to test out the new technique. Charlie Lewis was with us then, good old Tobacco Lew he was called, for always having a great big wad shoved in his cheek. Tobacco never left Charlie's mouth. He may have slept with it for all I knew. He was the only man in the Teams who took a chew with him on a dive. During morning Quarters, we'd be standing there at parade rest and Tobacco Lew would have a big mouthful of Red Man or Days Work chewing tobacco shoved in his cheek.

Lew didn't think very much of our officer back then. While standing at a perfect parade rest, Lew would suddenly spit and that officer would have to jump out of the way to avoid the stream. And Lewis was the platoon's leading petty officer then. "Oh, I'm sorry," Lew would say. "I didn't see you standing there, sir." Yeah, like he was fooling anybody.

But for this new cast and recovery test, Tobacco Lew was right out there along with the rest of us. All of the high-ranking officers were there, scrambled eggs on their caps and big ideas in their heads. For a high-speed cast and recovery, we were going to use PT boats now, not the old, slow PLs that had worked for decades. Forty knots, about forty-six miles per hour, was going to be our speed. And fifty knots was considered available if forty worked. These PTs hauling ass drove up a rooster tail behind the boat, like you see behind racing boats on TV. To cast off from the boat, we were going to run off the stern of the PT into the rooster tail.

This hadn't been tested, we were just going to do it. And the guy who thought it up wasn't going to be entering the water with us. I guess the higher-ups figured we were tough enough to face high-speed water that was known to rip a hydroplane to bits. Running us by the observing officers, we jumped from the boat and into the water.

The impact was so bad you had to hit the water with your life vest partially inflated to start with. The rooster tail would spin and tumble you around so badly you had no idea which way was up. By the time you could get yourself oriented, you would have drowned if the vest didn't take you to the surface first. Sounds a little like my adventure with the dam during SBI, doesn't it?

With the rooster tail built up behind the speeding PT boat, we had a good twenty-foot drop before we reached the water. Driving under the water from the impact, the currents spun us around like a damn toilet bowl. The life jackets were the only things that kept any of us from drowning. Going off the boat was bad enough all by itself without the rooster tail. To keep from injuring yourself on impact, you had to assume the high-speed cast position. This meant you cupped your groin with one hand and grabbed the back of your neck with the other. Cupping the groin kept you from becoming a soprano from the impact and grabbing your neck kept it from snapping.

We did this shit two times, and that included the high-speed pickups. The PT had a rubber raft tied to the side of the boat and you were supposed to grab a snare with your arm just like in a regular pickup. The pickup wasn't going as fast as the delivery, but it had its own problems. The PT boat sat high in the water, with the coxswain somewhere in the middle of the boat. And he was trying to pick up a string of swimmers in the water. Within fifty yards or so of the boat, the coxswain couldn't see us anymore. If the coxswain was off to the side too much, he would have plowed right over us, cutting us to ribbons with his screws. They wanted to cut back on the number of men in the Teams, but I didn't think killing us was considered an option.

Tobacco Lew was missed twice during pickups. Finally, after our second insertion, we were all standing on the deck to do this stupid stunt a third time. All of the brass were patting each other on the back thinking they had come up with the best idea since offshore bombardment. We certainly thought it was just as big a bomb. Lew was standing on the deck, his skin a bright red like he had been beaten on with a whip. Lewis threw his fins and mask down on the deck and shouted, "I want to know who the stupid fucking son of a bitch is who came up with this brilliant idea?"

All of us were being beaten to shit by the high-speed impact with the water. I heard Brice Adkins groaning in the water—he was almost unconscious. Calling over to Brice, I checked if he was all right. Oh, he was fine, he had just been kicked in the testicles by the Pacific Ocean. Brice was tough. He later played football at UCLA with 49er great Randy Cross.

Lew was voicing all of our opinions when he threw his gear down on the deck. And then he refused to do another insertion. "You want somebody to do this stupid shit," he said to the assembled brass, "you go up to San Quentin. You get those convicts on Death Row to do this. Bring them down here and let them go off all afternoon. If they survive, then I'll know this is fit for a human to do. Until then, I'm not your guinea pig anymore."

That was the last insertion of the day. Within a week, the whole idea was gone just like it had never happened. And it didn't take many more weeks before the rest of us had healed up from the injuries we had taken during the tests. All it had taken was an old-timer like Tobacco Lew to speak up.

Sometimes the Teams get to the point where they feel invincible, like there isn't anything that they can't do. And sometimes it gets to the point where defying death reaches

the point of stupidity. No matter how hard you train and
check your equipment and techniques, you have to be able
to stop and say, "This is crazy."

If the high-speed insertion was required for an operation, we would have figured out some way to do it. But
just for practice or experimentation, you don't go out and
try to kill men. Brice had been incapable of swimming
when I called out to him. But probably some of the higher-
ups got their ideas for this kind of shit from the things
the guys in the Teams did just for fun.

Some crazy guys used to do some crazy things while I
was in the Teams. For all I know, the tradition is still
carried forward today. When I was at Coronado, there
were these big building projects going on. All of these
condominiums were going up and there were these tall
cranes standing near the base.

Guys from the Teams used to go out on the arms of
these tall T cranes and do their death dives, rappelling
upside down from the crane. Letting out their rappelling
line, the guys would jump off the crane and fall headfirst
towards the ground until the line would start slowing them
down. This was a lot like bungee-jumping today, only we
were doing it with a rope and carabiner rings back in the
early seventies. "The sights of San Diego as you're falling
upside down at night are unbelievable," they said.

It was getting closer to the end of my time in service,
and I may have been mellowing out just a bit. As my ETS
date was approaching, Bruce Dyer pulled me into his office for a reenlistment talk. That was more of a standard
formality than anything else, and I think Mr. Dyer knew
it. For myself, the Teams had just changed too much for
me to consider remaining.

The morale of the Teams had fallen when the dirty
thirty were dropped for no reason that anyone knew well
enough to talk about. You felt lucky for a while that it
wasn't you who was sent back to the fleet. But then the
realization set in that it could be you the next time. The
cuts had come about because the military had been inflated
in size. We had been fighting America's longest war, and
now the war was over. Other cutbacks could come at any

time. It was the sword that hung over the heads of the military during the 1970s.

As far as my own reasons for leaving the Teams, it was enough that all of the chickenshit Regular Navy stuff had started. All of a sudden, the Teams were more worried about standing inspections than they were about going out and doing work. That wasn't why I had joined the Navy and come into the Teams. I was a Team guy, a pirate and a maniac. Raising hell was more along my lines than shining shoes.

My last six months in the Navy, I was even riding with a local outlaw motorcycle club to keep the adrenaline moving. When I left the area, I would put my colors on and go off on my Harley. When I came back later, I would take off my colors and put on my Navy uniform before returning to the base. Teammate Mike "Unc" Baumgart had started me riding Harleys and the outlaw life along with ST1 Danny "Midget" Horrell.

Later, Bruce Dyer told me that some of the other officers had been a bit worried about me. But the attitude they took was that Janos would be getting out soon anyway, just leave him alone. As long as I was doing my job and kept my hair cut, things were fine with them.

The local police saw things a little differently. When my club, the Mongols, was pulled over, I would be checked out right along with the hard-core members. But just like in the Teams, the members of the club looked out for their own. Whenever something even a little bit shady might be going down, I was sent out of the room. The club members knew that I would face double jeopardy, civilian court and then military court, if I was involved in any criminal acts. Whenever something came down, I knew what was going on because I would be asked to go and sit with the bikes. Just because I wanted to have my fun didn't mean I couldn't keep my head screwed on right.

The club had never seen anyone like me, so I earned their respect early on. As a prospect, they would drop me for push-ups, and I would laugh. "Push-ups—which arm?" Being a prospect was a lot like going through an initiation. But after BUD/S and Frank Perry's PT, they couldn't do much to me that hadn't been done by experts. These were fat bikers that thought ten push-ups were a major undertaking. The old-timers in the club thought I was great. During my time in the Mongols I moved into the third-in-command's place.

Finally, I did get out of the club some time after I left the Navy. One of my friends that I had been in with came to California and talked me into going home. That was the right thing to do, looking back on it. Being in that club would have been nothing more than a one-way ticket to jail. Especially in that era in time. Still, it had been fun to ride into Quarters in the morning on my Harley wearing a patch that read "Mongols South Bay."

All my friends had gotten out, so it was just a matter of time till I left. This was one of the only things that kept the officers from messing with me. Though you could live off-base, coming back and putting your leathers in your locker and changing into your uniform did raise a few eyebrows.

But the Team had changed for me a lot. Today, I've been told that the retention rate in the Teams, the number of men who reenlist, is like eighty percent. In the early seventies, that was more like the rate of those who left the Teams, at least on the West Coast. Maybe twenty-five percent of the guys would reenlist when I was in, and I just wasn't one of them. Besides, I wanted to grow my hair long again.

During my last year, I had gotten into weight lifting along with Kim Erskine. My intention was to play pro football when I got out, so the extra muscle would help give me an edge. It also almost helped get me out of the Navy early. According to the Navy dive standards, when you're six foot three, you can only weigh a maximum of 225 pounds. I had built on muscle to where I weighed 226.

Going into Mr. Dyer's office, I mentioned to him that I was over my weight limit and could I get an early out. Listing the dive standards, I suggested that he could give me an early out. Mr. Dyer said that if we took a picture of me and sent it into BuPers he was fairly certain that they would give me a waiver.

The extra muscle didn't get me into pro football. But it did help when I started on the wrestling circuit a few years later. So it is fairly easy for me to say that where I stand now came directly from my time in the Teams. And that is a time that I will never forget. You can leave the Navy, but you never really leave the Teams.

UDT-SEAL MUSEUM

The UDT-SEAL Museum tells the story of U.S. Navy special warfare from the early days of Naval Combat Demolition Units and Scouts & Raiders to Underwater Demolition Teams—better known as Frogmen—and today's SEALs. Outdoor and indoor exhibits illustrate the unique history of the men who fought in World War II, and those who followed them in Korea and Vietnam. Also part of the exhibits are recent operations in Haiti, Somalia, and Iraq.

The museum, dedicated to preserving the weapons, equipment, artifacts, vehicles, and valor of the country's most secretive fighting men, is operated by the UDT-SEAL Museum Association. For information about becoming an association member, contact the association at the address below, or call (561) 595-5845, or fax (561) 595-5847.

UDT-SEAL Museum
3300 North A1A
North Hutchinson Island
Fort Pierce, FL 34949-8520
(561) 462-3597